THE POOL OF MEMORY

The Pool of Memory

● ● ●

The Autobiography of an Unwilling Intuitive

● ● ●

MICHAL LEVIN

Newleaf

Newleaf
an imprint of
Gill & Macmillan Ltd
Goldenbridge
Dublin 8
with associated companies throughout the world

0 7171 2757 5

Print origination
by Carrigboy Typesetting Services,
County Cork
Printed in Malaysia

A catalogue record is available for this book from the British Library.

1 3 5 4 2

Dedication

To Tom and Ellie – love everlasting

With the exception of family, some public figures and a few friends who have been expressly asked and given their permission, all other names and identities have been altered to protect the privacy of the individuals involved.

Acknowledgements

Acknowledgement alone seems laughably inadequate for the love of my family. I trust they know what it means to me and how deeply it is returned.

To all those who cherished me when I so needed to be cherished, my profound thanks and love. So many have shown what they brush aside as 'nothing' — kindness. There are too many names, but they are, every one, noted.

Then, to all those I met, or will meet as our journeys cross — may we continue to learn to live, and to love, together. With time, I understand more and more clearly how we are all interrelated, each depending on the other, ourselves and the infinite. For that understanding, its inspiration and the reality it inspires, I am grateful.

Author Statement

The story this book tells is true. But, in some cases, names and details have been altered to avoid identifying individuals.

Throughout the story, there are sections which are taken from the meditation diaries I kept at the time — a small sample of the whole I received. The descriptions they contain are not easily accessible in the normal way. Like dreams, they don't conform to the usual dictates of time or space. Like dreams too, feelings and consequences do not follow the rules of the rational mind.

In this case though, the journey I was making in meditation had a number of very real results in the everyday world. I think it is more important for the reader to recognise those results, than to understand each twist and turn in my meditation journey. Of course, for those who choose to spend time with the meditation sections, I hope patterns and pathways will become clear. Pathways they may find in their own depths too.

Contents

CONTENTS

Chapter One

Los Angeles

31 March 1994 'Jem, oh Jem, this says that they may have to cut off my leg, or an arm or part of a limb, I can't bear it, it's too much, I can't sign this.'

He holds me as tenderly as he would hold his small daughters, clear blue eyes soft with love and concern, his skin, a shade paler than mine, taunt over his fine features. 'It's all right. It's really all right, I knew there would be something like this, it's America, they're worried about law suits. You have to agree that they can do whatever they think necessary in surgery. Of course, the chances of their having to amputate a limb are virtually zero. This is just a formality. But,' there's a muscle that twitches in his face, a slither of silver, 'they won't operate unless you sign.' He need not worry, the half whisper of despair has melted in the air.

For a moment, I am outside myself. Again, my consciousness is no longer with my body. From some other vantage point, I see Jem, my brother, seated beside me in the bleak hospital administration office. Hospital forms fan before us. I am tanned, frail and luminous. Behind me is a mass of Light. I put the word 'being' to it. Without my understanding how, or why. I am as certain of this Light, in this moment, as I am of my own existence — still — in the world. I have known it constantly in recent months. The guidance of this Light is what has led me on, and pointed the direction when doctor after doctor denied there was any real problem. It was this Light that warned of death, that pushed me to search for my physical salvation. I owe the possibility of saving my life, to this Light. I am immersed in it, I believe in it. But I do not understand. In the moment, I believe in my survival. I will live. But, more than that, whatever the outcome I will be well. It is the message of the Light.

St Vincent's Priory is on the crest of a hill, in downtown Los Angeles. It's a Catholic hospital. Across a busy road is the House Ear Clinic, where I became a patient yesterday. This Clinic is one of the few centres of excellence in the world that specialise in removing acoustic neuromas — the tumour rooted on my acoustic nerve, pressing its bulk, like a peach I am told, against my brain.

Jeremy, my brother and a British qualified doctor working in New York, identified House a week ago. With my life in the balance and British medicine failing me, he turned to Medline, an information file on computer. Who did the most acoustic neuroma removals in America, and with the best results?

Jeremy rang me at home in London early in the morning. Speaking tersely, 'Shel, I've found a guy, Brackmann, in Los Angeles, I think he's your man.' What time is it for Jem in America? Where is he? Managing Director of a biotech firm, with an amazing schedule to meet, he could be anywhere in the States, or Europe.

'I've spoken to him, he sounds impressive.' His voice is exhausted. 'Brackmann wants you to FedEx your scans today, so he can see exactly what it looks like. He'll shift his schedule to operate immediately, if that's what it means. I think he's the one. Let's not waste time now. We have to make a decision. Let me give you his number — call him and talk. And send the scans today. I'm very encouraged. I think we should go for it. Call me when you've spoken to him. You need to decide. Love you. Bye.'

He's right. Derald Brackmann feels OK. His published work, the number of patients he has operated on, all support the claim to his being the right man. Brackmann wants me to start taking steroids immediately, and come directly to Los Angeles. But it's my daughter's end-of-term play, she has a lead part. I can't come before the play, that's Friday.

'I'm coming with you, Mum. You're not going to America without me.' At ten, my daughter's certainty is impressive. Ellie is no pushover. 'You can't stop me. I won't let you go.' She puts her thin arms around my shoulders, my beautiful daughter, with her long dark hair and green eyes so like my own. Now filled with tears. She doesn't cry. She's hardly cried through all the months — years — of my being ill.

Long ago, when first learning to juggle her life between her divorced and so disparate parents, she learnt Pollyanna's 'glad game'. It has not been a device. In her sweetness, she will look for the good in every situation and be glad. She is certain I will not die. A certainty born of her desperate need for me to live? Or her conviction that this will not be asked of her? Or something else?

The House Ear Clinic surgeons operate at St Vincent's hospital. My surgery is scheduled for 31 March 1994, report at 6.00am.

Bumping in the back of a yellow cab, which cuts the corners and jumps the lights in the near deserted, early morning streets, I see derelicts around Echo park and smog rising. Even before 6.00am, in spring. Run-down stores, people on the sidewalk with no where else to go. I see the hills far away. I want them. I feel them. I am alive and I want to live. This operation will save my life, or take it. Or save my life at the cost of disfiguring my face. I will lose my hearing on the right-hand side in the process. The tumour pressing on my brain will be removed. What else will go?

Mostly Mexicans and other immigrants live in this part of town. The majority of buildings are two or three storey. The junky LA taxi draws up outside a tall modern building, a landmark. Jeremy and I enter the lobby. In the empty space, with its marble floor and black vinyl chairs, I see only the statue of the Christ, that stands beside the door. A plaque says this place is a Healing Centre. A non-Christian, joy and relief flood through me. It will be well. I will be well. How can I know? But I do.

I sign the forms. Jeremy's face relaxes, a little. 'Second floor, Lowther Ward, the elevator's on your right-hand side — they'll be waiting for you,' the unusually restrained hospital administrator directs us. No 'have a nice day'. Past a pair of double doors marked Chapel — how glad I am. Across the foyer to the lift. Second floor.

How strange the nurses at the central reception desk look. British nurses would not have their hair falling around their faces, or over the shoulders. The girl who takes my arm is wearing nail varnish. I feel my skin taut under her hand. My face is stretched tight too. This morning I did as instructed, showered for the second time with the prescription surgical soap, washed my hair and face in it. Applied nothing else to my complaining skin. Or wire wool, stripped hair.

Where is the ward, where are the beds? Instead, I see a row of doors. The nurse is steering us towards one, diagonally opposite the desk. She opens the door, I glimpse a tiny wash basin, I think, on my left, could be a lavatory. In front of me is a bed that occupies most of a tiny bare room. There's a double-glazed, blue-tinted window and a chair. Standing beside the bed, I turn back to the door and, looking up, see an enormous television screen. Not likely to want that.

'You get changed now,' the oriental-looking nurse with the nail varnish is saying to me, indicating a gown laid out on the bed. 'He can stay,' gesturing to my brother, 'you give him handbag, put clothes here,' a shelf I hadn't noticed.

'I'll wait outside, Shel.'

'No need,' no modesty left. 'Freedom's just another word for nothing left to hide,' nothing — I hear Janis Joplin's voice. He turns his back as I take my clothes off. The vast green gown drowns my body. No option now but to sit on the bed. I am tired. Tired beyond belief. Tired way past my too bright smile and quick movements. Let me lie down. How uncomfortable the semi-reclined bed is. It doesn't matter, don't let it matter.

Jeremy sits on the chair beside me, leaning forward. He holds my hand. A doctor, he knows more of what's to come than I do. Much more. A man, he grapples with the possibility that I may be about to lose the facial beauty that has been my birthright. The surgery may sever my facial nerve, which would cause paralysis to one side of my face, a stroke-like effect, depriving me of the ability to move my lips, flare my nostril or even to close my eye, though I do not know that. Yet . . . I am not thinking about it. Denial? Perhaps. My thoughts are concentrated in faith, and trust. The words of the Lord's Prayer run ceaselessly as a sub-text through my mind.

He needs me. My brother needs me to talk, to take some of the terrible weight from him. Loving him, I give him the only gift I can. My attention. We talk of love, his love for his wife, the central relationships in his life. Perhaps I will die. Then let me say what I really think, what might be of most use to him.

There's a knock on the door, which opens simultaneously. A Filipino-looking nurse, or nursing aid. 'I come to put on your stockings.'

'Surgical stockings, Shel, probably to prevent blood clots,' Jem murmurs.

She undoes a cellophane package, removing two long cream-coloured tentacles. Starting at my toes, she rolls the first one up my leg. 'It's very tight,' I say, 'and the seam on the toes, there, is in the wrong place. Could you straighten it, please.'

'Oh, no matter, good, very good and tight, no blood clot.'

In the days ahead, the wrinkled seam will come to be a saw across my toes, but for now I am too weak to dispute such cheerful indifference.

I am smiling, chatting, slower now, not much energy left. 'I don't know how to thank you for all your trouble, and it is such a busy time for you too.'

'It's nothing,' his eyes filling with tears. 'You'd do the same for me.'

An orderly knocks and enters. He is wheeling a mobile bed, like the one I am lying on; it fits exactly beside me. Single-handed, he moves me from one bed to the other. I feel so frail, powerless. Jem hovers. Will he come with me, I want to ask, weak in the instant, but say nothing.

'I have to go now Shel,' his voice is breaking. 'Good luck.' He kisses me hastily and, without meeting my eyes, turns so I cannot see the tears in his. But I know.

'Goodbye and thank you,' I wish him well, smiling with my voice and eyes.

Lying on my back as the orderly pushes the bed along the corridors, I see lights flashing by on the ceiling, and feel the motion in a curious, disconnected way. Am I in or out of my body? Is the Light above or behind me? I feel the presence nearby, but do not look for it.

Down the lift, through large swing doors, two sets, there's a crispness in the air. Gowned masked figures pass, one comes to take charge of me. Oh God, I am no longer a person, just a body on a bed. This place is bare, scrubbed and dingy.

'Hi honey,' the masked face leers at me, 'you still awake? It says here you haven't had a sedative 'cause you want to see the anaesthetist first. Well, he'll be out real soon, they're taking a little longer than we thought, sure you want to wait?'

'Yes, I'm sure, I'd like to see the anaesthetist,' the person I am, or was, replies. I know how important the role anaesthetists play in operations is. Somehow I am still clinging to control, as if it could matter at this stage, whether I meet the man. What difference will it make, his acknowledging me as a person?

'Right honey, just like you want,' and she moves off, leaving the trolley at an awkward angle to the wall. I sense no order in this space, no spatial relations I understand, is how I'd put it. No relations of any kind I can make sense of. Now I know why they did not want me to be conscious here. A ghastly groaning starts from some other bed I hadn't registered. No-one pauses to investigate.

The same gowned figure returns to me. 'I'm going to shave your hair now honey,' fingering the long tresses going down to my shoulders. 'Which side was it, the left one?'

'No, the right. I'd better have a sedative now.' And I turn to concentrate on the Light.

Chapter Two

Life

London, October 1987 The street light shines through the uncurtained windows and the screen of the year's last remaining leaves, into the crowded Bloomsbury room. I haven't got the hang of this — going to parties on my own, let alone dating.

'Scuse me.' A man's just emerged from the gloom, tapped the friend I'm dancing with on the shoulder and stepped between us. 'You're fabulous,' he announces to me, enunciating the words carefully, but with the air of a chap who knows that what he says matters, even when he's the worse for wear.

'Will you dance with me? What about coming home with me? No, you wouldn't want to say yes to that, yet, would you? Just dance with me, come on.'

What do I say? 'Hey, thank you, but could you have had a little too much to drink?' I'm used to being married. Since I was twenty. For most of the last fifteen years. People don't approach you like that when you're married, or at least they didn't approach me like that.

'Ah, come on,' the tipsy one shows no sign of fading away. 'I'm Simon Blue, I can get you into television, into places you never dreamed of going.'

My friend — not lover, past, present or future — is not looking comfortable. He knows very well who Simon Blue is, a powerful man, a man on the make, a rising star. 'C'mon baby, dance with me, you won't forget it, you won't regret it.'

In a clumsy parody, I shrink backwards, trying not to make it obvious.

He lurches forward, and peers into my face. 'You're so fabulous, all I want to do is dance with you, hold you, tell you you're gorgeous, because you are . . .'

December 1987 It is Friday night. I am standing beside the wired glass of our panelled front door, with the two troughs of trailing ivy and patch of woody lavender, long passed its prime, in front of me, waving her goodbye. A small three-year-old with shoulder-length brown curls, round cheeks and my green eyes. She is hurrying along beside the privet hedge to catch up with the tall man ahead of her.

Such are the realities of divorce. Am I glad or sad she is going away for the weekend? Will she be properly looked after? Can her father disentangle his attitude and feelings towards me and the failed marriage, from those he shows to her? Can any parent — without conscious effort? How do two parents who have failed to come to agreement in marriage agree on so contentious an undertaking as bringing up a child, especially after a divorce? How can a mother and a child not be regarded as a unit? Or a father and a child? I don't know. I do know I need this scrap of time to myself. This role, as single working mother of two — even without the hurricane of divorce — is too much.

I turn to go indoors, the familiar, once gilt-rimmed hall mirror shows my tension and fatigue. I sit at the round kitchen table that I painted a pale green to cover the polished black, with a cup of weak, milky earl grey tea. Then it hits. A nagging pain in my lower abdomen. It's a cramp, if I straighten out it will dissolve. Lie down, that will help, fetch a hot water bottle. The manner that has dealt with a hundred childhood ailments, soothed others a thousand times is turned on myself.

9

I need to go upstairs. My bedroom is on the second floor. If I hold the banister I can do it. I reach the first-floor landing and pass the open living room door. I see the trees and the terrace on the other side of the street, the gap that opens over a row of scrubby west London back gardens, with the church spire at the end. Now I am standing, holding my breath, on the last landing. The pain is cutting through me.

I go into the bathroom, to fill a hot water bottle. If I keep all my concentration on what I am doing, I will be able to continue to stand up. Then, I am holding the heat of the rubber bottle to my belly and crawling, curling beneath the duvet. In a minute I'll find a comfortable place.

Why isn't the pain receding? Let it go, just relax and let it go, I tell myself. But it won't. It has its teeth in my belly and it's tearing me apart. My knees are raised to my chest, I hear my breathing: it's erratic, wave after wave assaults me. Ridiculous, this is ridiculous, some everyday part of my brain reprimands. It cannot be happening. The pain is so intense I can't think.

Later Through the lines of the blind, I can see that the light outside has almost faded. How long has it been? It's as if I have reached an island in this sea of suffering. A doctor, I need a doctor. I haven't registered with one since moving, after the divorce. Morgan will help. I call her. A doctor's daughter, she doesn't just hand out a number, she comes hurrying in her long black coat, with the tenderness and solicitousness inbred by the black nannies of our shared colonial background.

'Dr Ruston is wonderful,' she says. 'The surgery's just behind Kensington High Street. I'll call.'

'I'm taking you to the surgery,' she says calmly, putting the phone down. 'Dr Ruston's just finished, but she'll wait for you.'

I don't know how she manoeuvres me down the stairs. Morgan has taken charge, with the confidence of an adult dealing with a childhood trauma. It's dark outside. I don't recognise the route. Lights pass. It's Kensington High Street, elements of normality beginning to creep back. Is the pain receding, or the simple practicalities reintroducing some order?

On Dr Jane Ruston's consulting table, it hits again as I try to straighten my legs. This is no chimera. Looking up into her blonde-rimmed face, I feel the confidence of a child — I know she will take care of me. When the injection comes, I welcome the sharp pin prick and dull, focused ache that follows. Within seconds, a diffuse molten warmth spreads from my buttocks through all my muscles. Its almost instantaneous. If this is what a fix is like, now I understand. Relaxation, that's the word.

'I think it's irritable bowel syndrome,' Dr Jane smiles, in her hazy, lazy Auzzie way, full of the joys of life. 'Nothing serious, but it can be real mean. The injection should take care of it for now, perhaps you better come back next week and we can talk about it.'

Monday and Tuesday I work at home, keeping quiet. Wednesday, lunch with Tobias Boxer and Steven McCloud, the managing director and editorial chief of T.S.L. Titles, the publishing house, who want to discuss setting up a film company under the T.S.L. banner. With my impassive mask and Max Mara suit, my pain has no place, where am I to put it?

We lunch at the Groucho club, media London's mecca. Piece of cake, I tell myself, stepping though the brass revolving door, onto the dark blue carpet. Like a kid going into someone else's den, walking through the contrasting turquoise and salmon-pink interior. Only I've visited this place often enough, and it still doesn't feel comfortable.

We walk through the open lounge, with its companionable sofas, club chairs and casually strewn newspapers, past the bar along one side, to the dining room. The chairs are high backed, our table just far enough away from our neighbours so as not to overhear, or be overheard.

'Let's meet again, when you have done a little more work on the idea.' Tobias and Steven are smiling.

Back to see Dr Jane. 'It's all emotional, you know.' I nod my head. 'It's stress — you have to do something about it,' she says in her sweet, blonde way.

What can I do? Life goes on.

22 December Tobias, Steven and I meet again, this time with T.S.L.'s accountant, in their airy headquarters. Down the street is a famous hospital for nervous diseases. Actually I ought to be there. But I don't know it. Tobias plays his role with energy and enthusiasm. 'I'll work on the figures,' I promise, secretly unconvinced.

Christmas comes and goes. It is not my year to spend it with the children. Adult jollity is empty. I take the children to Ireland for a New Year's Eve party. To Morgan's husband's family seat. Kinnock House stands unexpectedly on a corner of the Liffey, on the outskirts of Dublin.

When Morgan's husband was a boy, his parents remembered fields, stretching from the steep banks around the house to the curving hills in the medium distance. Where now there's an almost impenetrable beech glen, with the river and a dual carriageway below, was once fifteen gardeners' province, with the boathouse on the far side of the river. Today, stories of raids from local boys have a more authentic ring; the backs of terrace houses and thin wisps of smoke fill in the middle distance.

We approach past the cow parlour, and the redbrick farm workers' cottage complex. A wing rises up like a pink, painted institution, scaled by drainpipes. There's a scraggled fence and the ramshackle feel of a semi-neglected kitchen yard. Then we turn the corner to the front of the house and I see the orchard it faces. Gnarled trees, caught in every direction; softened by the gloom, dozens of greens, despite December.

Dark conifers shading the background, unclothed tree shapes extending ahead.

Later my host will recite for me, walnut, lime, beech, for the benefit of the horticultural blank my colonial transplantation has helped produce. But the pleasure more than amply compensates for my ignorance, with branches at every angle, forms organised to complement shapes. I recognise the landscape gardener's art, even under nature's rule.

Turning back to the house for a wider view, a gracious portico, hung with creepers, reaches out, doors half open despite the wintry weather. Proportion is restored in the windows on either side. A light shines, a token to the time, and a torrent of children run out into the evening and away, around the house.

Into the wide hall, with its shaded heights and depths, peeling wallpaper along with elegant prints. Whose father's father, or mother's mother, was responsible for the profligate layout — gun room, boot room, rod room, and beyond with a place for muddy riding boots beside the worn rush mat on the ancient flag floor?

Later in the evening, the old house comes alive with lights, as first the young bloods arrive, fresh from London for the party. The girls are wearing high heels, and short-skirted cocktail dresses, along with confidence and excitement. Men in black tie. Everyone knows everyone else. All, most anyway, are related to or married to someone. In my long skirt of many seasons' service, I take pleasure in watching, from the outside, for a while.

The dining room is a dull cobalt blue, the impression of the Japanese prints which almost paper the walls, in the flicker of the candelabra. After dinner, the party swells. Eccentricity is prized here in Dublin society. One woman wears a feather head dress, another an orange-lined cloak as from some dressing-up box, a drunken girl with jewels at her throat — too many people. A photographer from *Tatler* stalks the ballroom; its enormous fire place accommodating a blazing forest. A man

13

dances with his daughter, the honourable miss's dark head below her father's waist, her tartan skirts swirling.

A staircase winds to I know not where, another to the landing beside my cold damp bedroom, unchanged since early in my hostess's mother-in-law's time. The walls are stained. I escape the conflagration, but not even along these corridors and around these turns, the sound, entirely. It is a very successful party.

11 January 1988 Today, I drive from London to the Berkshire headquarters of the Laura Ashley organisation. I am working as a management consultant for an international operation, in a job that materialised along with the end of the marriage, and grew. Surprisingly, so it seems to me, with my background as a television reporter, I am good at it. It suits me because it pays well. Even more important, because it pays well it enables me to work part time, to make home and children the focus of my time as I want. My boss, the boss, is Rupert Hamilton.

Rupert, tall, blond and jovial, loves driving, and sailing his boat, or piloting his helicopter. The firm's headquarters are outside London. Working from outside London suits him. I hate the drive. I dislike all drives, and always have since childhood. Driving, or being driven, makes me feel ill. Fine for men in their Mercedes, I think petulantly. Rupert loves his Merc, he purrs along with real pleasure.

My diary continues apace, my glittering, privileged, full life. Still. Dinner the following evening with Richard, of recent advertising agency fame, and Suzie. Her make up is impeccable. Friends matter.

Another T.S.L. Titles meeting follows. This time a friend, a figures wizard (chairman now of a public company) accompanies me, as financial adviser. Supper with an old girlfriend from America. The past seems so long ago. Lunch with a film actress. Then the final T.S.L. Titles meeting. The figures do not add up. Am I glad or sad?

Dinner with a new boyfriend, a psychiatrist, and friends of his, in a gothic house in Barnes. The friend, I discover, is a so-called international 'glamour' photographer, whose wife works with him. I suspect this relationship won't last long. Tea for my daughter and I with another working mother and her daughter.

Work steams ahead. I am supervising a film being made for a national newsagent's chain. There's a meeting where a colleague and I present to the unresponsive board of an international food company, then a much more successful presentation to a high street retail chain — I am in charge of a piece of research for them — and an encouraging meeting for Rupert with a supermarket group. I know that it would be interesting to work there, to see how the company plans to re-launch itself. I pitch for business at an international oil company. I think the deal will come off.

At the same time, I handle head teachers, class teachers, speech days, school assemblies, sports days, tears, troubles, bedtimes, night times, mornings, weekends, bad times, good times.

Divorce was deadly. A core of friends remained, others scattered like hail. 'I'm so sorry — I was coming to help you move house, but I've been invited to a party down in Sussex on the same day and there's someone coming I particularly want to meet.'

To my surprise, a well-known London hostess told me that she knew of cases where clairvoyance had been helpful in similar circumstances. Accurate even. Her future husband had been described to her right down to the detail of an old foot injury. (Do people assume a future husband to be my solution? Is it?) She gave me the clairvoyant's name. His address is in Knightsbridge. Behind Harrods.

In response to my timid ring on the doorbell of a large redbrick building, a quiet, civilised voice asks my name over the entry phone. I am shown into a room filled with furniture, *15* masked by half light filtering through the net curtains. What seem like a dozen small Jack Russell terriers hold sway, colonising the stately chairs and firm sofas that fill the room.

'How nice to see you, Mrs Harvey,' he greets me with a distinct Irish accent, hauling his bulk to his feet as I am shown in. His manners are impeccable. His style, from his waistcoat to his neatly trimmed grey hair, is old-fashioned. At a word from him, two or three dogs leap to the ground, circle the central, circular piece of furniture and disappear for the nether regions, the others settling on an assortment of chairs and sofas. Every surface is covered with nick-nacks, papers, stones, ornaments, even what I take to be a collection of African figurines.

He seats me before him, a carved, dark wood table between us, a matching escritoire behind him. His back is to the window, a Royal photograph (Princess Anne, I think) and a bunch of artificial flowers to his left.

'Now, please, if you'd put your hands on this,' he places a crystal ball in front of me. Pause. 'Thank you,' moving the crystal ball away, 'that's enough. Please let me give you some paper, and do be sure to write everything down. You'll want to have a record.'

Hard to say if, or how much of, what he tells me is accurate. 'Nice gates, the place you'll be working there's a nice gateway,' But he's comforting and I like him.

In my despair, and desire to know what to do, I go again. But, heart of hearts, what I am looking for is not here. It is not a question of whether or not I believe in clairvoyance, or even in what is said in this instance.

Perhaps astrology could help? Long ago, I decided that Jung's words, from the foreword to *The Secret of the Golden Flower*, 'Whatever is born or done this moment, has the qualities of this moment of time,' were true for me. Astrology, I believe, has little to do with the columns in the back of magazines. At the same time, I have always been pleased my mother could not remember the time of my birth. So, no definitive chart for me. Free will rules.

A while ago, a friend told me of a Jungian astrologer. I went to see her, in a ground-floor flat near where I was living. I remember orange, was it the walls, or the colour she wore? Her eye shadow was dark, brown perhaps, and marked, her voice low. She swallowed her words. I remember little. Nothing resonated. I could not connect with the person she talked about. I didn't recognise myself. Perhaps I didn't hear. Failure, I thought.

Now, another friend, a writer, gives me the name of a woman he knows, who's been helpful to him and of whom he's had good reports — Anna Balfour. Her husband is a lawyer, apparently. Interesting. 'This is Anna Balfour. Leave your name and phone number and I'll call back.' No please, no thank you. A slight antipodean drawl.

Our first meeting takes place in Clapham. The address I have turns out to be an old redbrick mansion block, one of several, facing the park, with an external staircase. Anna Balfour opens the door to me. If I had any expectations, they're confounded. She's very attractive, with blonde hair cut in a bob, green eyes and a face that moves as she talks. She is a bit older than me. Late thirties, early forties perhaps.

'Hello, how nice to meet you,' a professional but kind-sounding greeting. It is a beautiful, large-roomed mansion flat. The yellow-painted room she shows me into overlooks the common. The room doesn't look like her — square cane furniture, painted elephants and peacock feathers. Someone must live here, but whoever it is, they eradicate their traces very well.

Anna Balfour sits on a small sofa, opposite me. She is wearing a navy blue jacket with white trousers, a scarf holding back her chin-length hair.

The chart she has drawn for me is interesting. 'Of course, we can't know the house placements because we don't know the exact time of your birth,' she tells me, 'so it's pretty general, but I think it's accurate.'

I think it may be too. As a character analysis, some of what I learnt from the Freudian analysis of my late teens and early twenties is alluded to. Her interpretation of the chart also seems to fit with certain ideas that I have picked up since. But how to proceed, where to go, what next? How do I know what is true anymore? Neither Anna Balfour nor the chart can answer any of those questions, but I will come again, I think.

1988 I left management consultancy. Driving, or something, seemed too much. I was constantly tired. Oddly disconnected from the world. Perhaps, if work was the problem, and it was certainly an element of it, I should return to my first love, television?

Over a decade, in a patchwork of freelance reporting (interspersed with consultancy) I had covered political and financial stories, social issues, the sexual abuse of children. I'd travelled up and down Britain, and abroad, taken up cudgels against multinational drug companies, fraudsters, government ministers, in short fought for what I thought of as social justice. Much less financially rewarding, but satisfaction of a different kind. Perhaps that was what I needed.

So I went back (can you ever?) first to the BBC. Then, I was offered a job with a company producing a novel idea for Britain's new fourth television channel. The programme's brief is to look at the press, find the stories behind the stories they are running. Expose reality, I think. It is a tremendous success. But, having my kind of scruples, and some experience of television as well as the world, hasn't served me well.

1989 'Michal, all I'm asking you to do is to read the commentary, surely that's not too much? You're the programme's reporter, remember?'

Not that this looks like a television production office, I think, noticing how the wires hanging down on the landing behind him seem to spout from either side of Pete's head. We are standing in a sea of cardboard boxes, in a jumble of office furniture, probably from a bankrupt's auction. This is cheap space in the clothing wholesalers' district around Whitechapel, pressed into service by a money-wise man for his television production company.

'I'm sorry, but I still think there's a problem. Of course, I'll honour my contract, I'll do what's required, but I still don't think this story is OK.'

'Oh come on, this is ridiculous. This story is being handed to you on a plate. You haven't had to research it, you haven't had to film it, you haven't scripted it.'

It is a joke how a programme like this one, a huge success, in its second season, is run from hand-to-mouth. As ever, the pressure to perform, to find stories, is immense.

'What's the problem? We've got two very plausible victims — a middle-aged woman looking after her invalid mother. The mother's been put onto this pig's insulin stuff and they're both frightened out of their wits by the scare stories the tabloids have been running. Then we've got a little boy who's a diabetic too, and his parents have been given the heeby jeebies by reading all this rubbish, and now of course they don't want him to go on the new insulin. And we've got two docs, one hundred per cent OK, who say pig's insulin is totally safe for diabetics. It wouldn't have been okayed if it wasn't. The tabloids are just filling space, running stories like this . . . It's scaremongering! What more do you want?' Pete asks accusingly.

I can see he thinks I'm being difficult, but he's worried too that I know something he doesn't. There's a coffee stain on   **19** his blue jeans and I know his wife is close to breaking point with a new baby. 'Pete, they said thalidomide was safe.'

'What's that got to do with anything? This isn't thalidomide.'

'No, it's not thalidomide. For all I know, giving humans insulin made from pigs is a great advance. Could well be completely safe. Or it might not be. Of course the majority of doctors will say it's safe. Just like they said thalidomide was safe. But it was only because some journalist kept asking questions that they found out the real truth about thalidomide. Look at the way that was withdrawn and the huge compensation the manufacturers had to pay.'

'Come on, this isn't thalidomide, you said it yourself.'

'No, probably not — the chances are very slim indeed. Like I said, it's probably absolutely fine and a great invention. But it's also absolutely fine for the newspapers to question it. Their methods, and they way they play on people's emotions with over-coloured stories is another matter. I abhor that as much as you do, it's not honest. But I'll always defend the press's right to question new drugs or medical advances. If we run this story, like this, what we're doing is no different from what you say they're doing — filling air time.'

I go back to the half-glazed booth that's my office. I want to put my head on my desk and cry. But, of course, I don't. What worries me doesn't seem to worry him.

When I started working in television, reporting seemed much clearer. I thought it was about showing what was, or is, happening. True, that seems increasingly difficult to capture. But, have the goal posts moved subtly too? Consumer hunger is our concern. How to feed, how to tempt and lure viewers. What do the viewers want? Remember it's not the same as what you and I would want. 'More accessible.' In other words, simpler, snappier and further from the truth?

My mind set, and some experience of the world, aren't serving me well in this situation, although there have been some coups, stories I have been delighted to uncover and excited to have a chance to tell. But I realise what I am fighting for cannot be achieved in the way I am working. Or by taking up arms. Over and over I see not the truth, but the truth of the moment, the truth for the benefit of this side or that, the truth of a pinhole perspective. 'What is truth? said jesting Pilate, and would not stay for an answer.' Bacon was right in 1597.

It seemed that whatever life's lessons by the late Eighties, I no longer fancy them, and I haven't learnt to make the journey comfortable. I plan to resign from my role as a television reporter, when my current contract expires. For what? I don't know. I make the relevant financial plan, adding the figures up over and over again. The children and I can last for so long without my earning. Then the house would have to go. Irresponsible action for the mother of a five- and a twelve-year-old? No, imperative in a way that only addicts know, but then resistance is their route to salvation.

'Sorry luv, got to do a set-up in here.' It's a man carrying lighting equipment. This office is about to be used for filming an interview, and I am needed in the editing suite, a land of permanent gloom, coffee and smoke. But highly professional. The man who's making the money from this outfit has had the sense to pay for a real pro to run the editing suite.

'It's not my job to say anything,' he tells me. 'I just do as I'm told.' It would be so much easier if I could.

Chapter Three

Dowsing

October 1990 'Come to dinner, do,' Suzie and Richard are good to me. I need goodness. We sit in a newly designed dining room. The stylish cutlery grates on the glass dining table. The surfaces are hard, walls reflective — brown-washed and glazed. Sound bounces back with a clear edge.

'More salad? Just a little radicchio and some bits and pieces.' The salad bowl is heavier than I can handle comfortably. My stomach refuses to relax. It won't accept Suzie's delicious, grown-up cuisine. My autonomic nervous system seems to have switched off. I concentrate on making sympathetic responses. My hands are cold, the habitual exhaustion hovers.

I sit with my back to the glass patio doors. Turning my head, I can see the garden in the gloom. It is prettily planted with white petunias, glowing in the semi-dark. The front pathway is laid out in small stones, like specially chosen *petit pois*.

Suzie is spiritual. Spirituality isn't part of my bag, I judge. Not that her spirituality — whatever it is — seems to interfere, as far as I can tell. I am stuck in a groove. What am I going to do?

'Why don't you go and see this incredible woman who's a dowser. She's really amazing.'

'What's a dowser, remind me — what does she dowse for?'

'Oh, love, don't be so silly,' a mock sharpness from Suzie. 'She uses a pendulum, you know, and goes down this list of everything that could be the matter with you, or that you need, and tells you what to do.'

'Sounds a bit odd to me.' I'm trying to be polite. I hardly know what I think about anything anymore. All I'm certain about is what I don't want, and that there's a weariness that troubles me. More than simply my distance from life.

'Go on, go and see her, she's just in Camden Town, and she's really amazing. Tell her I sent you.'

'Actually, I don't think so. I don't think I can bear the thought of hocus pocus, even if she might come up with something.'

'Honestly, she's altogether genuine, and frightfully high powered. She just does this at night, in the day she's a scientist I think, working for the government. No, really, you'd find her very interesting, whatever you thought.'

The journalist in me rises. Curiosity killed the cat.

Friday, 2 November 1990 Sheilagh Brownlow lives in a blue house in a tiny street behind the railway arches in Camden Town. It's hard to find her, I know the way, but not that night. No entries, no right and left turns, traffic intercedes. Finally, arriving.

A woman answers the door. 'You must be Suzie's friend.'

'Michal.' My name again, no-one knows how to say it, 'I'm sorry I'm late, the traffic.'

Her skin is pale, red-brown hair, light eyes behind cold-rimmed glasses. Wrinkles, smile lines, no make-up I notice. I like something about her.

It could be anybody's house, Seventies 'modern' furniture and a swirly brown carpet. Thin curtains, more brown, floral. It's clinically tidy, and strangely characterless, as if someone has just moved in, or out. Empty cream walls. We sit on the sofa and she waves a pencil over a typewritten sheet. This is it, what I've come for.

'I don't know how this works,' she tells me.

'What is it?'

'I dowse,' she says.

'Dowse? Like a water diviner?' Mystified at what a process appropriate to the Australian outback could have to do with me.

She blushes. She is no more comfortable with this procedure than I am, but gripped by it somehow. She seems reluctant to speak, eager to complete the purpose of my visit.

'Let's just go through it and then I'll try and explain.'

Sitting side by side, if I look down I can see the top sheet resting on her clipboard. I spy with my little eye, but the words make no sense. Four squares, each with a list: etheric body, base chakra, star flower, gemstones, I glimpse at random.

Sheilagh wants me to talk. 'Why have you come?'

Years of psychoanalysis dance by. So many words to choose from. I am trying to focus on the sense of my malaise. Such good fortune from the world's perspective, why the malaise? What symptoms have I to tell, beyond a sense of not belonging, worries, fears, exhaustion and disenchantment at every finger tip, along with hope. Like some inherited condition. Persistent, but more powerful.

Does she want to hear? I don't think she is listening, I'm the background music. She's concentrating on the clipboard, but the pencil isn't making any marks. She flips the sheet, same thing again on a fresh page, only this time the list looks longer, and without the squares. My voice trails . . .

Does she live alone? The room looks too neat. Messy hallway, but no children's clutter. Is she shaking slightly? A squint of concentration, and could it be distress, blood so close beneath the white Celtic skin?

'It's funny,' she says, 'but I can't come up with much. Only osteopathy really, it seems.'

'Osteopathy? That's one thing I don't have — physical aches or pains. My body's OK, it always has been.' My mantra,

'I get tired, have done for a few years now, but that's life. What's this about, can you explain what you've been doing?'

She sighs. 'Really, all I've done is write down every possible treatment, or diagnosis, that I know for all four realms, and then tried to see if any of them come up for you. You could dowse each one separately, with a pendulum – it's quite a common practise, putting a question to a pendulum.'

Yes, I think I know about that, I've seen people playing with crystals, usually on chains. I've even tried it, not seriously. But it hasn't worked. It never seemed to me a very profound process, a little like newspaper horoscopes. But what's this about the four realms?

'It's very simple. It's the physical, emotional, mental and spiritual. Those are the dimensions of the whole body, including the energy body around us, and I'm simply looking for any treatment you could need in any of those realms. I don't know how it works.' Lamely. Pause.

I've heard a bit about these sort of notions before. I haven't judged one way or the other. Usually they have simply seemed a little flaky, or even mixed up with quantities of dope, which has never appealed. Fringe I'd say, but fringe weird. Sheilagh Brownlow isn't weird. Her face is open. There's a clean plainness in her hands. I trust that.

So, gently I ask, 'Are you trying to decide from what I tell you what's the matter, or is it something different? I know about pendulums, but I don't quite see how it fits.'

'No, that's not it.' My rationality almost embarrasses her, could be it's hers too. 'My pencil is my pendulum. I tried it by chance and found it worked. I've done this lots of times, which is how I came to draw up the lists. It was much quicker than trying to decide what could be the matter, then using a pendulum to confirm it and decide how to treat it. I use homeopathy too.'

Homeopathy, I've recently started using that. The homeopath Anna Balfour recommended seems to have cured my irritable bowel condition completely. But what do I think about the rest of her explanation? 'Four realms' sounds like a metaphor of sorts that's perhaps not very relevant. What her diagnoses or treatments could be I can't imagine — star flower! I'm curious, she's no flake.

'How did you come to this, how does it relate to the rest of your life, to your job?' I am reluctant to ask directly what she does, it seems impertinent. I sense a certain reticence, along with compulsion in her manner.

'Oh I just do this at night, when I can. But everything is a little difficult right now, personal things, and I'm under quite a lot of pressure. It's got nothing to do with my work — they'd be horrified if they knew I did this, I'm a scientist, you see. People aren't very tolerant. I'm sorry I haven't got much time now — when you called, you sounded as if you needed it so much, I agreed to see you.' I'm nodding, the pieces are coming together.

'I don't know why so little has come up,' Sheilagh continues. 'Usually people get a lot more, but you seem different. I've got a funny feeling about you, but I don't know why. Osteopathy would be good though, did you say you had back trouble?'

'No.'

'Well, I don't know why, like I said, but it's usually right, if you know an osteopath I'd go and see him, or her.'

'I know an osteopath who's been recommended. Funny, because I got his name only recently, for my mum, and he works just around the corner from me.'

Driving home from Camden Town to West London, all the lights are green and it takes no time. Sheilagh Brownlow has something, but I don't know what. I recognise this feeling. My journalistic nose tells me that there is something here. This feeling has led me into trouble before, opposing others, seeing issues or angles, often unpopular, no-one else recognises (or wants to). Usually it's been correct, which hasn't always won me friends. Now I know there is something here, but what? Osteopathy for me? Why bother? That's one problem I don't have, or need.

My sleep is disturbed. I dream a dream repeatedly that makes no sense to me. I am showing a property to prospective purchasers. The property is close to where I live in real life. I have no actual experience of selling property — at least not professionally. It's an unusual building, largely made of wood and like a place of worship, or perhaps a New England picture-book barn. However, its potential as a dwelling place is not immediately obvious. But to me it is clear that this is the most astonishing opportunity to occupy a magnificent and vast space. The prospective purchasers seem uninspired. I am amazed at their lack of insight.

Two, three, four times I dream this dream. Then, in the dream it occurs to me — why not buy the property myself? The finances would be easy to arrange. I myself could live in this wondrous space. What bliss. The dream does not reoccur. But a few nights later, another stays with me. I am living in quite cramped quarters, with my children, in what looks from the outside as if it should be a large home, but somehow isn't.

I am worried about having enough space and about our finances. I walk up and down the stairs and through the rooms as if there is some solution to be found in the activity. Then, pressing on a wall, it gives way, revealing a low and lovely attic area. With room beyond room visible. I am overjoyed. Why did I not realise I owned all this space already?

Chapter Four

Past Lives?

Saturday, 3 November 1990 'It was really interesting Anna, I just don't know what I think about it.'

'Oh, you're such a sceptic. Of course it works. There is so much we don't know. Why do you have to understand it to believe that it works. What's electricity? Do you know exactly what that is?'

Warming, she continues, 'You use electricity every day, without a second thought,' her plain, square hands shake the air for emphasis. 'You just know that there are people who understand it, and you don't question it, it just works. You intellectuals, you're all the same. Academics are just as bad, don't believe it unless you understand exactly how it works. Scientific realism, it's a plague.' Annoyed, she picks up a dish from the table and walks over to the kitchen sink.

'Now now, darling,' the plummy tones of her husband, 'we are all quite prepared to accept the unorthodox here, but it is always interesting to question the whys and wherefores.'

'What do you think, Anthony?' I ask.

'All sounds jolly interesting to me. But then, I'm old enough to have a little perspective. I remember a time, twenty-five years ago, when I wouldn't have given Anna's astrology the time of day. Fortunately, that's one of the benefits life has brought. I'm a little wiser than I was, less inclined to hurry with judgments. What your dowser lady says certainly sounds worth investigating to me.'

Anna has stacked the lunch dishes carefully on the counter, I rise to help her.

'No, don't worry about that now,' she says, 'let's start.' Anna has been working on a new breathing technique. 'It's marvellous for relaxation, for rejuvenating the whole body, right down to the cells,' she says.

I'm going to try it out. We walk down the corridor to a small spare bedroom. The walls are wood panelled, the only window is rather high and small. There is just room for a bed and a chair, with a clock hanging on the wall above the bed.

'You have to lie down,' says Anna.

So I take my shoes off and lie down, noticing the time, 2.35.

'You start like this, little shallow breaths, only filling the top of your lungs, then . . . '

It's a bit like prenatal classes. I am concentrating really hard, following the instructions of the voice, which is fading away.

I open my eyes. The clock says 3.56. There is a sound in my ears, lapping and washing like the sea.

'Welcome,' Anna is bending over me and smiling. 'What happened to you? You looked so peaceful, where were you?'

'I don't know,' smiling back weakly, as an image from childhood passes before my eyes. Early morning, and the marsh mist hovers. I am twelve, bicycling to school in Rhodesia, now Zimbabwe, Central Africa. Down the hill, up another, down a little way, across the flat. Past the avenue of tall gum trees, the bungalows set well back in the lush gardens. The benefits of cheap labour on show, everywhere.

Then the houses recede, scrub land, with hummocks of coarse grass waiting to cut your fingers on its blades, takes over. The tarmacaddam cycle path makes my way easy. Because I hardly know any comparison, I do not recognise the network of cycle paths as a sign of this third world economy. I am rich in the piercing loveliness of the sky reaching to the bare hills, and the damp ground in this dry place. My legs move rhythmically, at one with my machine. I am invincible on this unopposed path, loving living.

In the same moment, I see a red spot ahead. Focusing my attention, I see a red bishop bird. It is perched on a stalk of sage-coloured grass, growing from a marshy hollow. Now I am close enough to see the beady eyes and spotless carmine breast. The bird remains motionless while I pedal past, the energy of its scarlet breast exalts existence in the silence of the morning.

A moment later, refocusing on the panelled walls, the glory of my memory fades, pushed out by another image, grey and cold. Snow. Oh God, it's death. There's a man lying on the snow. He's dead, or dying. It's so cold, biting biting cold.

'Michal, what's the matter? Don't cry, tell me what's happening.'

'I don't know Anna,' my voice is low and broken. 'I can see these pictures, I'm there Anna, I think I'm this man, lying on the snow, I'm dying . . . it's so sad.' I feel the snow, the elemental winding cloth. I am bound and wound over, I have always had a dread of snow, the cold is death and now I feel it.

Then Anna takes over in a low and steady voice, the tone she uses with clients, 'Don't be scared, tell me everything you see. Who is the man, what has happened to him?'

It is 4.45 and I have told Anna the whole story, as I learnt it myself. And two others, less detailed tales that followed. The stories are real. I am sure of that. I saw myself there, each in another time. In each I recognised many of the characters as figures from my life here, now, only playing different roles, sometimes different sexes too. My certainty that what I have seen is somehow 'real' shocks me.

'I think what you may have seen are past lives.'

I have heard the expression, but hardly know anything about what it means, or could mean. It's not something that has held much interest for me.

'I've heard of cases like this where people spontaneously remember the past. I think you should write it down. You're lucky, very lucky, I've been doing the breathing for months and nothing has ever happened to me. Do you know anything about past lives?' Weakly, I shake my head. This is really foreign territory for me.

'Well there's a man who lives in America, one of the real authorities on it, he's coming here at the end of the month and he's giving a lecture at the Whitehall Centre. I am planning to go. Why don't you go too.'

'Thank you Anna, I'll try, I need to think about all this a little more.'

Early December, I'm having lunch in a small cafe close to Whitechapel tube station with Peter and Dora Hatchard. An academic, he is immersed in psychoanalysis. Dora paints. I want to talk to them about the idea of 'past lives'. All else has faded out of my mind. Sheilagh Brownlow and her dowsing seem unimportant, compared with my own experiences.

'So, you say this lecturer actually called someone from the audience and had her relive a past life on the platform?'

'Yes. She got terribly upset, remembering a life in Japan where she was being raped, and all sorts of ghastly things happening. I found it quite upsetting to watch, it made me feel really uncomfortable — he had to arrange for her to come back and see him afterwards.'

'From a therapeutic point of view it sounds pretty dodgy. You say he's a Jungian?'

Peter is sceptical about the idea of past lives. My account of the lecture does not seem to convince him any more than my own experiences. Those have been built on by a further session, where the same thing happened again. But I find I do not want to talk in detail of what I have seen. I cannot tell the tales. It is as if they are etched on my heart, for me to see and   31 feel through. Just for me. I know they are true. In some way. They are like the ground beneath my feet, part of me in the way that the ground is — we share the same mineral elements, the same reality. That reality defies this conversation.

'It sounds to me as if you are having spontaneous fantasies.' Dora looks thoughtful, but she does not comment on her husband's assessment. I have to go back to work. It is the last week of my television life.

11 December 1990 I am being pulled. It's as if events are leading me. I have come to see George James, BA (Hons) DO MRO, cranial osteopath. I am not sure why. Anna gave me his address, behind Paddington station, a brutal place. I walk through a few streets of railway no-man's land. Social security hostels, immigrants, multiple occupancy hold sway here. Around the corner, polite W2, with town houses, mews and even a riding stable, blends into Hyde Park.

Some months ago, my mother had trouble with her shoulder. She asked if I knew of a good physiotherapist. I didn't. A little later, talking to Anna, she mentioned that she was seeing a fantastic osteopath, a real miracle worker. I took his name and passed it on to my mother, noticing how close the address was to my own. True to his reputation, George James cured the shoulder and its owner's scepticism. Now, if seeing an osteopath is my next step, why travel any further?

George James's waiting room, which he shares with two others, is no more than six feet of corridor. Walking into his room, when he calls me, the first thing I notice is the many-armed oriental deity in red above the mantel piece. It is surprisingly spacious. There is a couch, like a massage table, in the centre, a *chaise longue*, a wash basin, desk and two chairs.

Formalities complete, he asks why I am there. I take the plunge. I tell him the truth. 'I don't have any aches or pains, a dowser sent me.' Silence.

He has very blue eyes, with dark pupils which seem to widen, looking at me, old eyes for a young man. His crinkly hair is still almost blonde, with no trace of grey.

'OK, I'm open to all sorts of stuff. That's a new one on me, but that's fine,' reassuring himself as much as me.

I lie on the table. There is a wonderful lightness in his hands. I feel as if I am dissolving. I no longer exist. Neither does he. My body is being moved in the gentlest, slowest of ways. Somehow, my attention is outside my limbs. I am free. Now the lightness is concentrated on and around my head. Nothing is said. Briefly, I open my eyes, re-entering reality, his eyes are closed, chin raised, lower lip protruding as if concentrating, almost meditating I think, and close my eyes without analysing the thought.

Again the sense of lightness. The hands on my head are mesmeric. A crazy thought — the hands are loving me — floats through my mind, as the need grows for the quality of the hands on my upper chest. A warning flashes by hazily: avoid any sexual touch, my habitual fears are surfacing. No need, the interchange is quite without, beyond, I later realise, carnal contact. Simultaneously, the hands move to the very spot that craved their presence. Honey flows through my chest. Peace enters my heart.

Later, I rise from the table slowly, replace my jeans, jacket and pumps.

'What was going on? What did you find?'

'Well,' he says, 'you tell me. Funny that you've never had any back problems, you spine is twisted a little.'

'When I was seventeen I was in a car crash, I was sitting in the passenger seat, I hit the windscreen, had some stitches here on the side of my jaw. I was lucky it wasn't worse, but surely there's no trace of that, it was more than seventeen years ago.'

'I don't know what there is or isn't any trace of, but there are certainly a few things I could help with if you come again.' 33

The peace I feel, alone, would bring me back to him. There's more, but it's beyond my grasp. His words tell me little. His level of explanation leaves me altogether unsatisfied: is this all from someone whom I felt held my soul? Was it simply my perception? Was this what was supposed to happen? What always happened? Is this what cranial osteopathy was all about? If so, what, in down to earth language, happened? Questions without answers that day.

'Make it a week or ten days, please,' he said. 'I'd like to see what happens,' the only indication he gave that what took place was of interest.

That night I phone Anna. 'George James, he's very spiritual,' she says in her New Zealand accent. 'I really go for him in a big way.'

'What do you mean spiritual?'

'He's a Buddhist, very devout. You'll be fine with him, don't worry so much. Sorry, but I have to go now, I've got a meeting. See you next month, I've got the date in my diary.'

A Buddhist. So that was it. What did being a Buddhist have to do with anything?

Chapter Five

Seeing

1991 The year started quietly. Only when alone did I feel real. I sensed the phoenix and hurried to throw off the ashes of my old existence. Too soon of course, but death was overdue. A lover went first, I think the word implies more than was the case. For a while he and I had passed pleasant interludes together. An art dealer, I accompanied him once to Italy when my children were away on holiday. In London he gave civilised dinner parties at his Hampstead home. He liked my looks, perhaps other qualities too, but they were not discussed. I appreciated his gentleness; he was wounded, each gave the other a long rein. We circled at a distance. I let two weeks, then three, go by without meeting, and found that the waters closed quietly, no ripples troubled me. I let it go.

I drifted out of the city's social life simultaneously. Dinner with a Euro MP — not to be repeated. Supper with a dear, but somehow distant friend, unable to explain what I did not understand myself; I was not real. Just terrified. I could not be specific about my sense of malaise, exhaustion and distance. I certainly could not talk about the experiences of seeing what I believed firmly, somehow, to be my past lives, nor even about Sheilagh Brownlow or George James. Silence seemed the most sensible option. I had stopped working. I planned to take six months' break, the money would last that long. I needed to rest and to think.

I went to see Jeanette Joliff, the homeopath who had cleared up my irritable bowel where my GP, and the consultant who followed, both failed. (Or perhaps the cramps just stopped?) I sat on the train to south London, watching suburbia pass by. Why did I find myself drawn to the alternative, the unorthodox?

Mrs Joliff worked from a converted wooden garden shed with a concrete floor and electric heaters, in a semi-rural suburb of small detached houses, most with good-sized gardens. Her neighbours, and others who came from much further afield, filled the simple waiting area, where a jolly, ample receptionist presided. The wait was endless. She was running late. She always was.

'You need to meditate, that's what you need.' Oh no. Images of eastern mysticism. 'You'd be able to do it very easily.'

'I don't see what the point would be. I've never understood the attraction, the whole idea just seems boring to me.'

She looks down. She's plump and fortyish, with an almost demure smile. 'I wouldn't say that. Just try it. I am certain it's right for you. This is what you do . . . ' She gives me complex, precise instructions.

'And remember, write down everything that happens afterwards. No matter how unimportant you think it is.' She smoothes the skirt of her stiff, royal blue suit and turns to fill in her case notes laboriously.

It is drizzling when I leave. The receptionist smiles, and wishes me 'God bless' in an old-fashioned sort of way. The walk back to the station is invigorating, I don't mind the wet. Well, at least I'm enjoying one aspect of the trip. Meditation really doesn't appeal.

I am enjoying being at home very much. I dismissed the last of the nannies. Without working myself, I did not need or want her, nor could I pay her. My daughter luxuriates in my captive presence on the walk to school. So do I. Day rolls into simple day. Domesticity is bliss, and 8.30 till 3.30 is mine. That the clock might be ticking on this blossoming idyll, I refuse to consider. Finally, alone and quiet, it seems my tension is starting to lift.

There is another boon. A few lines in the local free magazine advertise painting and drawing classes with a Royal College of Art instructor. I call, and agree to try a class.

Sandie Potter welcomes me into her unexpected studio. It is hidden, a relatively modern extension built on the side of a large, divided house. I enter a kitchen, Sixties pine beams overhead and too many pictures pinned to the walls to have much other impression of the space. From the moment I smell the open turpentine standing by the kitchen sink, mugs equally for coffee or washing brushes, till it's time to leave the clumsy easel and hurry to the school gate, I am in seventh heaven. I haven't drawn or painted since I was a girl. Now it flows from me like some underground renaissance surfacing. Shapes I didn't know I could master, colours I feel, not think, fit.

Sandie, freckled like her name, stands by. There is very little help I want, just her space, and the occasional line. I arrange to come twice a week. I paint the models who come to the studio and sit for us. A fat woman comes first, repeatedly. She curves, I play with contours. She glows, her dark skin set beside bright silks. The colours fascinate me. Then comes a breakthrough. A boy, a young man sits one day.

'I want you to try using just two colours, and black and white of course,' Sandie says. 'Try and see what you come up with.'

He looks around twenty, and less than comfortable, in front of eight ill-assorted, some-time painters. Nice wide shoulders, compact hips, legs a little short, a small penis he very soon gives up trying to hide.

'I want you to sit here, in this chair,' says Sandie, 'with your legs sprawled like this,' moving his limbs firmly, any modesty stamped out. 'And then, if you could lean on your elbow, no the other one, that's right. Just a minute, I want to mark your position,' as she picks up a chalk to mark the places on the floor and table where the model's legs and arms rest, so that after a break she can easily reposition him.

I choose blue and yellow. There are shades in his youth. The picture shapes itself quickly, 'That's lovely, very nice,' says Sandie, looking over my shoulder, without offering a correction to the layout which has given me a little trouble, unaccustomed as I am to figure drawing. I work through the break. Difficult to say whether I enjoy more setting up the structure, or working with colour as I am now. I study his arm. My concentration is intense. Almost automatically I squeeze a little scarlet onto the reject china plate I'm using for mixing paints. Not thinking of Sandy's stricture — two colours only. I see red at the model's elbow, where he is leaning on the table, probably stiff from the position he's held for nearly two hours now, with short breaks.

'That's fantastic,' Sandy says. 'Actually, the proportion of that arm is wrong, but by using the red, you've completely drawn attention away from it. Why did you use it?'

'It's only what I can see,' I say. Which is true. When I look at the model, focus my attention on him, I see a red haze around his elbow. Suddenly I realise, it's not my imagination working for me, a logical deduction, or simply my creativity in some form: it's reality. It is what I see. I close my lips firmly. Not another word. I need to think about this.

I walk home through the streets lined with gaunt trees. My daughter has book club after school, so I have another half an hour. I realise that if I look very closely at the passers-by, I can sometimes see faint colours around or even inside them. It is not automatic, but it seems that when I choose to 'look', then I can 'see'. Is this real?

A memory from university days floats past. A page in a scientific journal, 'What the frog's eye sees'. In an experiment on frogs' visual cortex, electrodes are placed on the brain while images are passed before their eyes. It was found that the visual cortex is only stimulated by shapes which approximate frog food. In other words, show a frog a flower and there was no apparent sign of mental activity. Show a frog a shape like a fly — potential food — and the brain registered a response, or something like that. Is it relevant, I wonder, as I reach home and the phenomena has faded, on the simultaneously empty street.

A message on the ansaphone tells me that my daughter isn't feeling well and would like to be collected straight away, where am I? Oh the automatic guilt. Fancy phenomena vanish, briefly.

'You certainly seem well, something's shifted, hasn't it?' Anna's sitting opposite me across the ugly glass and cane table in the Clapham apartment. Behind her I see the green shapes of the common. I say little. I don't want to talk about 'past lives', or this new development, which hasn't gone away. When I try, I can see colours or light around or through people. From flicking through the esoteric section in my local book shop, I suspect what I am seeing is what people call 'auras' or 'energy'. I would like to talk to someone, but I know I can't.

Instead, I settle for hearing Anna talk. I made this appointment to see her for an astrological reading. Her interpretation of the current trends and celestial developments tells me little. Then I mention George.

'So, you like George, he's lovely isn't he? Marvellous energy.' Enthusiastic as ever, Anna's nothing if not wholehearted.

'Yes, I am really enjoying seeing him. I have been three times now, but I haven't a clue what he's doing. Whatever it is, I'm feeling wonderful. It's also such a relief to have stopped work. But tell me Anna, what do you think is going on when one sees George?'

'Ah, good question. It's powerful, very powerful. I don't know exactly what he would say, but he's definitely working on the energy, aligning the chakras, it's very deep.'

Which tells me precisely nothing, and nothing in language that, frankly, I distrust. So why come back to Anna? Why am I drawn to people who cannot, do not, meet my rational criteria? Like Jeanette Joliff, with her instruction to meditate. Could it be relevant? Perhaps I'll try, just to make sure.

Jeanette told me about the chakras, energy centres she called them, through the body. She told me how to visualise them, and what colours to put to them. For a week, I follow her suggestions. Twice a day, morning and evening, I sit on the side of my bed (she said in a chair, but that means bringing one from downstairs) and light a candle on the chest of drawers beside me. I face the window, with the trees across the road, a gap in the terrace opposite, and a church spire a few blocks away. Then I close my eyes and go to the first chakra.

Surprisingly, it's easy, and pretty ordinary. Words seem to fill my mind.

I see colour clearly, there are no other specific images. 'Hold onto honesty and humility' the words tell me. 'Love yourself, God loves you, love yourself, you are loved.' I am not religious, but this reference to God doesn't seem to bother me. Then, 'This is the time of blood, but it will pass, it is necessary. Be firm. Don't cancel the feminine. Be female.' On and on they run, colours replacing one another fluidly, words ceaseless, effortless and soundless.

When I finish, I am well. And somehow reassured. About twenty minutes have passed. I don't question what has happened. It seems peaceful. Perhaps the words are not very important, some release mechanism, I think. Interesting, the references to God. I am probably an agnostic. Religion has never troubled me much, one way or the other. My family is Jewish, not practising, and I had a pretty average exposure to the Church of England through school assemblies, etc. Being Jewish was a good excuse to get on with homework, instead of sitting through religious education classes. Though I grew up in the Sixties, when it was all around in London's hippie circles, Eastern religion and mysticism never appealed. It always seemed mixed up with drugs and incense, neither of which I cared for. That's why I am surprised this meditation seems to work.

Jeanette was right. To my astonishment, it is easy and relaxing. Would I want to do it regularly though? Would it have a cumulative benefit, or would it start to be boring? She has given me another exercise to do when I have finished working with the so-called chakras. She said I would know when that was. A week later, the lights come on as has become normal, but there is silence, then a prompting, 'Go on, go on to the next.' That does strike me as a little odd. Is it my subconscious, or unconscious, urging me on to the next stage? I decide I'll try tomorrow. Make it a birthday treat.

19 February 1991 The night of my thirty-ninth birthday. These are the notes I wrote in my notebook, afterwards.

I sit down in my usual place to meditate. Tonight I plan to focus on a new image, as suggested. What happens takes me quite by surprise.

It is blue. With light purple lines spinning around it. They spin and spin, pulling me in as they become a funnel to the blue star, which is water. I enter the water in a white shift. (Funny that in reality I had put on a long white night-dress beforehand.) I am washed, anointed, and my hair is cut.

Then I am called to meet the Light. I leave my body behind, and join the Light. For a while, I simply enjoy it: the love. Such a pure pleasure. Then I am shown the world and told, 'This is for you to enjoy — take it in. And for you to help.'

'What am I to do?' I ask.

'*You will find out. First you are to solidify your personal life. Your foundations need to be a little more solid. Then you will work for a while directly, write and teach, and then more.*'

I stay for some time. Finally releasing a long breath, I know it is time to leave. I go back to my body, climb out of the pool, and return into life on earth. Dazed.

Afterwards, I note that throughout, my feet were burning, pulsing with energy. Also, to begin with, my hands, head and trunk were throbbing too.

What has happened to me? What is happening?

Against my expectations, I slept deeply that night.

Chapter Six

Meditation

Without question, I am following this meditation.

Evening, 20 February *With closed eyes, I begin to meditate. Instantly, I am pulled into the pool, and out of it again, leaving my body behind. Don't quite remember the order of what happens then. It is all very quick. Going into the light. Try to slow it down — not much good. I have a form, the same form as my body, though differently dressed, wearing the white shift.*

There is a presence, a being, with me. He is from God, not God. I am to know him as the Disciple, for now. He is a relatively young man, thirty to thirty-five. Very kind. I am shown the world again from the clouds. The message is, 'You are to love everyone, that is an important part of your work.' I see flickery pictures, like old movies, or old negatives, lots of people walking.

The Disciple tells me I am to speak to many people. I am to teach 'the Wisdom of the Ages, you have the ability to communicate it'. What's the Wisdom of the Ages? Then it is over. I go back to my body, reunite with it, splash into the pool, and emerge on the other side.

Opening my eyes, I am sitting on the edge of my bed. Physically, I note that my nose was very itchy towards the end of the encounter. Again, tingling and throbbing in my whole body from the start, almost as I sat down. Tingling in the soles of my feet was particularly strong. Is all this egotistical nonsense? What is going on?

Evening, 21 February *Quickly into the water. I want to linger, but somehow dare not. I leave my body and immediately join the Disciple. He seems impatient. 'Whatever took you so long? There is so much you have to learn, so much I have to teach you. You must learn about the wisdom of the sky and the stars.'*
  'Why?' I ask.
  'Because it is part of the unity of the whole, and you need to understand it.' (So, I think that means I have to learn about astrology, which is as far as my limited understanding can take what he tells me.)
  'Should I learn the Tarot too?' I ask. (It is my idea of the arcane or esoteric, at this point.)
  'If you really want to,' comes the somewhat cool answer, 'but it's not necessary, and takes up time.' I am not to waste time on an 'outside to inside' type of process. He says I know all that, and must press on. I am not sure quite what he means, but guess that if I am not to work on processes that come from the outside to the inside, then perhaps I am to concentrate on processes from the inside to the outside? Whatever they are.
  There is birdsong, beauty and ease. 'Enjoy it,' the Disciple urges. I am rather slow and bemused. I feel this is becoming a bit of a soap opera, right down to the music. Then the Disciple says he must go and vanishes. I return, slowly, to my body and leave the pool.
  Again, there was pulsing and tingling in my physical body throughout the episode, but it wasn't as strong as yesterday.

I need to think about this. What is going on? I think I am afraid.

Morning, 23 February *Wake in the night, feeling my soul racing. The Disciple is there. Comforting me. Trying to help me* *to dwell only on the moment. Still, it is hard to go back to sleep. (Bread and honey and tea would help, but I daren't risk waking the puppy in the kitchen.) Awake again at 7.00am.*

Is all this predestined, or am I choosing it? If I'm choosing, what am I choosing? Who is calling the shots?

Evening, 23 February *The Disciple is waiting for me, welcoming me. I am glad to see him. He is reassuring.*

I walk with the Disciple among the trees in the sky. 'Soon it will be time for you to go back to the trees, but not quite yet.' I wonder just what he means — that I am to live in the country again?

I ask 'Where do you come from?'

'The world that watches the worlds.'

'Are there other worlds, then?'

'Yes, but you cannot know now — after this life you will know. But now you have much to do.' I see the flickery pictures again. 'The pictures of all the past. You have knowledge, your problem is to know that you know. You have much to do. Right now you are tired.' He embraces me and leaves. I wait, standing there, then wander in the clouds for a short while — where is this place? Finally, I go back to my body, and return to the so-called real world.

I need someone human to share this. Is it some super ego playing tricks? What is it?

'Sue, you go to church, who's the best vicar around here? I mean the one who's the most clued in?'

'Well, do you want somebody to instruct you, or to talk to, or what are you looking for?'

'Talk, really, that's all.'

'Father Kevin, at All Saints in Kensington, is supposed to be very good. He's been the adviser to all sorts of religious programmes. Are you OK?.'

'Fine, thanks. See you soon.' A good neighbour.

I arrange to see Father Kevin on Monday.

Sunday, 24 February *I sit down to meditate and find myself by the pool in a black bathing suit. It is lovely and sunny, but a black bathing suit! Seems inappropriate for the high seriousness of the occasion. I try mentally to replace the bathing suit with the white shift. Failure. Then I haven't time to bother anymore because the Disciple is waiting.*

I join him, asking, 'Why the bathing suit?'

'Because this world and the other are meant for pleasure too. It is not all high seriousness, even though it is so important. You have had your share of pain. Now there is pleasure. Go out and enjoy. Be in the air and among the trees. See the sky. Feel the beauty and be joyful.' Then he leaves.

I go back to the pool, look around. It is beautiful. It is anything you want it to be — sandy beach, forest to the edge of the water, anything and everything. There is a sense that a great many people, shades in a way, have passed by, but not come into the water, or through it. It is almost as if they came and then went back. I see the flickery pictures again, people marching, marching.

I lie down in the sun. It seems as if I am with the part of me that I recognise as my body. Rolling over onto my stomach, right side slightly raised, I see George James coming towards me. Somehow I am not surprised. An image of me, my spirit perhaps, leaves my body to greet him. But what form is he in? Is he in body, or spirit? There is some kind of fundamental mingling — as if I go into him and then come out again.

I open my eyes and cease to meditate immediately.

Sunday, again, later *I leave the pool in a white shift and go to join the Disciple. George is there again. The Disciple urges me not to worry, saying that George is doing exactly what I am*

*doing now, meditating, and that he, the Disciple, is with him
also. He urges me to rest — I am very tired.*

Monday *My meditation is unsettled, my mind wanders. The
Disciple is very calm and understanding. He tells me that the
wonderful morning I woke up to this morning, in the physical
world, was a gift, 'Enjoy the beauty and delight of God. You
will find richness and beauty wherever you go. Enjoy it.' He
goes on, 'Your job is to understand, as well as to act. By the end
of this life you must understand.'*

The number fifty-two bus pulls up at the corner of Kensington
High Street and Palace Gardens. I cross the High Street and
turn off into a square, with All Saints Church in the far corner.
Father Kevin's study is up the third floor of the rectory. The
worn stone steps are uncarpeted. I enter a small room —
there's one book case and a table overflowing with books and
papers. The walls are bare except for a large crucifix. Such a
painful image, I think.

'How do you do? Thank you for seeing me.' His hands are
surprisingly hot. Pasty face, with pale eyes behind large glasses.
Kind or not? I wonder.

'Well, what can I do for you?'

'It's a bit unusual. Perhaps I should begin by saying that I
am not a Christian, and I'm not really interested in becoming
one. At the moment anyway. But . . . ' I hesitate, 'certain things
have been happening and I am trying to understand them, and
I wondered if you might be prepared to discuss one or two
things with me.'

'I see,' he looks serious, he looks away, 'What sort of things?'

'Well, meditation really.'

'Oh,' brightening, 'have you read anything about Christian
meditation? There are some excellent books I could recommend
as a good way to begin.'

'Right, yes, I could do that. Does anyone go into the subject of visions, visions in contemporary life I mean?'

'Having visions are you?' he says, looking decidedly distracted. 'Well, that would be very unusual indeed, given that you tell me you haven't entered the fold yet, so to speak. You have a rather long way to go, I think.' He's shuffling papers and looking down. He asks, without enthusiasm, 'What are these visions, then?'

'It's a little difficult to say,' I'm clamming up, 'I wonder whether they could be connected with religion, the divine, in some form.'

'Of course, there are all sorts of reasons for hallucinations. It's a rather different subject from Christian meditation. Look, if you're interested in meditation why not borrow these,' handing over two lightly worn paperbacks. 'Then, perhaps, if you want to make another appointment, we could discuss them?'

Monday, much later, after a difficult day *I am almost pulled out of the pool by the Disciple. He is furious. There is thunder in the air. 'How dare you doubt! How dare you!' He rages at me. I feel contrite, but how can I be sure about what is going on?*

'How can you not listen? Didn't you see all the shades by the pool? People who came up to the pool, but didn't listen — couldn't hear. You must never doubt again. Use your strength and ability,' he begs. 'Soon there will be another master to take you on the next part of your journey. Don't mess this bit up for me! The master who is coming is much more senior than I. Don't doubt — just carry on. Go back and sleep now, so that you have the strength for tomorrow.'

Tuesday I go to see George. He is his usual smiling, slightly shambolic self. I notice that his eyes are avoiding my face. He starts his usual routine, hands on my head, as I lie on his couch.

'George, Anna says you are involved in Buddhism. Do you meditate?'

'Oh yes.'

'Forgive my asking, but what is it all about? Do you have visions, or what does it mean to you?'

'Well, it's difficult to say. If people are interested, there's a centre that deals with enquiries, I'll give you the name. If you could raise your knees, please.' He moves his chair to my side and shuts his eyes. That is the end of conversation.

Later, I get up to leave, feeling extraordinarily renewed and relaxed.

'Your spine is straightening out nicely. Here's the address of the meditation centre and please make an appointment for two weeks' time.'

This evening, I am going to listen to a woman who works with the voice lecture, at a church which is used for alternative forums, off Piccadilly. Her work is clearly well known, St James' Church is full. The speaker, Anne Peel, has spent several years working with Tibetan masters on the use of her voice, for what is called chanting. She makes an extraordinary sound.

Theoretically, I think I understand the significance of the voice as an expression of oneself, as an individual or as part of a larger group. Releasing a sound is an emotional experience, an aspect of giving vent to your feelings. That sound could heal, in some sense, seems a perfectly reasonable proposal. Tone, volume, cadence, all speak. From experience, it's clear that the quality of sound touches my feelings, and feelings are integrally involved in well-being. Then, singing as a group is strangely moving. So, I am interested in Anne Peel's work, as one way of exploring these issues. (Kiri Te Kanewa or Chrissie Hynde may make the point in other, more enjoyable ways, I think.)

Then, something else catches my attention. It's more interesting to me than her words, or the sounds she makes. Anne is sitting on a stool, at the front of the large church. The lights are dim and she is wearing dark-coloured clothing. But, as she shifts her weight, or as I turn and slightly alter the angle at which I see her, I notice a red beam of light at the base of her spine. The lighting is odd, I think, taking it to be some form of stage lighting. But, that cannot be the case, can it? Still the red beam of light shines in a long arrow from about the level of Anne Peel's coccyx. Once I have noticed it, it does not go away. It's like pain, I think. Then comes the certainty that it is pain, that Anne Peel suffers from a back condition and I am seeing it. Surely not?

Wednesday *The cloud land is empty. Then a deep ruffling in the sky and an older man appears. 'You have to choose now, will you go forward and take on this task? It is your destiny, but also your choice.'*

'I will go forward and take on the task. Who are you?'

'A master.' Then he leaves.

I wait. The form of George comes to me. He is in despair, unable to stand up straight, black and grey shadows surround him, and a heavy burden. Somehow, I am not surprised. Nor do I enquire. I comfort him.

Later, Wednesday *When I arrive at the pool, I see a strange thing: two bodies, two images of me — one in the swimsuit and one in the white shift. I try to reconcile them, but it is no use. I can feel the master calling, so give up and go to him instead. He speaks, 'It is done. You don't understand why. You are on the path.' Then he embraces me. But it is not him. It is somehow as if he draws the world in with his arms, and sends me back with the love and acceptance of the universe.*

Yet later, Wednesday *This time there is a new master waiting — M, he says his name is. The other, he tells me, was K and there are many masters looking after different aspects of my life. I ask if there are women.*

'Women too,' he answers with a special smile, 'you will meet soon. The next few days are to be restful — it is my job to help this.' So, I am being looked after, protected and loved. Even now, after all that has happened, it is not easy for me to accept what he says.

Thursday So much is happening in my everyday life. I am painting and exercising and feel utterly engaged on all levels. I feel life in a way I have not known before. Tonight, I visited the address George gave me, a Buddhist meditation centre. It was pleasant, but not, I felt, of especial relevance. It certainly did not explain what has been happening to me. We did two meditations. The first for beginners, then when they saw I was quite comfortable with meditation, I was invited to join the more advanced class. Actually, I gave up following the images and procedures they were prescribing and just allowed myself to go to my 'other' world.

I noticed a name on the centre's notice board — Sara Jones. I went to university with a Sara Jones, apparently she's a co-ordinator here; I wonder if it's the same person? I haven't seen her for at least twenty years.

There is not enough time and space to express the joy I feel. Physically though, I know I am becoming very tired. I am spending many hours every week, early, before anyone else is awake, and at night, in meditation.

Thursday, later *My body enters the pool, joyfully. What I think of now as my 'soul' leaves the body, playing in the water. I ask M for some practical respite. He says this place is my home, I can always come here. He sympathises with my tiredness, but points out that I have offered myself and that the work is great.*

Friday *I leave my body self peacefully in the water, with a book, while my spirit — it has occurred to me that it is my* 51 *spirit, not my soul — goes up and on. I find M in a grove of trees, which at the same time is a plain. It is extraordinary the quality of the other world to be a specific place, but also, simultaneously, not. We talk.*

Then M gently reminds me how much I have to do in the everyday world, the clearing (I am clearing out many of my material possessions) and the learning.

Saturday, 2 March Despite my joy, despite all that has happened, I cannot be rid of my doubt. I go looking for people who say they know about esoteric, psychic or spiritual 'things'. In particular, I have been given a set of insights into my own future which I question closely. Apparently, so I am told, one is never truly given much insight into one's own future, so why am I receiving it? What am I receiving?

Saturday night *I leave my body at the pool, reading. M is there, furious, with thunderbolts. 'You are being given so much information, how dare you doubt! And as for consulting other people, stop!' he rages. (The soles of my feet — in the physical world — are burning.) He says it doesn't matter how I meditate — sitting cross-legged or on a chair — I am quite strong enough to receive the message. He confirms information I have been given about my future work, but cautions that it is not to be all at once. Then he leaves.*

An extraordinary process unfolds around and over my eyes. Waves of colour, alternating with waves of darkness and light, wash over them. I understand that I am being prepared for a different sort of vision, because I will need it in my work. Perhaps I will sleep now.

I can't sleep. I have to go back.

Through the pool and on up. There is no-one there. I wander around a little and call out. M appears. There is another being

*with him. The newcomer is covered up so well that I am unable
to see his face. M introduces him. I can't make sense of his
name — D something. Finally, I settle on a version, D . . . i. He
(perhaps 'it' is more appropriate?) touches me, my shoulder,
then my arm. But his hand is not a hand. There is no flesh,
only bone. He is a skeleton. I feel no fear, only slight surprise,
then tiny feelings of revulsion.*

*I turn to M, but he has gone. D speaks. He says he is
checking whether I am OK to help him. I ask, is he OK to help
me? Yes, is the answer. I understand that I am to work with
death. I am given a little more information. It is difficult for
me to hold onto, to really understand what he says.*

Sunday, 3 March *I am met by M and D. M advises me to
learn from D.*

*'Embrace death in all its forms,' D says, 'because death
leads to life. All ends are beginnings.' He leaves.*

*For a while, there is nothing. Then there are colours — turquoise
and blue light, with a shape emerging from them. It is a Buddha
figure. The soles of my feet, in the physical world, are burning.*

*D returns. He seems sad, an almost tragi-comic figure. 'No-
one has reverence for death anymore,' he laments. I hug him,
feeling sorry for him. He says that after death, I will encounter
the life forces which will be much more difficult to handle. (I
don't understand, of course.)*

*I see many scenes, a gold Buddha in the sky, many different
places. Then the gold Buddha reappears. Now he seems to be
pulling me to him. Suddenly D speaks. He tells me there are many
gods and masters, and right now I am being pulled to the Buddha.*

*'Go!' So I do, for a while. Then the scene fades. I feel pain in
my chest, in my physical body.*

Monday *This morning upon my arrival, there seems to be a
staircase rising up from the pool. I follow it, only to be grabbed
by a huge black figure lurking on one side, while D stands on* 53

the other. Strangely, I am not afraid. I order the black one to leave me alone and go on up the stairs. They lead to a pleasant meadow, with a convenient garden bench where I sit down.

The black one addresses me, saying that he is death, doubt and all negativity, that he has been plaguing me in 'real life'. Then D, who has continued up with me, speaks, while the black one still hovers, huge eyes glowing, in the background.

D says, 'It is good that you am not afraid of him. That is how it must be, for then he is transformed into all positive qualities, just as I change from death to new life.'

While we are talking, I see the golden Buddha in the background, on my right-hand side, in the sky.

I ask, 'Am I to understand him, D, as part of Buddha?'

'Yes,' he answers,' he is one aspect.'

Then they are all gone.

I notice that the field is full of flowers, as a new figure approaches — a middle-aged woman, wearing a gown and a hood. Her name is A. She tells me she is motherhood and fertility. She is good to me. We talk. I lie on the ground, on my back, with the flowers rising above me into the sky. A says she will be with me always. She enfolds me in light, repeatedly. I press to know more detail about her.

In reply, she tells me I have been part of her before. How? 'As a healer' is all she will say. She is all healing and female skills. Then, repeating that she will be with me always now, and adding that there is one more teacher to come, she leaves.

Tuesday, late *I find myself in the field of flowers. A joins me, smiling. I lie down on the ground, on the flowers. Flowers are everywhere. It seems as if I am small and the flowers grow above me. Smiling always, A holds my hand for a while. 'Soon it will be time for your master to appear.'*

Again, I feel this is all too much for me — my mind is drifting, I am very tired. A advises sleep and leaves. I lie on

my back in the flowers, loving the beauty. Then it's time to
return to the pool, where I find my body asleep in the sun.

In the everyday world, I am constantly mulling over what is
happening to me. I have read very little about the esoteric.
Later I understand this is good and am forbidden to read
anything on any related subject unless I am told to do so
specifically. I know little about formal religion.

Many years ago, at university, I stumbled on the ancient
Taoist text, the *I Ching*, so esteemed by Jung and others. I
have read certain sections several times. Some sort of spirituality has always been part of me, whether its form has been
a love of trees or simply a sense of justice. But does that relate
to this? And if so how? And just what part, if any, is cranial
osteopathy playing in it all?

'George, we've had at least ten sessions now. What do you
think we've achieved, and is there more to come, or any need
to go on?'

'Well,' he hesitates, pulling words is like pulling teeth, 'Your
body has begun to unwind.' This is true, the third or fourth time
I saw him, his usual gentle movements resulted in a furious
spontaneous whirl of all my limbs, which he called unwinding.
He said it was a well-documented phenomenon. What I
noticed was that afterwards a great feeling of stillness seemed
to descend.

'We're working on your face, relaxing the right-hand side,
and matching the two halves.'

'Yes, you've made me much more aware of the difference
between the two sides of my face. But I think I've told you,
they always have been at least a little bit different. I do feel
the right-hand side is veiled in some way.'

'Well anyway, there's that, then your back seems steadier.
You seem to have reached a place where you feel stronger
now. Generally you seem better than when you came.'

'Yes, that's true. It's fantastic not working and I'm loving painting. And I do find meditation very interesting.'

I've told him what's happening. He's the only one I have talked to about it. Characteristically, he's greeted what I have told him — and I have told him most of it — phlegmatically. As if this sort of thing is prone to happen. The words he says do not reflect the bond I feel when he touches me. His hands seem to speak a different language, as he stands at my head holding my temples, or steadying my spine. Again, I wonder at the bowed image of him I see in my meditation. When I mentioned it before, all he would say was 'interesting'. I suspect, I know, that what he says is not the whole truth of what he thinks.

'George, what do you think is really going on in my meditation? How does it relate to reality?'

'Well,' he hesitates. Will he answer or not? 'OK, I think it is reality. Somehow, I don't know how, you seem to be having experiences that a lot of people spend a lot of time trying to get to.'

Silence.

'What makes you say that? What do you think I should be making of it all?'

'Look, you say you've seen me. Well, this isn't something I'd normally say, but a while ago there were some very difficult things that happened to me and it was Buddhism that saved me. Especially one particular teacher. And I guess I am still working with what happened, the aftermath in a way. So, it's right when you see me bowed. In some ways I am. Not on the surface of course, or all the time, but somewhere. I don't know why you see it.

'But it sounds to me as if you are accessing another level of reality — and that doesn't surprise me, because I take it for granted that this everyday level is just one level — that there are other levels where there are other beings, other realities. I don't know why you've been allowed to enter the other levels now. But I'm pretty sure that's what's going on.'

It's the longest speech I have ever heard from him on his philosophy. The only one.

'Who was the teacher? Is he someone at the Buddhist centre you told me about?'

'No, that's just the place I tell anyone who asks about Buddhism to go. It's a good enough place to start if you're interested.'

'Well, I've told you what I think. It's OK. I've been a couple of times, but I'm not particularly interested in going back. And actually I doubt whether I'd really want to get involved in Buddhism, although from the little I've seen it does seem to have a lot going for it. But I guess I find all those rituals rather off-putting and it's difficult to make sense of it.'

He looks away.

I hurry on, 'Anyway, if you felt you could say who's helped you as a teacher, I'd be really glad to know.'

'My teacher is Orgyen Rinpoche, but he's in France. He's written a few books though, you could have a look at those and see if anything takes your fancy.'

'I will, thank you.' He clearly wants to end the conversation, but I must go on. 'There's one other thing. Have you heard of Anne Peel? She seems quite involved in Buddhism.'

'Yes, I know her.'

'Well, I went to hear her a week or two ago. What struck me wasn't so much her voice, but a beam of red light I saw at the base of her spine. I didn't understand what it was at first, but then it seemed to me that she was in pain, a lot of pain, which she felt particularly at the base of the spine that evening. Does that seem like a crazy fantasy to you? What else would the red light have been showing me? Anyway, it wasn't as if I just saw it, I knew it. What do you make of that?'

'Michal, Anne Peel has a long-standing back problem. It fits with the rest that's happening to you.' And he turns away.

Chapter Seven

Teachers

March 1991 Orgyen Rinpoche. I'm rifling through the shelves at Compendium bookstore on the bridge at Camden Lock. They have the best selection of 'alternative', or is it 'esoteric'? books of any place I have come across, though the crush on the pavement outside is overwhelming. There is every description of facial ring — noses, lips and eyebrows, as well as multiple earrings on display. Green or purple hair shades are common, and black the uniform of the crowds on the street. But none of the more fashionable characters seem to come in here. So many of the books in the esoteric section seem to have clichéd titles, gushing references to 'Awakenings', 'Joy' or 'the Divine' . . . You can talk, I think.

There are three books by Orgyen Rinpoche. I buy one. It's very short and fairly easy to read. In parts, familiar almost. I'm not tempted by the meditation or practices described — partially open your mouth, curve the tongue backwards and gaze straight ahead with eyes semi-closed. But, I'd like to know more about the man.

Apparently, the teachings that he gives belong to a school that transcends sectarian limits and man-made barriers. It seems he is not setting out rules for the route to so-called enlightenment (however that is defined; it is not a state I had ever given any thought to before), but instead instructions for seeing. It seems that what I see, in meditation, and when I 'look', is different from everyday experience. Different perhaps from what other people see. Certainly from what I saw, or acknowledged, before. I want and need to understand it.

At the back of each book, there are a number of addresses. One in France, the home community of the Rinpoche (I've learnt that's an honorary title, meaning 'precious one'), several in other cities around the world, and one in London. Supporters of Orgyen Rinpoche. I send a postcard.

A couple of weeks later I receive a phone call. 'Hello, are you Michael Levin? I got your postcard.'

'Thanks for calling. Actually, it's Michal. I'd like to know more about Orgyen Rinpoche, can you help?'

'We're not a big group, but we do practice together regularly, and there's a newsletter, all the details are in that.' Apparently, there's a practice next week, I'm welcome to come.

I park carefully. I've never seen this north London square, almost a small park, before. It's unfenced, crossed by several paths, tall trees interspersed with street lights along the outside. The pavement is wet, and the winter gloom at 7.00 could be 11.00. I have left a babysitter at home to give me an evening out.

The front door to 57 opens onto the pavement, but there's a small sign behind one of the door's glass panels: 'Entrance through back,' with an arrow. Following the arrow, I open a gate into a plant-filled yard. There's a pine door, with panels again though which light shines, in the side wall of the house. I knock. No answer. Though I can hear voices inside. Knock again. Still no reply. So I turn the knob. Inside, rack upon rack of assorted, mostly well-worn shoes greet my eyes, and beyond them a bearded, well-padded looking man, with a string of beads around his neck, seated at a long pine table, deep in conversation with two women. The light is soft and warm.

'Welcome, I'm Humphrey,' he has a wide, kind smile. 'Take your shoes off and come in. So, what brought you here?'

'Well, I looked at a couple of Orgyen Rinpoche's books and I thought I'd like to understand what he was saying a little better.'

'Right, that's all it takes.' A meaningful silence follows, which they all observe, but I don't understand. 'You were attracted to him, then?'

'Well, you *could* say that . . . I'd like to know a little more.'

'We have all been drawn to him, in different ways. According to the teachings, sometimes you just have to hear the master's name and the connection happens. Are you going to see him?'

'Actually, that hadn't occurred to me. I thought I'd find out what I'm interested in by reading, or something similar. Presumably there are transcripts of his talks, or people who can explain the same things?' They seem to be looking at one another. Could Humphrey be trying not to smile? 'I'm just at the exploratory stage,' I finish.

'Well, you'll see. Rinpoche says that some students only need to see him once, to establish the connection, and others go on coming to all his teachings for years.'

'I saw him three times last year and I'm hoping to do the same this year. I'm off to France next weekend, to Majorca in September and America if I can in October, then maybe to France again at Christmas.' I hadn't noticed the entrance of the newcomer who announces these plans. He's a solidly built man, probably in his late thirties, wearing jeans and a dark shirt. Around his neck he has a series of trinkets (several up on Humphrey) and what I think I recognise as a Tibetan-style bag over his shoulder.

As he finishes speaking, the door opens again to admit a party of three. No-one takes any more notice of me.

They begin a heated discussion of which 'practice' to do tonight.

We move out of the room with the pine table into an inner hallway and enter a little room directly ahead. It's dark, with Tibetan, I think, pictures on the wall, and what I take to be a larger-than-life photograph of Orgyen Rinpoche occupying one entire wall. There's a scarf draped over a table lamp, creating a purple-tinged gloom. Humphrey goes to light a fat candle with a complicated pattern of wax drips down the side. A woman lights a stick of incense, and Teddy (who visited Orgyen Rinpoche three times last year) motions me to sit beside him on one of the cushions that form a circle on the floor. There are not enough prayer books — I think the name is appropriate — to go round, so I share with Teddy.

Then the chanting starts. It's all in Tibetan, I'm told, but there's a phonetical translation, or perhaps just a translation into Western script, beside the Tibetan. The voices of the group rise unselfconsciously, as the chant continues. Humphrey rings a bell from time to time. The sounds and the smell of the incense together have a certain mesmeric quality. Does this have anything to do with my meditation? Could I join a group like this?

I know the answer to the second question is no. But I don't know, for sure, the answer to the first question, though it seems unlikely. I am not uncomfortable with the proceedings, but not engaged either. One thing I do notice, though, is that the allegiance to Tibetan culture seems central to this group, and at the Tibetan Buddhist Centre I've visited, too. Of course many foreign cultures are interesting, the plight of different countries sad or compelling. But, I cannot imagine wanting to identify with Tibet as these people do, however I might wish to support it, or anywhere else. Then the chant is over.

I am glad to step out into the night air. To go home to my meditation in the silence in front of my uncurtained window. And to wake to the same in the early, early morning.

Wednesday 6 March *I lie down again in the grass, among the flowers. A comes. She sits beside me and holds my hand. I try to analyse her face and find I can't. She is wearing a hood and a wimple, that's as much as I can be sure of. She repeats several lessons that I have been taught. That I have to own my strength, that I have to take up my power. That it is the path and not the goal that matters. Finally, A reassures me that 'up here' is my home, as I feel it is. Finally I have found a place where I feel at home.*

Thursday *I am afraid this other world will want more of me. But I am drawn to A, although I try not to enter further into her world, and simply to meditate remaining 'empty', as the Buddhists teach. The flowers growing around me seem to rise taller and taller, until they become a ladder up into the sky. I know it is the way I must go, into the apparently empty blue above. I tell A, desperately, that I don't want to move up, I am not nearly ready. Gently, she says I have to, though I can come back. So, slowly up the ladder. With each step, the sky is filled with light, till I am consumed in a blinding embrace. I am broken up and integrated with the Light.*

Thursday, later *I sit with A for a few minutes, then the ladder grows and I have to climb it. Into the enormous Light. After a few moments, two dark shapes, Shadow figures, come forward, storming. I try to disregard them, but they stay. It seems they are part of the Light. (The marriage of the Old and the New Testaments comes to mind.) Then I understand, the Dark is an essential. From now on, this space, the space of the Light and the Dark, is where I have to work. I hardly begin to understand the implications. Then it is time to go back, down the ladder, past A, to the pool. Rejoin my body and leave.*

In the physical world, my head is throbbing and the soles of my feet are tingling.

Friday Past A. Up the ladder to the place of Light and Dark. A Shadow figure immediately materialises and ravages me. I am curiously impassive. My body, as always, is left at the pool, but the form I usually carry — the same shape as my body — is not there. I seem to be no more and no less than a 'space'. The Shadow is a cross between a huge man and a panther. It tears strips down me, savages me and still I stand impassive. Then, slowly, I begin to fill with Light, from my feet upwards Golden Light infiltrates me, defining my form, hesitating briefly at the top of my legs, but then quickly continuing.

A very old, grey-bearded man materialises ahead of me. He speaks, 'You are ready to start some work.' I see a Buddha in the corner of the frame.

'Am I to become a Buddhist?' I ask.

'It is a useful framework, all religions can be useful, you have them all,' is the matter-of-fact answer. He says that I am too tired to go on, I'm to return in the morning.

Saturday, early The field seems empty. Then, in a far corner I see the ladder of flowers. I hesitate. I am not sure whether I am going towards it or it is coming towards me. It is beside me, I mount the treads. The Light is very strong, as usual. Reaching the top, I do as I am told and lie down in the Light. It is like a 'booster' treatment.

The old man is there, beside me in the Light. I wonder who he can be — surely not God? When I ask, he tells me he is known by many names. For now he has become a Buddha. Suddenly, my consciousness is pricked by the knowledge that then, as always, the Dark force is there. The old man seems to know my thought. 'You wouldn't want it any other way,' he says, 'you are ready, for work. Soon it will come.' There is no elation. I am strangely heavy and flat.

Saturday *I ask A, 'Do I have to go forward?' In her presence, I feel comforted. I have come to feel love. I'd like to stay, in just that situation.*

'Ultimately, yes,' she answers. Then I see the ladder behind her, and the gold Buddha hovering in the sky. I realise that whatever my passing desires, I have already made the choice: sadly, slowly, up I go, to the Light, and the Dark.

The old man is waiting, sitting on an elaborate throne-like chair. He tells me, again, that I am ready to work — I am to pass on what I know to others. I am mystified — what do I know? Who would want to know whatever it is? Then I feel the Light beginning to enter into me. I see myself somehow as a glass or crystal container, filled with the purest liquid. It is for me to pour out the liquid, and somehow, as it flows out of the container, so it is refilled.

Then I see the Dark force close in around the glass. It grabs hold of the container. The glass breaks where the force closes around it, but the pieces do not fall away, nor are the contents spilled. The Dark recedes, only to come again. Meanwhile, the glass has reformed. This time it is stronger. It only cracks, it doesn't break. Again and again the same attempt is repeated, but the glass seems to become stronger and stronger, until it is absolutely unbreakable.

I and the container are still one, but before the gold Buddha now. Then a conversation I had with A, earlier, comes into my mind. She told me that all the characters I have encountered are part of me. But that they also have objective reality. I understand now. The scene dissolves. I am back with the old man alone, with the Light from above streaming into me. It is time to go.

Sunday *I go to the pool as usual, but find that it is no longer water. Instead, it becomes a sort of implement which, as I stand there wondering, crashes over my head. I have a fleeting vision of my body being left behind, before I find myself high up in a* *strange mountainous place, beside a huge overhanging rock. Which way am I to go? And where is this place? On one side, there is a little hollow in the rock filled with muddy water. Nothing invites me. So I turn in the other direction, to the left; though I cannot see anything at all ahead, this seems the only way. I take it.*

Then the old man appears. I am not exactly delighted to see him. Somewhere far in the distance I begin to see a 'golden building'.

'Just what is all this?' I ask the old man, who is walking beside me.

'An initiation,' he replies, 'you are starting a journey.' I look closely at him, as if for the first time, and instantly recognise his face. He resembles a much revered Tibetan lama of the past, whose picture I bought recently because it struck such a strong chord with me. I ask his, the old man's, name. V, is the answer. The coincidence of the similarity between the faces sets me wondering again — what is all this? Doubt and the need to understand enter. Instantly, V disappears. Then I reaffirm, and mean it, my desire to follow with all my heart whatever is being put before me. With that statement of trust and belief, V reappears and we continue.

We come to a deep chasm filled with water. I must jump in and swim across. It is terribly cold. I hate cold, but there is no time to react, I am pulled down into the icy depths. There is no fear. What will be will be. And I reach the other side. V has walked across the water. Soon afterwards, a chasm with a rope strung across it appears. This is a little more difficult — I am afraid of heights — but reaffirming my trust in God, I manage it. Then another chasm, wider, but now it is easier. Then a third, with a terrible fat snake at the end. No problem. I step over the snake.

V praises me. We are at a mountain pool. It is beautiful and clear. He says we have to stop here for the time being. I touch the water with my feet (which aren't there). I long for the comfort of A. V says I may call her. I do and she comes into my head, with love and reassurance, but only briefly. Then it is time for me to leave too. I crash back through the barrier, the same way that I arrived, with a fleeting vision of my body hurriedly leaving the pool to join me.

Monday, 11 March I wake at 5.30am, reluctant to get up and meditate. Want to sleep for another hour. An awful pain develops at my rib apex. Know I have to get up. Within instants of sitting, the pain goes.

Again, the shape that previously was the pool, crashes over me and I find myself beside the mountain pool, where last I was. It is rather desolate. I think V is there, but I can't see him. I paddle in the pool. It is both beautiful and hideous, now I know V is not there. My feet go cold, they are freezing, then warm again. I don't know if I can endure this pattern. I look closely into the water — it is full of horrible crawly creatures, but under my gaze it clears. I feel I am being asked what I want to do. The answer comes: go forward. So I set off with a rucksack on my back.

Soon, I face a huge crevasse which I have to climb down and then up again. This happens several times. Past a rotting corpse of an enormous animal. It's very bleak. But there is also a particular kind of beauty. V joins me. He is elusive. I feel lonely, I call A. She comes, then D arrives too. I am pleased to see him. My pleasure triggers a question from V. Do I wish to leave my body now? I think he is asking whether I want my life to end, to face physical death. Immediately I answer no, I do not want to leave my children. Also, I have not yet done what I must do.

A has left us. We are coming to the Light and D leaves too, just before we step into it. V tells me I am facing my work. I experience the most beautiful sensation, walking into the Light. We walk some way. I am diffused by light. At one stage, taking handfuls of light, I reach down and stuff it into the chest of my body which is sleeping beside the pool. I am conscious of a dimming on my right-hand side, the brightness is not even.

I have a feeling that this time, or place, links back to Egypt. I sense, or remember myself, in a place of great stone slabs, invoking enormous powers. 'Taming evil' are the words that come to mind. V says it is enough for now.

Tuesday *Into the pool, and then I find myself back in the place built of slabs of stone. Linked with Egypt. V is there. He urges me to take up my power: there are two black snakes wriggling on the ground, he tells me to grasp them, to hold them up. It is horrible. Awful. They are fat, firm and venomous, I am sure. Black with yellow mouths. I bend to catch hold of them, and instead of turning in my grasp to bite me, or wriggling out of my hands, they behave like rather unstable rods, wobbling in the air as I pick them up. Finally, it is too repulsive — I fling them away.*

Again, V urges me, 'You must take up your power.'

'But how?' I ask, 'What do you mean?' Over and over again, for no particular reason, I say that I do not want any sort of prominence.

Disregarding what I am saying, he tells me to call forth snakes from the shadows, all the snakes. So I do. Huge numbers seem to come from nowhere and writhe before me. Automatically, I flick my hand dismissively. The movement destroys them in a flash of fire.

In the space where the snakes were, there is a clear, almost singing cool. It is as if it has been cleansed. I don't understand.

Then V tells me that 'flaming evil' is what I am to do. I am really concerned. I have been through the illusions of 'fighting' my idea of social inequality or 'wrong' (if that's what he means) in my journalistic life. It is a power trip and I don't wish to go on it. V says that the effects of this power are quite different — and that I have to use it. I feel a movement in my body.

67

'It is a force,' V says. I am half-excited. I can hardly think about power, snakes, or evil. I don't see how it can be right, but perhaps it is? How can I know?

I prostate myself on the floor of the stone place. A kind of 'force' is moving within me. I am faintly radiating. Vibrations are starting in my physical, real-life body. I am not sure if power is being beamed at me, or if I am giving it off. There is a problem with my right side — I must go back to the pool.

Tuesday, later I go straight to A's field, the flower field. I find her and ask her to come with me. Together, we go to the cave of stone slabs. She explains that it is not her place; joy and fertility are her domain. But there is work for me here, she says. V appears and asks me to follow him. A comes too.

We go to a beautiful, though slightly menacing, pool set in the rocks. I am to immerse myself. The water fills me with 'sparkling'. When the effect diminishes, I step out of the water. I do not know what is happening, let alone its significance. A leaves us and I follow V down a narrow and treacherous rock passage. We reach a tiny black cave.

'You are to spend three days here,' he tells me, then leaves.

It is very dark, but my body is Light, through and through. Two tiny creatures, like miniature winged horses, appear, and pull a line from the end of each of my eyebrows, up through the sides of my head, to make a funnel shape, leading down to the crown of my head. A massive dose of Light pours into the funnel. Afterwards, I am truly very radiant, sitting peacefully in the cave. When I feel I have to go back to the physical world, because I am tired, somehow only a part of me seems to return to my body, while yet another part remain in the cave.

Wednesday, 13 March, 6.45am I wake before 5.00am, but lie in bed, my thoughts roaming. Then to the pool, past the flowered plain, through the domain of Light and shadow into *the cave — where I still am. Part of me, or is it me? is still there and has not left.*

In the physical reality, my feet are tingling slightly; then my physical body starts twitching — slight but distinctive twitches. As it goes on, my spine becomes straighter and straighter, but with no sense of stiffness. Instead, I feel physical ease, or lightness. The 'me' in the cave is relatively motionless, a light body in a small triangular space. I imagine my chakras as lights coming on from the bottom to the top. When I reach the top, light begins to flood into my corporeal body. The body in the cave becomes more and more radiant with light, which seems to push the walls of the cave back. My corporeal body rocks from side to side. I feel increasingly tranquil.

A Buddha image floats across the picture of me in the cave. My neck is a little uncomfortable. I can't quite settle the position of my head. Then it is time to stop — the light is fading. I switch off the chakras. The sexual chakra resists, fleetingly (my physical desires? I acknowledge them, sympathise and the light goes off directly). My body in the cave stays where it is, cross-legged on the floor, but where before the head was bowed, now it is upright. Again, some part of me leaves the cave to go to the pool, while my main, non-physical self remains in the cave.

Afterwards, I feel as if I have had cranial osteopathy, or something similar. I stand very straight on the floor.

Chapter Eight

Whose Will?

March 1991 My meditation has become immensely complex. New characters have entered and the guise in which I see myself has changed. I seem to exist in two forms. Much of the time now my image is golden in colour, or there is a person who in some way relates to me who is golden. So, there is me, in my bodily form, and then there is the Golden One. I know the old man as V, and have to come to recognise him as a most benevolent teacher. I find him most often under a tree, in a place with rich grass covering the ground, close to the edge of a cliff, a glorious ocean below. Trees grow in scattered clumps and birds of every subtle colour weave through the air.

What I think of as the Force is common now. It is an actual physical force that runs through my body, or parts of my body, at certain times. It seems associated with realignment. On occasion, while in meditation, I have been led to hold a picture postcard in my hand and watch it flutter simply from the energy running through me. Once, the fluttering was accompanied by a loud crackling noise. All this I write in my notebooks, trying not to need to understand it.

Am I to be a healer? I have started to wonder. I don't see how, but that would be an explanation, of sorts, of events. In meditation, I ask V.

'You could try healing,' comes the answer.

'Well, if I'm not to be a healer, but am to work in some way, what exactly am I to do?'

'You are allowing the Power through you, you are accepting your Power back, soon you will hold the Light too, then truly you will See. You are to be a Seer, but what else I cannot say.'

I do not know what to make of it. I run through my friends and acquaintances — who would understand? Who would I dare reveal all this to? I am sure they would think I had lost my grip. Except maybe Anna, but I don't feel it's right to talk to her. George seems to have said all he can. Instead, I go to see Jeanette Joliff. What did she expect when she suggested I meditate? Did she know this would follow? What's going on?

She looks at me calmly, crosses and re-crosses her plump, stockinged legs, 'It will unfold, it's God's will,' she says. 'Don't be afraid — just let it happen.'

'Do you know what's happening to me,?'

'I know a little, but I can't tell you, except that everything will be all right, just let it happen, stop worrying.' She bends to write her notes, in her neat longhand, adding 'These are interesting times!' With that, she hands me a packet of homeopathic pills. Constitutional remedies, to strengthen my general well-being, a sign that it's time to go, but I have one last try.

'Jeanette I'm not even religious.'

'That doesn't matter, just trust.'

'What about the physical stuff, are all the things I am experiencing just part of this process, whatever it is, or are they symptoms of something else?'

'Don't worry,' there's a note of emphasis in her voice, 'It'll be all right. There're very few people who have experienced what's happening to you — be sure now to write it all down.'

The ample receptionist wishes me God bless again, and it feels good — I don't know whether to laugh or cry — can all this be for real?

Wednesday, 27 March, 11.30pm I prostrate myself on the ground before V. 'Please help me. Guide me.' As I lie there, I see a cloud of some sort, mushroom shaped, emerging from my body. Energy? I can't identify the colour, there are many colours, but none. I am aware though of a rosy band close to the edge. Then the mushroom flower, as it has become, detaches to float over the world. In its place, another grows.

Meanwhile my physical body, sitting on the side of my bed, has been doing gentle circular movements , which become less and less, until I am still and the Force takes over again to pull me upright.

There is something beside me. I look down. It's a snake. I recall being in the stone room, with V ordering me to pick up two black snakes and use the power. It comes to me that the snake is wisdom, whatever else it may be. A vision comes of myself as an Egyptian with a golden snake band wound round my head. A healer, a seer. What did I see? I saw into people.
The vision fades and I am back at V's feet. I look at the snake. It has become a golden cobra in front of me. I am afraid and uncomfortable, but there is no question of moving. Gradually the feelings lessen, though I am still most uneasy.
'Place the snake around your neck.' I hear V's voice with great reluctance. It is only as an act of faith in him that I am able to bend, lift the golden snake and put it around my neck, concentrating all the time on V so as to contain the horror of what I am doing. It hangs there, heavy. I am so aware of it, but also that my absolute fear is lessening.
Then the serpent seems to float in and out of existence. At times, I know it is there, or think it is there, but it has become weightless. 'Go to the seashore,' V orders, and so I do, still with the cobra around my neck. It is lovely by the shore. I am at peace and present, even with my strange adornment, or companion.

Suddenly the snake is no longer around my neck, but dancing in the air in front of me. A magic golden, dancing snake, and we are in some way friends.

A sharp pain grows in my left shoulder, real pain in my corporeal body. The snake floats around to my back and bites the shoulder blade, digging deep into it to reach the pain. There's no immediate help, but the snake says it will come. Then I am told to stand up (my physical body) which I do, to move my arms up and down, around my head in every way, exploring all dimensions. When it is over, the Force pulls my body down to rest. Relief. The pain is gone. V says to sit, in the physical world, cross-legged on the floor, so I make the shift. Shaking and twitching takes over.

Later, when I am quiet again, I see myself sitting in front of V. Looking down on the ground before me, I see a tiny, golden snake ring. I pick it up, as V tells me to, and watch it grow in my hand to become the real thing. I suspect it is a lesson, but struggle to formulate the meaning. I am very tired. It's time to leave, V says.

Thursday, 6.55am *Peaceful, sitting at V's feet. The Force pulls me upwards. At my feet, I see the small gold snake again. It stretches out like a tiny river of gold, disappears, and reappears slightly larger, as a cobra again, rearing up on my left-hand side. I recognise again the swaying movement of the serpent's raised body — it is the same movement I have sometimes found my physical body making, or being made to do, by the Force.*

'Put the snake around your neck again,' V suggests. It's heavy, then light, then heavy again. Anxiously, I concentrate on V. Now the snake puts its mouth over its tail and is a perfect circle around my neck. For some reason, this increases my anxiety. I long for the snake to dance in the air and at the same time wonder about the mythological significance of the shape it forms with its tail in its mouth.

73

Then the creature begins to have 'radiations'. Instead of being just a snake, it seems to become largely a band of energy, still around my neck but a couple of feet above the body, radiating upwards. It forms a very strong wall of radiation. Blood begins to spurt from two, three, four places on my shoulders where the wall reaches down and touches my body. The blood gushes out in mushroom-like fountains. I wonder if it is energy, because it does not seem to spill or run over anywhere. Then the colour of the 'blood' turns to blue. I feel sick in my corporeal stomach, a very strong physical sensation.

The fountains change back to red, and some flowered bushes seem to be sprouting from the place where the fountains emerge from my body. Now there are two flower covered bushes growing from the base of my neck. They rise and rise, they are taking my body over. Is this a death?

V says it is time to put my body in the earth. There is no emotion. My head must go in too. The earth opens to accept me. Now in the place where I was sitting there are only two beautiful bushes, live, growing and covered with buds. I cannot find my consciousness under the earth. I am no more. There was no struggle. The plants are beautiful. Soon the buds will open — they do. Inside each is a tiny image of me as the Golden One. The whole picture is extraordinary.

A faint vibration begins to grow in the air. As if responding to the sound, the tiny figures at the hearts of the flowers seem to join together into the image of me and grow. I grow and grow, towering into the air. I become a huge giant, overshadowing V. He smiles.

'That is your strength, be careful how you use it. Now come back.'

Slowly, I reduce to normal size, till I am sitting beside him again, perhaps just a little smaller than before. There is radiant white light all around me. Time to go.

Thursday, 11.30pm 'Golden radiant one,' V smiles, as I *prostrate myself on the ground before him. We sit together and enjoy the loveliness all around. Then the small golden snake appears again at my feet, and almost simultaneously I find the serpent with its tail in its mouth around my neck. V tells me to stroke it. I expect it to an unpleasant sensation, but instead discover it is smooth gold. Then there's another live snake swaying on my left-hand side. 'Stroke it too,' V says. This is a little more difficult, but I do, repeatedly.*

The snake, which I see as a female, lays its hooded head on my arm. Suddenly, without warning, it seems to change, and strikes out at me, biting close to my heart. I don't appear to feel anything, but say to V in some perplexity, 'What's going on?'

'Nothing,' he replies, 'nothing at all.'

Well, nothing has happened to me, it is true. The snake has struck and absolutely nothing has happened to me. My simple mind tries to make out if this is the meaning of the event — that in one part I am greater than the snake, it cannot harm me? I cannot grasp what is meant. We start to move on, but I'm too tired and have to return to the pool.

Friday, 8.05am Joining V, the snake is there too. I am golden and *radiant. Not exactly pleased to see the snake, but I will accept whatever I have to. I am feeling low. The Force pulls me upwards with my breath. It is a good feeling, though I am still sad. Suddenly, the snake darts forward and bites my heart, she eats and eats, leaving the cavity empty. What is going on? I collapse onto my back. Another death. I am not going to resist. What is the snake — good or evil? Triumphant, she stretches herself out over my body. I have given up. Gleefully, she urinates and defecates on me. Surely I am not expected to put up with this? I jump up and rush down to the sea, to wash. I realise that it is impossible to make sense of all this — it is beyond logical analysis. Perhaps I will understand it in another way. Or not.* 75

When I return, the snake has gone. On V's instruction, I move my physical body to sit cross-legged on the floor. I feel warmth radiating from my back. Great shaking and twitching takes hold of me, including my head and neck. (I have had excema at the back of my neck for many years, sometimes more, sometimes less. Now, meditating often irritates it and this last week it has been particularly aggravated.) I begin to cry. On and on. Afterwards, I am clearer.

Because he asks, I tell V my crying is the pain of wanting earthly happiness, not this. I realise I am being self-pitying, but cannot stop. My life seems so strange, I complain. He is furious. 'Look around! Look at the beauty! How can you feel empty or joyless? Relax, do nothing except the jobs it is your duty to do. Stop searching so frantically,' he orders. I sit a little more peacefully, and then the Light comes down onto me. It is very good.

Am I, as the Golden One, to die now? I am, or can, V says, or will take up 'the body of Light' — that is, integrate with the Light. What does it mean in terms of my physical life? Is he talking about physical on-earth death? It sounds as if death, ordinary death on earth, may be a possibility. I am afraid. Does it have to be so extraordinary?

'Can't I have some ordinary life?' I ask.

'No, not on your path,' V replies, leaving. I sit for another few seconds. The Light fades to a single beam and I hear a voice. It tells me that the beam will stay with me.

Saturday, 8.40am *As I go up to V, I realise the serpent is with me, she is holding onto my heart. I prostrate myself before V, as usual, and she lets go, lying down on the ground. V tells me to go to the sea, leaving the snake behind. It is beautiful and calm.*

The Force pulls my physical body upwards and I shake. Now it seems appropriate to sit on the floor. My lower back aches on the left-hand side. On and off, I have a deep ache in my right ear. As soon as I move onto the carpet, huge, wild shaking begins in my body. It is followed by the need to move my arms up and down. There's a swirling sensation in my head, accompanied by darkness and light. I am hot, have been hot ever since the Force came as I was sitting on the bed. I imagine the heart and base chakras of my physical body as open. From my heart, I try to give out love, peace and light.

From time to time, I see the Golden One and the sea. As the Golden One, the serpent comes to me, dancing before my eyes, it dissolves into lines of light on the sea. Peace comes to my physical body, with one or two big breaths. I am standing on the sand, the snake has come down to earth beside me and seems to rest, coiled by my feet. I pick it up tenderly and hold it to me as I go to join V. All pain has left my back. Time to go back.

Afterwards, I notice that my right eye is very big, much larger than the left one. This has happened before. Random thoughts: first, about cranial osteopathy. I have experienced an energy there which the osteopath moves within me, but the Force which I experience in meditation replaces that altogether. It is of a different order, much stronger, much more intense. Also, I wonder about the serpent. Previously, I considered whether in some way she represents my ego. Now what strikes me is the transformation — in her and in me dealing with her.

Saturday, 9.45pm *I approach V, carrying a small basket which contains the serpent. It is rather as if she is an infant, asleep, and I am terribly careful not to disturb her, partly because of the hassle that will result from her being awake. I prostrate myself on the ground before V. I know there is no other way for me, I could not be different. But I am afraid I am too weak to follow my path.*

77

The Force has been pulling my physical body upright. V tells me to sit on the floor. I start to shake and sob. My arms move all around my head. At one point, I seem to be massaging the area around my heart chakra, and almost screaming, silently. I am very hot, the activity is fast and furious. I am rubbing my 'third eye', then pulling 'demons' or 'impurities', as I think of them, out of my head.

At the same time, I see my golden self prostrate on the ground before V and a white light entering me. V says simply that the Force is working. Then my legs begin to shake. Finally, my corporeal body is still. *As the Golden One, I turn to V and say, but with less vehemence than before, 'I am afraid I am too weak to do what I am doing.'*

He reassures me, 'Your foundations are being strengthened.'

Almost immediately, I am asleep and as I sleep V sings to me, a curious high-pitched song. I do not hear the words, and anyway who is it who is observing what is going on? How am I able to report watching myself asleep?

As the song ends, there is a movement from the basket on the ground beside me. The snake leaves the basket and rears up, growing very tall. She seems to be checking all over and around the Golden One for 'enemies'. At one point, she leans over the Golden One's face, with great tenderness, before moving towards V, who embraces her like a much beloved woman. She sits on his lap and speaks in his ear. Together they watch me, the Golden One, wake. 'It's time to go,' V says very gently. 'Take the serpent with you to help you.' And we go. To the pool, to my body. The golden snake wraps itself around my waist.

I know that this existence dominated by meditation is curious, but it is also imperative. I am drawn to it several times a day, some days. I have no desire to look for work, or do anything beyond what I am doing. I am lonely, I long for someone human to share it with — but who would want to, or be able to, share this? Beyond that, I am peaceful and quietly happy. Painting is a joy, pictures, with names, come. Perfecting my tiny world, I feel a little constrained in the city; I miss regular access to the country, so I treat myself to a ride. Having spent my first thirteen years in Africa, horse riding is something I learnt to love early, though I rarely indulge it now.

I drive to a riding stable in Hampshire. The thrill of the space almost makes up for the discomfort of driving (do I dislike driving more than ever?). I mount a beautiful, highly strung liver chestnut and work in the large outside menage. She bucks with the excitement of the raw morning, which I share. It is a boundless pleasure to be at one with an animal again, part of a much larger unit, thinking and feeling in a different way, trying to read the chestnut's mind and mood, to steady the wildest of her temperament. How blessed I am.

But my mind, ever active, would like to discuss what is happening to me in a rigorous, discursive format. Not for my experiences to face disbelief or dismissal, nor to be fawned over as marvellous or magical, but for them to be talked about, properly discussed. Then the name Sara Jones comes up in my meditation. *Go and see Sara Jones.* Is that the Sara Jones whose name I saw on the notice board at the Buddhist centre? The Sara Jones I knew briefly at university was a tall elegant girl, with long auburn hair. If she is involved with the Buddhist organisation, perhaps she can shed some light on my meditation experiences. Interesting that the meditation is instructing me to contact her. Is it a subconscious desire, masquerading as meditation?

23 March Sackville Road is a nondescript street in north London. The buildings are small and a modern block of low-cost housing rises in the background. Typically of London, a few roads away there are comfortable Victorian terraces, 79 where the streets are lined with tall trees. Investigation proved it was the same Sara Jones I used to know, and she's delighted to see me. Apparently, she's a psychotherapist now. I find that hard to imagine. But then how would I describe myself?

The woman who comes to the door oozes warmth, which emanates from her like a blanket. Lines that were spare at nineteen, have gentled into curves now, more than twenty years later. But there's the same openness and sweetness in her face, along with this quality of enfolding one into her embrace. Do her patients feel this? I wonder as I follow her up the stairs to the first floor sitting room.

'Don't mind Podge,' she says, scooping a large black and white cat off one of the two armchairs by the fire. 'He's very old and deaf. Do sit down.' The room feels a little like a country cottage, with old-fashioned cotton lace curtains at the windows and a white cotton cloth bearing the crisp lines of an iron on a pleasing old wooden table in the corner.

Sara brings tea with chocolate biscuits.

'I remember how sweet you were to me at university. Do you remember that night when you found me crying in the kitchen of our Hall, and you made me supper? What happened to you after that? I don't remember seeing much more of you.'

'Oh, lots of things,' I answer. I am much more interested in hearing about her, than reminiscing about my past. Is it calculating of me? I want to find out how much, if anything at all, I can tell her of what is happening to me and to have some sort of background from which to evaluate her response. It isn't a thought-out strategy, but it is the case. 'Tell me about you. I saw your name at the Buddhist centre, running voice training workshops was it? Sounds great, I'd be keen to do some work with my voice at some point. What's happened to your own singing, and what're you doing now?'

A long story follows. Sara shifted from classical music and her training as a putative opera singer to jazz. But immediately after university, she did a two-year post-graduate training as a social worker, specialising in psychotherapy, simply because she wanted a professional qualification behind her before trying her hand as a professional musician. She says she also knew that one day she would return to take it further. Then she became a professional saxophonist, travelling the world with a group who did rather well.

All that changed when a family disaster, the suicide of a beloved sister diagnosed for many years as a schizophrenic, struck. It sparked a search for meaning and comfort. Sara gave up music and returned to further training as a psychotherapist, and to take up the discipline full time. Simultaneously, she turned for spiritual comfort to Buddhism. For twelve years now, she has worked with the Buddhist centre where I saw her name. She has never married, or had children, but her present long-term partner is also a Buddhist.

At the Buddhist centre, Sara became close friends with an older woman called Comptesse de la tour de Chene. Dorothy de Chene, as she was commonly known, combined a devotion to Buddhism with a whole range of esoteric and other interests. She was an art historian, a specialist in Episcopal embroidery, a member of the Spiritualists of Great Britain and deeply involved in colour therapy.

Sara has to interrupt her story to explain to me what colour therapy is. Apparently, it is the study and use of colour to interact with the emotions and also for physical healing. The therapy is based partly on the premise that colours have a vibrational frequency; that is, the notion that as energy they emit a frequency, which can be used for treatment.

Accustomed to the Buddhist concepts of energy and working with your energy, Sara was fascinated by Dorothy's energy work. For the last year, she has been doing a part-time course, with a series of teachers, on colour, exercise, music and meditation. I'm not sure exactly what the focus of the course is, but then things New Age do tend to elude me. What the outcome of the course will be is similarly unclear. But, fortunately, my own experiences are teaching me a little caution. I can accept that this course might be useful to Sara, or that I might not understand what it's about, or even the possibility that it is of no long-term use, but important to Sara at the moment. Or something completely other.

Six months ago, sadly Dorothy died. It was a painful, slow death from cancer. Sara was deeply moved by the dignity and spirituality with which she handled her death. It seems that Dorothy worked through the process in an almost textbook Buddhist manner. (I am not sure exactly what that is, but I don't want to interrupt again.)

Sara is working as a therapist and also a lecturer in psychotherapy at a well-known therapy centre specifically for women. At the moment, she is involved in a new project on brief psychotherapy. Eating disorders and sexual abuse are areas she specialises in. I am impressed. She sounds pretty competent in her sphere.

'Where does Buddhism fit in?' I ask.

She pauses, 'Oh, it's the centre of my life, I love the Dharma,' she says a glint of tears in her eyes. Dharma means Truth, I recall. 'It just seems so important to work for the benefit of all beings.'

I remember the words I have heard said at the end of each Buddhist practice,

> By the power and truth of this practice, may all beings have happiness and the causes of happiness, may all be free from sorrow and the causes of sorrow, may all never be separated from the sacred happiness which is soulless and may all live in equanimity, without too much attachment and too much aversion. (Or almost that.)

I was touched by the beauty of those simple phrases when I heard them.

Apparently, neither the form of the religion, with its complex rites of worship in a foreign language, and obviously culturally conditioned visualisations, or the notion of devotion due to a guru whom you take on as your teacher — a concept I find particularly difficult — worry her unduly. However, she is clearly well versed in the philosophical aspects of Buddhism, has extensive reputable experience as a psychotherapist and other esoteric interests. Above all, I am conscious of her sweetness and her genuine care for others. I can tell her what has been happening to me.

Chapter Nine

Then

'Well,' I said, 'you asked how I came to be at the Buddhist Centre, and I rather dodged the question, but only because I wanted to hear what's been happening to you first.' I explain how eager I am to talk, to try to make sense of what has been happening to me. And how investigating Buddhism was just a way of trying to explore this. Sara smiles encouragingly. I can just see what a sympathetic therapist she must make.

'What's been happening?' She asks the obvious question.

'Partly to do with meditation, and partly to do with sight, all issues of sight, I guess,' I explain. 'For example, I may be deluding myself, but I think I can sometimes see what I can only call energy.'

'What do you mean?'

I tell her the story of Anne Peel, the voice worker, or chanting lady as I think of her, of whom Sara has heard. 'Since then, I have learnt how to control what I see to some measure, and even, I think, to understand or read it, up to a point.'

Sara is silent. 'That's incredible, I've never known anyone that's happened to, but of course there are loads of people who make all kinds of claims about seeing energy. There're so many questions I want to ask, but tell me first about things happening to you connected with meditation.'

'This is hard for me to say, hard for me to really get hold of,
84 except it's completely real for me. Real in a way I can't

explain. You see, I started to meditate, not that it was anything I was even remotely interested in before, and I entered another world. With people, or beings, presences anyway, and events, and what I think of as teachings, but I can't exactly formulate what I'm being taught. Sometimes I hardly even understand what is happening.'

Sara is silent, momentarily lost for words, then, 'What sort of meditation? What do you do and who taught it to you?'

'I see this homeopath from time to time — she's been helpful on children's things, and a few others — anyway, she's the one who insisted that I try when I stopped work. She told me to start by concentrating on the chakras, from the bottom up, in a particular way — nothing special. That's when it started, but I hardly knew it had, it was so gradual. Then she gave me an image, and told me to concentrate on it, and that really started the journey. It brought the first being and everything went from there.'

'Michal, that's absolutely amazing, when did it connect with being able to see energy?'

'Oh, quite soon after the meditation started, it's all linked, it's as if I'm being prepared for something in some way.'

'What sort of things happen in your meditation?'

'So much it's hard to say. You see I find I want to, or I have to, meditate at least twice every day, and masses seems to happen.' I tell her that there are all sorts of different presences, with particular roles in teaching me, different places, and a great deal about Light.

'I could go on and on, and it feels as if this is only the beginning. At the moment, there's all this stuff about Power and taking up my power and working with it — I know it sounds ridiculous — and work with a snake, which is somehow symbolic. It's beautiful and extraordinary and has brought me great peace and happiness, in its way.

'But on the one hand, I don't want to attach too much significance to it. Obviously it's important to me, but quite likely it's nothing more than something, a phase, I'm going through at the moment. On the other hand, I'd like to understand it as best I can, to make the most sense of it.

'Clearly, when it started I found myself looking at it analytically, exploring it from what I know of a Jungian perspective, or a Freudian one, but none of that seemed to make much or enough sense. I don't think it is my unconscious fantasising, I can see elements which could correspond to archetypal figures, or ways in which you could say I'm connecting with the collective unconscious. But, fundamentally, I simply can't see what the source of it all is, nor can I explain the form. What do you make of it? Does it seem possible that I could be, to put it bluntly, going nuts?'

'No, absolutely not. You're not going nuts in any way. What's happening to you is obviously very extraordinary and special. Perhaps because I've spent so long working in the Buddhist tradition, it doesn't seem so strange to me. We're taught to do visualisations, to imagine things happening, we're given figures to see. For example, there's Tara, who could correspond to the female being or presence you are describing, and all sorts of different deities who have different powers. We learn to do visualisations aimed at filling ourselves with light and healing.

'But what seems amazing to me is that you're telling me these things are just happening to you. You obviously don't know anything about visualisation, or deities, and you're seeing things happen spontaneously — that's amazing. They're happening to you directly, without any teaching, or without any attempt to make them happen, even without your understanding what's happening. From what I've learnt over the years that's very special indeed. You must have earned this in some way — it must be your karma, the result of your past lives.'

Past lives rings a bell, but I am not going to bring that subject up now.

She's going on, 'You need to be helped and looked after — it must be very frightening — and if there is anything I can do, I will. I think you should talk to someone who knows a lot more than I do.'

'Well, you make it sound so incredible. It's not really. In a funny way it's very ordinary. I can't believe it's something very special, except that it's important to me right now. I can't imagine anyone else would be interested. All I've been trying to do is find someone who could help to make a little sense of it, you know I come from a very strong rational, logical tradition, which is hard to just let go. But I've sort of agreed, in my meditation, not to look for books to try and make sense of it. It's good knowing that anything that happens really is authentic and not the result of someone else's experience I've read. I can't help doubting, though. But I am better now than I used to be. It's wonderful to talk about it to you, I'm so grateful.'

'Please talk to me anytime. I'm fascinated, apart from anything. But there are people you could talk to who know more than me.'

'Who would be interested, or know more? Also, it might not seem it because I've just blurted all this out to you, but I'm not really keen to go round talking about it. It seems as if it's either boasting — amazing things are happening to me — or it's advertising I'm going nuts. I feel I should be very careful about talking about all of this.'

'Yes, I understand — well, I can't really understand because it's not happening to me, but it must be terribly confusing to be going through. All the same, it's really important, I can't impress that on you enough. I think you should talk to my teacher about it, Tsering Rinpoche.'

My face must have fallen, because she adds, 'Dorothy had a great friend, a medium called Iris Malcolm, who channelled a spirit called Ree-mor. Iris did a lot of work with the Spiritualists Association; and she wrote a rather good book about what it was like living in the spirit world and ordinary everyday reality at the same time. You could go to see her, she's retired, in Brighton I think.'

'Oh gosh, that seems very extreme, I'm not a medium or anything remotely like, surely it would be presumptuous to go and talk to her on the basis of a few months unusual meditation?'

'Don't be silly, something is happening to you, why not try going to talk to Iris? I'm sure she'd be pleased to see you, or if you call her and explain a little on the phone, she can always say no if she doesn't want to. I wish you'd see Tsering Rinpoche though, and talk to him too.'

'Oh, I don't know Sara, I feel reluctant to get into that one. It's not that I don't respect the discipline, but somehow it just doesn't feel right. I don't think I can put it better than that.'

'Well, of course you have to do what feels right for you. Maybe you'd come to some teachings with me one day. I'm sure you'd enjoy them, and then you can see Tsering Rinpoche, and you might change your mind. There's just something so wonderful about hearing the teachings, but anyway it might not be your thing. What about your homeopath though, have you talked to her about what's happening?'

'Yes, a bit. She's amazingly elusive. All she says is 'trust' and 'God will work it out', I don't think she really knows what's going on or what it means, or if she does she definitely won't say anything to me. I can't thank you enough for being so understanding.'

'Oh it's nothing, I really sympathise with you, and I'm very excited. Shall I give you Iris's number?'

'OK, if you really think it's not ridiculous to bother her, that would be good.'

'No, not ridiculous at all. I think what's happening to you is important.' I start to qualify her statement, but she immediately interrupts, 'OK, I know you obviously can't bear the idea that it could matter to anyone other than you. I think it does, but I am not going to push that on you. I'll just go and get Iris's number.'

It's the end of the afternoon and Sara has to go back to work. We agree to have dinner one evening before too long.

My visit to Iris is disappointing. Our initial phone contact is unsettling — she says she's happy to see me if I really think it worth the trip. The journey itself is wonderful. I take the train to Brighton, enjoying the strong undulating lines of the south downs, the drama of the supposed Roman figure, the Long Man, etched into the chalk near Wilmington, and the bustle of Brighton itself. Iris lives in a small flat on the grey sea front. The day I visit her the sky, the pebbles on the beach, and the water itself, all seem shades of the same steely colour.

Iris has little to say to me. It almost seems, I think, as if she can't see me, or see anything about me. Maybe she sees something awful and doesn't want to say it? Instead, she asks if I can see anything about her past lives! I hardly know how to answer, it seems such an extraordinary question. Then, as if it follows naturally, she tells me she has a statuette I might like to see. We move to a small adjoining room and Iris takes a well wrapped parcel out of the cupboard. Removing the covers, I see it is an off-white, stone figurine of an Egyptian-looking woman. My flesh creeps. I look intently, the energy around it seems to me to be dirty and ugly. I don't want to touch it. Iris seems a little surprised by my reaction. Apparently, she regards this statue highly — a sort of Holy object — but nonetheless she takes my muted reaction with good grace.

Finally, she says there is nothing she can tell me, wishes me well and refuses payment. I don't know what to make, if anything, of our conversation, and leave very puzzled.

My daughter is on holiday with her father and things are not going well. I am worried, she is such a beloved, sensitive creature. Inevitably battle overtakes all three of us. My body shudders. My need for peace is very great, it is as if a physical weight descends on me at the thought of more stress or strife. I send her father love in my meditation. The strife continues.

I have never thought of my body as weak. On the contrary, my boundless energy and physical endurance have been a source of strength for so many years. Any aberrations have seemed to me just that — due to exceptional circumstances. Now I wonder. Again, I feel so tired, my need for quiet so profound. Negativity overtakes me and I battle with it in the other world.

Dinner with Sara helps. We talk of past lives, their validity and significance, and I tell her the outlines of my own experience. But not the histories themselves, I do not wish to share them. I am increasingly confident of her benevolence and I say more about my other reality. I agree to go with her and hear her teacher talk, but I have serious reservations — I'm sure it's not for me. When I do a couple of weeks later, my reservations are confirmed. My world is my inner world.

Monday, 1 April, 6.50pm *The snake and I travel up to V and, as usual, I prostate myself. This time he asks why I do it, why I lie on the ground before him?*

'To be utterly humble,' I reply.

'Well, there's no need,' he says, dismissing the matter.

We speak of many things and then he asks me to sit on the floor, in the corporeal world. The Force has already straightened out my spine. Now an enormous shaking sets in, accompanied by a very curious series of hand movements over my 'third eye', and great heat in my entire body. I massage the heart chakra, bringing a strong response, and seem to be patting or smoothing the air around me, about an arm's distance away from my body.

Then there is some shaking in my legs and I rock on my seat. One arm stretches up. The right-hand side of my face is bothering me. Also deep down in my right ear and in the shoulder I feel something. Then there are a few twinges in the lower back, right side again, and the right arm comes up over my head. At the same time, my body leans to the left. It is as if I am moving, or being moved, to reach some point of balance. A still point. I do not quite reach it. But I do achieve somewhere near.

Afterwards, my eyes, particularly the right one, are very twitchy and feel as if splinters are lodged in them, or moving.

Tuesday Awake with a dream of just having sold some old stuff at auction for £24,000. Nothing that I wanted to keep or valued. In fact it was chance my entering it into the auction, and I would not have been surprised to receive £5.00 for it. So I wake feeling rather pleased.

My morning meditation focuses on my physical body, as it did last night, with change after change taking place. During the following ten days' meditation sessions, many things happen. I am made to change my form from the hard shape of the Golden One, like a golden Eastern statue, to a Western female with flowing hair, a long dress and various ornaments. At times, I experience wings growing from my back, and use them. I am also given an outline of my work, which does not make much sense.

Thursday, 11 April, 7.20am *I am happy to see V. I ask for his help to do the will of the Creative, and then relax, lying on the grass in front of him. Casually, I look at him. It is unusual for me to see his face clearly, or to focus on it, but this time I look and look. Something is happening. I look away, but he tells me to look at him again, into his eyes. I do, and am pulled right inside V. We are one, or perhaps two in one.*

Before I have time to consider the situation, he moves. He travels upwards. A long way. We arrive at a huge area, filled with 'shadows' of beings, but substantial shadows, somehow. I understand they are the shadows of people who lived on earth recently, waiting to be reborn. I see a dear relative, who comes rushing up to V and asks how I am, saying how wonderful it is that he is looking after me. He tells her I am well, and asks isn't it time for her to be going soon. I look out, all around, noticing that the whole area is very crowded, then we move on.

This time we stop at a different place. The air feels menacing. The place is empty and chilly. It is not a neutral void, like the place of the beings waiting for re-birth. Looking closer, I see a shape, a sort of jellied lump emerge as if from nowhere. It is huge, with what look like parts of organisms inside it. Gaping out of the lump nearest to us, is a terrible mouth. Ugly and decaying, open, with rotten teeth, set in a hideous staring face that becomes apparent as we watch. The eyes are full of aggression, and behind that, despair. Nothing more. 'This is the realm of the Undead' V says, as we leave.

Back at his place, I slip out of his body and return to my own. 'Why am I being shown all this?'

'Because you need to know,' is the reply, 'now relax.'

The sky is enormous and beautiful. V tells me I am beautiful and I feel it. We are both wearing particular ornaments, my hair is loose and a shawl I know well from my life on earth is around my shoulders. It is dawn, which strikes me as a little odd, as I would have expected it to be later in the day. I remember a similar wonderful dawn when I was twelve or thirteen, alone on a patch of marshy ground watching a red-bishop bird in the tall grass. I was stung by the beauty then. V remembers it too. Time to leave. I nod and pass through the gate.

Thursday, 9.50pm We deal mainly with matters in my life. I ask questions and am finding out how much information I can elicit, and when it ceases to feel accurate. V says I am going so fast that events do not have time to catch up.

Friday, 10.00am I am taken back in time.

10.45pm I join V, feeling relatively calm, a little tired. He tells me to lie down on the ground. Two snakes come and play, dancing in the air above my head, then a whole network of others join them. It frightens me. I feel paranoid, sit up quickly and they recede. Simultaneously, Ra (a name I have discovered for 'my' snake) appears. She is obviously much bigger than the rest. 'Rest against her,' V tells me. So I sit with my back against her upright body. (I feel an effect in my spine — my physical body.) I feel warmth too.

Then I feel the need to relax even further and V takes me on his lap. I look up at him as if I were a child, watching his face as he speaks. We talk of my life on earth, practical matters. I ask if he will tell me things about the world. Yes, he answers, but at the moment he says I know all I could be told. Then, referring to my tiredness, he carries me to the gate.

Saturday, 13 April, 3.30pm I go to V and ask, as always, for his help. I am very vivid, the colour of my clothes and skin both are unusually strong. He takes me in his arms and onto his lap.

'You are tired, so tired,' he says. (My back hurts.) 'It is the end of a phase,' he continues, 'now you are to see George again. Contact him.'

I am amazed. 'Why?'

'The time is right. It helps to clear the channels.'.

Saturday, 10.45pm I have been feeling very tired all day, with a low headache. Calm descends on reaching V. I have just watched the television news, awful news of people killing one another. V says it is the evil that is fighting hard.

'Has it always been this way, 'I ask, 'or is it any different?'

'It has always been this way: Evil versus Light. But it has intensified and quickened and will continue to do so.'

93

'Can I do anything?'
'What you are doing — be a channel for the Light.'
'Am I a chaneller?'
'Of course.'
How surprised I am by this.

Monday, 15 April, 6.30am Wake with a dream of an owl coming to fetch me. I am afraid, but take control of it.

I sit before V and as ever ask for his help. We talk about what that means. As I understand it, it is help to allow myself to be led by the Creative. 'Look at me,' he says. Again, I feel myself drawn into him , into his eyes, then I am inside him. Quickly, he goes to the Place of the Undead. 'Step out,' he says. According to V, I can draw the Undead, he cannot.

We stand. The ghastly globule in front of us moves. A shape rushes out. It tries to batter me. I stand quite still, still on every level, till it subsides and a man, a thin grey figure, emerges. Pathetically, as if giving up, he asks to die. All my pity is engaged. Comforting him, I pass him over to V, who leads him away. Almost immediately, a new huge shape emerges and tries to swamp me. It seems to grow larger and larger. As before, I stay still and quiet. Eventually, the shape starts to subside. It shrinks to become an aged human, tears flowing, muttering. Instinctively, I comfort the 'person', and V takes him away.

As I turn, I am practically hit by a furious form. It is black and swarms all over me in the body of an enormous panther. It rips at my stomach. The red dress I am wearing is torn, blood oozes from just below my rib apex. The 'panther' seems to diminish a little in size and crouches to lick the blood from my diaphragm. I stay still throughout — all feelings are quiet. I look down at him sucking my blood. He looks up, huge green cat's eyes meeting mine, my composure. Then the creature's eyes begin to change. It cannot look at me, it shrinks down, shrivels. Where once there was a furious panther, now there is a man, crying. As before, I offer comfort as best I can, and begin to travel to the Place of Waiting with him.

On the way, we meet V, who takes my companion from me, and orders me back to the Undead. I do as he says, but I am tired now, exhausted. (I feel it in my physical body.) I am waiting for V — surely I cannot deal with any more now? Yet a small grey creature slinks out of the globule. It is an old lady, weeping. She is ready to die. V is there, I pass her to him and he tells me how pleased he is. Still, I have no feelings, except fatigue.

Back at his place, I rest under the tree. Light begins to pour into me. More and more. Then wings grow on my back, ornaments glow around my neck and the snake is there. V tells me to move in the physical world. I sit on the floor and shake, while light fills my body. Then he tells me to fly over the sea. So I do. Over the ocean in the blue and gold of the air and the water, I fly towards the Light. The sun is huge suddenly. Light floods the horizon, I am drawn towards the Light. My torso is somehow pulled right into it. Then sounds, words come from the Light. I forget the words as they are said, remembering only that the power of the Creative is pleased.

Totally exhilarated, I fly back to V with that news, which he knows. He kisses me on both cheeks, before disappearing, leaving me with the snake. Perhaps it is time for me to go? No, V returns. At first, I am not sure whether he is on his own. But it's quickly clear that he has another figure, similar to himself — a robed, grey-bearded man — with him. Only this figure is larger. V introduces him as T. He has a full moustache and a beard which is thicker, with slightly curlier hair than V's. It is a European, not an Asian face, but with no eyes. It is a blank face. He is very large, and seems to grow larger and larger. V and I grow too, trying to keep up with T. Then I stop, and return to a more usual size. So does he. He runs his hands over 95 *my face and shoulders (perhaps he is blind? Why does he have no eyes?) and seems satisfied. That is all.*

Monday, later *Meeting with V, there is an odd phenomenon — I feel that I am both facing him and that he is simultaneously on my left-hand side. Also, is someone else present? Is the large personage, whom somehow I cannot face, there? Who is in shadow? No answer, or explanation.*

Monday, later again *Rush to see V. He is very happy and kisses me. It is good. I realise that again he is somehow behind me and there is a figure in front of me. Is it T? Yes, it is. I am to speak to him.*

'Are you leaving me, V?' I ask, most anxious.

'No, but T is a higher master, address him.'

Curiously, I am still not clear on V's physical position — is he behind or in front of me? I ask T a practical question — but I cannot understand his answer — it seems to be yes and no simultaneously. V speaks out from behind me, repeating T's answer. Then T asks that I should take off an article that I am wearing on my head and put a particular ornament around my neck, as it is in keeping with the power that, he says, is coming to me.

I understand what he is saying, but am also rather wary about it, and him. He suggests, commands, that we walk together. Soon chairs appear. He wants to sit down and look at me (but how can he 'look' when he is blind?) He sits, I choose the ground instead of a chair. Then after a while, he leaves, walks away without saying anything else. I watch his back receding. A huge old man with a stick.

V reappears, very pleased. Apparently, it is a great privilege, a very good sign, that T is interested.

Monday, 10.10pm *I find myself with V on my left-hand side. (Sharp twinges deep in my left ear.) Before me is a great shape:*

T. I address him, instead of V, and ask for his help to enable me to yield and allow myself to be led. I ask if he is to replace V as my guide, if that is what V is. The answer is no, V is to stay with me, but T wished to see and consider me. One or two more words are exchanged. He suggests we go to the Place of the Undead, so we set off. The snake joins me. T tells me that she does not come to everyone by any means, I am fortunate. I realise how immense he is. He offers to carry me. I am tiny, and carried in the crook of his arm.

We come to the Place. It is its usual revolting self. Two grey 'things' crawl out and cling to my feet. I try to comfort them — they are ready to die — and turn to lead them to the Waiting Place, but V is behind me, and takes them from me. The procedure is repeated. Pandemonium breaks. A terrible leopard rushes at me from the lump. It savages me. Attacks my throat, my heart. I am on the ground, it is gorging on my innards. But I am silent, although the effect is ghastly.

Finally, when it is finished, it sits satisfied over my decimated remains. Then I rise up out of my body. The leopard is overwhelmed and shrinks before me. I forgive, offer my heart, and the shape of the leopard becomes the figure of a terrible but beaten man. He submits, he says, brokenly, and accepts death.

I feel weak and faint (equally so in my physical body) hoping nothing else will happen. But T says stay. As we watch, the lump which is kicking and screaming within, divides in two. The smaller part dissolves and the constituents rush towards me. They all want comfort and contact. They are all 'grey beings'. I give what I can, and ask why they have come. They say they did not, could not, believe, but now they have seen and admit the power of God. They are ready to die. V takes them all.

Then T picks me up and takes me to a place on the mountain tops, among the very high peaks. Again I am amazed at how large he is. The idea dawns on me — is he, could he be God? The question seems to amuse him. In the end, he settles for a *precise statement, saying that there are many faces of God and he is one of them.*

I ask if I am to be told about the world, the nature of the universe, and he says no. 'There is nothing useful you could be told right now,' adding that he would like me in his world, but I cannot come yet. In the meantime, he will have to think how best to use me. Then, with a movement of his arm, he puts me back in V's place.

*V is there, I turn to him, as I think. But in addressing him discover, confusingly, that I am not facing him as I thought —
he is standing on my left and I am at T's feet. Then T leaves, and I talk to V again. He is utterly delighted with T's involve-ment and warns it may change everything. We walk on the beach, much more as equals than we have ever been.*

V tells me he was asked to guide me. That he is to continue to do so, but he does not know everything, although he has many powers. This is a critical point. He walks with me to the gate. I have a wonderful afterimage of the two of us, on the seashore, in the nearly dark. We part affectionately.

Afterwards, I am rather unhappy. I am suspicious of references to me, delusions of grandeur, as I put it. 'Comforting' Undead, 'doing well'. Sounds like an ego trip. Why does it all seem to concentrate on me? Why am I not finding out about the world? Being given information about the nature of 'things'?

Tuesday, 16 April, 7.35am *Joyfully to V. I am glowing. I sit in front of him, but then find that in fact he is on my left-hand side and I am in front of a great shape, again. T? Confusing. At one point, I turn to V — it is so difficult to be sure of what is going on — to find V's face has become like T's, not that he looks the same, but his eyes are now round, staring blanks. I could not say for certain whether it was V's face or T's., V* *cannot tell me. He says something to the effect that he is part of T. It is impossible to converse.*

Eventually, physical things begin to happen. Shakes, then my arms begin to move out slowly, then upward. When they reach shoulder level, my torso sways to one side and then to the other. A pressure point which had begun to exist in the small of my back has gone. Arms are up above my head, hands over eyes, then tracing my 'third eye' and on. Feel flooded with light. See light pouring into my body.

Would it be possible, I wonder, to have the 'other' world and some of my former everyday reality? Could I find a way to combine the two? Not to be so strange, so isolated? A smart drinks party presents itself. A maid opens the door for me and takes my coat, before showing me upstairs to the first floor salon.

'Michal, how lovely to see you, you're looking wonderful.' My hostess greets me with a peck on each cheek, impeccable as ever, not a hair out of place, an ageless elegance. 'Do you have a drink?' signalling with a many gold-ringed hand for a waiter with a tray of champagne, and scanning the room simultaneously, whom to introduce me to? For an instant, I see the tall, blonde girl she must once have been, struggling to do the right thing, but just for a moment. The assurance of several hundred (thousand?) cocktail parties asserts itself, as she takes me over to join a small group.

'You know Hector and Alexandra, and this is our dear friend Augustus R—.'

What to talk about, my last trip, my next trip, gossip — I have none, I don't like it and I can't. If I could talk from my heart, I know there would be a response to my words, but my lips are frozen.

Dinner at Morgan and her husband's London home is more successful. It's easy to be comfortable in their large, bohemian   **99** house. A developer would see six or eight 'luxury' units. I see an enviable indulgence — space. The light from the candle-sticks in the candelabra up and down the long refectory table is reflected in the glazed ochre walls. The waiters are two out-of-work actors, the guests painters, writers, a bookseller and a gambler.

I am seated beside a writer, a homosexual with AIDs. He lowers his voice to talk to me in dark satirical terms. It seems to me I am not able to say much, but nor am I uncomfortable. In fact, leaving a little early when the call to the other world becomes too insistent, I realise that I have enjoyed myself and my spirits soar.

But the other world holds its grip. Angels have become part of my reality there and new locations have been introduced. In particular, a solid beam of light — a contradiction in terms, but no other description seems to fit — which travels to a site that seems to me a place belonging to the Rainbow. These, and others, claim me. That night, T tells me that it has been difficult to decide what to do with me, because he would like me with him. To die. *I say, 'Yes, but I am not yet ready to come, there are my children.'*

He walks out into the sea, with me seated at what has become the usual place, the junction of his neck and shoulder. He asks what I want. I tell him, again, I want only to work and to do his will and God's will. There seems nothing else to ask for. A flicker of concern about my children passes my mind. I trust God will handle the situation. All I really want, all I ask for, is work.

Then T sends me to the place on the hillside where the Ray, like a ladder, reaches. I travel away from the land on the Ray, to the spot I call the Rainbow Place, and sit down. The Rainbow surrounds me. I am pulled upward (corporeal sensation). Then I become aware I am surrounded by angels. I think they are singing. The sense of the sound and the setting fills me with joy.

I am radiant, yet again, in another, new way. Peace is mine. Then two of the largest angels come for me. One on either side, they go with me back to the gate between the worlds. They are leaving with me, they will stay with me in the physical world.

It is difficult to describe the bliss, it is so intense and permeates my every fibre. But it is not part of the everyday world. Next morning, my daughter and I drive to Hampshire to see my son at school.

My wonderful son is undergoing a transformation of his own. Not simply growing up, but confirmation. His unprompted choice. Today is his confirmation ceremony. Chomedley is a great English private school, or public school as they are curiously known. We drive into the school grounds through a massive gate, with gate houses on either side. The drive, even though it's only a couple of hours, has as always been draining. Is it my elderly car, I wonder? I am acutely aware of the suspension as we proceed up the three-mile drive, through the woods. When we reach the car park, Mercedes, Range Rovers and BMWs take the lead roles — how nice, I think.

'Mrs Harvey, lovely to see you,' it's Tom's house master. Strange being Mrs Harvey again. Summoned by the church bell, we join the throng for the service in the school Chapel and then move on with the confirmation group to a private ceremony. Tom is quietly jubilant and asks me to care for his confirmation candle. I am proud of his self-possession, overjoyed, as ever, simply to be with him.

We lunch at the local hotel, The Crown, roast beef and Yorkshire pudding, or the vegetarian alternative, and then walk along the muddy path on the bank of the river that winds through the school grounds. There's no-one rowing today, despite the promise of spring all around. Only one game on the endless, well-cared-for playing fields.

'There was a dance last night,' Tom offers, 'and everyone's recovering.' Our puppy is in seventh heaven, exploring every cow pat in sight. I remember this note so well — couldn't I live in the country with the children and just forget the rest?

Chapter Ten

Planets

The space offered by Hampstead Heath is quite different from the river bank and fields of Chomedly, Hampshire. Hampstead Heath is well trodden. Too well trodden for my taste. The core has been common land since before medieval times, before memory. It's as if old London and the darkest shades of times past live in the shadows of the trees or bushes. The quiet or hidden places I long for don't feel safe for a single woman. In my mind, it's a male province, or tribal territory. A woman on her own should beware. For three women, though, there is no problem. I agree to meet Sara, and Heather, a friend of hers, on the Heath.

We meet at Kenwood House. Approaching from behind, it's set on a slope, multicoloured now, in late spring, with rhododendrons. The existing house dates from the end of the eighteenth century, graceful, in mellow stones with beautifully proportioned rooms and windows looking out onto elegant walkways. It's built on a site where I am told there has been a dwelling since pre-reformation times. Inside, there is a collection of paintings bequeathed by Earl Iveagh, the previous owner. We have not come to see the pictures, though, but to walk, maybe to talk too.

Heather is a graphic designer, who is interested in spiritual development. The Buddhist path does not appeal to her, but for some years now, she has been steadily applying herself to cultivating her integrity, authenticity and what I summarise as trust in the benevolence of the universe. I appreciate her sweet, steady qualities immediately. It's hard to find a language to talk, however. Like Sara, she has investigated a wide range of alternative work, and is particularly adept at a series of exercises which she believes are helping to clear, or stimulate, the flow of her energy. I know nothing on the subject and cannot comment, but I am not drawn to participate.

Together, the three of us wander amongst the surreal colours of the acid-loving plants, oranges and pinks against glossy dark green leaves, past the still, stagnant pond and through to the wilder stretches of the Heath below. I appreciate their companionship, their openness and willingness to explore. I have little to say, but it's pleasant being in such non-judgmental company. We agree to meet again.

It is nearly six months since I stopped work. How am I to earn a living? All ideas of returning to the television world have left me. Physically alone, I feel I would be unable to meet the demands of those schedules. (I hardly question why though — things change, don't they?) But the physical practicalities are far from the only considerations. There is a way in which I am leaving this world, for another. My journey continues, at an ever intensifying pace, immersing me deeper and deeper in this other, symbolic world, where joy of a sort I have never known meets me.

19 May 1991 *The jewel at my throat is blazing as I prostrate myself before T. Go to the place where the Ray strikes the ground. I am asked to go up the Ray, alone. I do, into the light. There's a figure waiting for me, a man, but I cannot make out who. Ra is with me. Dozens of little snakes appear dancing in the light, and suddenly the air is full of angels. The largest two* come for me. They lead me, alone, over the Rainbow. I am a little afraid.

Then, my vision is filled with the sense of crystal. At the other side, there is an enormous Crystal Place — a huge cavern, that seems to grow bigger and bigger. I walk to sit in the centre. All around darkens. Suddenly, I know this is part of me. Yes, I belong in this other world; being with A, I feel profoundly at home, comfortable, loved, but here I have found a core of myself. This Crystal Place is part of me. I have been here before, a long time ago. I have spent a long time here.

I sit in the centre of the huge, darkened cavern, the jewel blazing. I feel there is only a little, little way to go and I will break through and understand, as I so long to do. This place is connected with my work. The angels take me to the edge of the cave. Below, all the world is laid out. I am dizzy (corporeal sensation as well) and pull back. V and T materialise, both assuring me that this is my rightful place.

The Cave is like an eye, offering special sight on the world. Now, it seems to me that I understand the ambiguous phrases V and T use when they describe my work, 'teaching ancient wisdom', 'seeing those who come', 'counselling counsellors'. I think they mean I am to be a clairvoyant or medium — a 'seer', as they say, of some sort. But how to achieve it?

I long to know, to know what it is I feel there is to be known. If only I could push my understanding, or is it my energy? that last bit. Strong corporeal movements, involving my arms and my head. Frustration, what is it, what is it?

The angels are soothing me, confirming I have found a part of myself here. And, now that I have found it, I will return often. They take me back, over the Rainbow. By the gate, I almost shout in rage and frustration — what is it I sense but somehow cannot articulate, or know? Then I pull myself together. The angels are with me as I pass into the human world.

If I felt myself drawn before, then the pull is doubly strong now. The enchantment I feel in the Crystal Cave defies expression. In the morning light, it is beautiful beyond comprehension, light reflecting from all its facets, all colours present in shades so refined as to be almost imperceptible. The softness and strength of angels that surpasses any human quality known to me. The sound of their voices in the subtlest of songs, which is and is not present, along with the beat of their wings against the yielding air, reminds me of the memory of my children, as infants, sleeping, and the quality of my passion for them in those quiet moments. If the images are clichéd, the emotions are not.

Now, I feel the angels with me in the human world, particularly Angel, as I call him, at my right shoulder through the day. The stillness of the nights is filled not only with the images of the other world, but the reality of the angels around me.

Often I walk in the hills formed by the clouds, the cumulus clouds. The Latin words *cumulus, cumulus-nimbus* hint at their fullness. I remember the view, at dusk or dawn, from the window seat of the jet moving silently across Africa. The fields of pink-tinged clouds hinted at what I know now. I dance with the angels. This is bliss. This is purity. But still the questions . . .

In the following days, I see the entire world far below. I see all places. I see into the lives of some whom I know. And it seems as if people begin to come to me in my meditation. People I know in the world. I understand it is their spirits I see and our contact is of the frankest sort. It is what appears to me as their pain, anger, hatred and what I think of as separation from God which emerges. I learn I am able to help clean their souls, to infuse them with fresh spirit before sending them back to the bodies with which they work, to help them fulfil their potential. This work — if that's how it can be described — expands to what I think of as the Tree of

Life, where souls are impaled by their deeds. I use coloured beams, as well as simply offering myself. Is this the work I have been prepared for, and promised? If so, it's difficult to see how it will pay.

Throughout, I am very clear in my mind that what I do in the other world, what happens, what is said, is not the reality of everyday. It goes without saying that I accept the language and events as metaphor of some sort. But more, it seems to me that any relationship between events in my meditation and the everyday is purely speculative. Logically, I accept it could all be my fantasy. But I know with my heart that some, at very least, is not. All this is exhausting, but peculiarly satisfying. Above all, it is uplifting. I believe. I feel joy. Profound, intense joy, and I am regularly filled with glorious, radiant light that brings a special peace and calm.

The shape of the inverted triangle becomes important. I begin to learn about the energies, which are coloured, and come from particular planets for the purpose of working on different sensitivities. At the same time, T continues to give me lessons, as I think of them. Again and again the nature of evil is explored. What is it? How to deal with it. Relationships and sexuality too are major topics. I struggle to understand what is meant, or only do so later. There are many homilies associated with the sea.

7 June T and I are in a rowing boat with no oars, on a fine day, on the sea, or perhaps a large lake. In an earlier session, he advised me to learn to swim, and warned against the dangers of relying on a craft, and on the acquired skill necessary to handle a craft. Instead, he urges, swim, depend on yourself. But this outing, apparently, is acceptable. He wants me to understand that it is all right to take time out and take advantage of an available craft, in certain conditions, like these which are placid, peaceful and playful.

It is not the same as in stormy conditions, or when trying to get somewhere. Apparently, there are times when a craft can be used, it's not always a mistake. Just then, a huge Egyptian ship with rows and rows of oars is skimming by. He asks if I'd like to ride in that.

Appalled, I reply, 'No, it's propelled by slaves.'

'Quite,' he agrees. 'However efficient it would be in getting you to another place, you could not and should not use it — it's tainted. But there are other alternatives.'

I see a sailing boat, a small one with a figure aboard it, the man who came part way with me the first time I went to the Crystal Cave, whom I could not identify, but who has helped me on several occasions. The boat is hardly more than a dingy with a mast, but he is clearly a good sailor.

'Well,' says T, 'what are you waiting for?'

New information and experiences constantly follow. A planet of flames, where all that is superfluous is burnt off, becomes important. When I am filled with Light, I realise a new shape has come into play: the sides of the inverted triangle are extended, the shape comes closer to a skewed cross. Later, my father and a grandmother, both of whom are no longer alive, appear. And more.

While I am utterly absorbed and satisfied in my other world, the same is not true of the everyday. I realise I am isolated in my inner world, without any way of earning a living for my family, and engrossed in a reality that most other people would call fantasy, even dangerous. I live in a society I no longer seem to be part of. It worries me, in one way.

T wants to know why my sadness. I try to explain as best I can: my fear of the worldly consequences of pursuing this path, and loneliness. He is a little dismissive. How can I be lonely with the other world, this world, around me? But I explain that I have to live out my life on earth — I cannot

literally escape to this other world all the time. That T understands. We talk a little about my fears. Then he asks me what
I fear most — and of course what comes to mind is nothing
earthly: it is losing my faith. When I realise this, there is a
curious kind of shift, as if this is something so profound that I
have not yet assimilated its importance.

11 June *T raises me up, tenderly, and steps out into the ocean
with me. We see two birds flying — a seagull and a dove. For a
moment, I feel I am both birds. When T asks which would I like
to be, I reply whichever he wishes. The dove, he says. I try to
understand the birds' significance. It seems the seagull is well
adapted to water and uses it as a larder — it lives off the sea.
The dove, on the other hand, was used to give guidance to those
at sea in the ancient story. It brought the symbol of land and of
hope to those who were in peril on the water. So the gull is a
symbol in a sense that it lives for itself off the sea, while the
dove brings hope to those on the water. I ask about the dove as
a symbol of peace. T tells me that was not its first significance.*

20 June *The disparity between my two lives is strong today,
and physically somehow I cannot, or do not, feel well. We are
standing in the sea. T is reminding me of the changeability of
the weather. It's choppy, but soon there will be sunlight. Then
the dove flies in to join us. Again, T reminds me of my role —
to carry the olive twig, as a sign of what is, what truly exists,
not as a messenger of peace. Still I am low.*

*With no warning, I am pulled into T — it is as if I merge
with him. (Much physical shaking accompanies this.) Then,
having been pulled in, I am pulled upward into a vast plain of
light. To begin with, the light is yellow white, then it changes to
a mixture of blue and yellow, then blue, grey and yellow, at
which it begins to snow, till everything is snowflakes, deeper*

and deeper, higher and higher. Now my body is covered by the snow.

Another death and a resurrection follows. But my concern about my on earth life stays. It seems there is nothing I can do, though. The summer holidays are approaching. Later, we will have a week's holiday in Wales with another family, old friends, with children of similar ages, with whom we have spent a week in summer for some years now. My former sister-in-law, with her sons, is coming to visit too. I half look forward to, half dread the time as a test — can I still belong to the human world? Meanwhile, events in the other world race ahead.

22 June, Midsummer's Day, 8.55pm *I tell T I want to merge with him. He urges me to use his strength for whatever I do — he tells me again and again how powerful he is and that his strength is mine. He is truly affectionate. I ask, yet again, what am I to do, on earth?*

'Counsel, teach, then more,' is the reply.

'Who? And what am I to say to them?' I ask.

'They will come,' he assures me, 'and you will know what to say when you see them. Each one will be different.' I cannot make sense of what he says.

I travel to the Crystal Cave with the angels. There, I am filled with light and much physical shaking takes place. Then the light stops, and I am dull, which surprises me. I suspect I must work to induce the light effect. I concentrate on opening my heart chakra and trying to pour love into the spaces of the Crystal Cave. It produces a brief effect. Then I realise I cannot do it myself. The angels help me to lie on the floor of the Cave. (At the same time, I need to lie on the floor in the physical world.) The shape I seem to take — I later realise — is the cross. My head to the south, or south east. I see rainbow coloured flashes entering my body. Then a phrase comes into my mind, 'Knock and ye shall be asked to enter.' So I do. I ask for God's help to let me in.

Immediately, a light leaves my body — is it my spirit? It's escorted by angels and drawn into a stream of golden light that seems to appear from directly above. And I am at a table and He is there. I have seen this figure before. At the start of this process, in my encounter with those of my past lives that were shown to me. He appeared to me between lives. It is the Christ figure. There is a table. Exactly as I saw it before.

I approach on the right-hand side, kneel before Him and kiss His feet. He pulls me up. I am not certain of the order in which things happen. He tells me that I have only to call and He will be with me. That this is the end point of this stage of my initiation. He pours wine — like blood — and then oil over my head. The blood is to symbolise his blood, his body, the oil, sustenance. Then He tells me I am ready to work. I ask what He wants me to do and He says it will present itself. Then I am to go, but He reminds me I have only to call and He will be there. The angels take me back to the Cave. I am utterly affected.

It's difficult to make clear, after so many extraordinary happenings, how much this session affects me. How I feel connected and dependent on the Christ figure, altogether. My final thought afterwards is that it is impossible to do anything on your own. I take to praying to the Christ specifically, as well as to God, my version of the Creative force behind life. Now there is even more work with the Undead and the dark forces. A new planet too. I am often with the Christ. Then another great figure enters.

29 June *Behind the Christ, on his left-hand side, is the Golden Buddha. The Buddha I saw so long ago. I note the patterns, shapes, made by our configuration and the colours of the lines*   111 that appear between us. The Buddha explains that he and Christ are from the same source, that there is no difference. That Christ's will and the Buddha's will are the same. Then I link hands with the Christ and the Buddha and there is a tremendous sensation of energy flow. Together, we go to work in the darkness of a dark place, establishing Light.

1 July 1991 A Wrathful Deity, as I believe he's called, appears, connected with the Buddha. I understand that in some sense he is there to offer me power, but am not sure what is happening. He does a dance; the pattern he makes on the ground brings to mind the sign of Aries, or perhaps Capricorn the goat. Or, a figure eight. He brings fire with him. He asks me to go with him into the sky, so I do, standing on his back, which is also his shadow. We travel to a place which could be, as I first think it will be, deep in the earth, but is in fact a corner of the sky, unknown to me till now. It is all ablaze. It is a vast expanse, fields and fields of the sky on fire — and poor wretched souls burning in it. We separate and walk in this terrible place.

The wrathful one seems to cut a hole with his presence. It is as if in some way his mere presence cuts a swathe. But I act a little differently. Simply standing there, arms outstretched. There is a pale blue light around me. I see drips of water coming from my arms and disappearing in the blackness, in their place steam rising. Then angels flock to the vast burnt-out areas, collecting souls, bodies. The Wrathful One turns away, and I am with him again. Together, we return to the Rainbow place.

It appears that with the Buddha's help, I have been offered the Wrathful One's strength and powers. I thank him seriously and say I will call on him. With that, he seems to sink away, face down into the earth. I do not know what to make of the experience. The other world has taught me that on occasion, lessons are connected to events in my life. They may sometimes be understood in terms of what I face. I ask the Christ.

In everyday life, I am wrestling with a question about action: when is it appropriate to act and when not? And how to act? I know it entails the issue of desire, and wanting something particular to happen. Attachment to outcome. I know, too, that my teaching in the other world seems to have been towards letting go of the desire for a particular outcome. I cannot better God's will, only surely, learn to follow it? Also, I know that often action is not called for. Rather, the wisdom of understanding that a storm is, as T put it to me, no more than the wind, which is air, acting on the sea. Now it seems as if the presence of the Wrathful Deity is connected with action. He appears to take action most forcefully. The action of cutting through. Is he creating the outcome he wants? How am I to understand it?

The Christ's answer is very simple. (Is he addressing my question, I wonder?) He says that being your truth is the first essential, but it is also necessary, in some circumstances, to explain it — that is, teaching. Which is what he says I must do. How does it relate either to the Wrathful Deity, or to my question?

It is not the end of the Wrathful Deity, he comes on many more occasions. First, he offers me a lump of rock which he says is a diamond. Apparently, it is to be sharpened and then used to 'cut through', his action. He teaches me how the power to hone the lump of rock that is a diamond rests in my eyes. Then I learn to merge with the Wrathful One, so that his strength becomes mine.

Other beings, other places, more planets, symbols, come and go. Symbols, forms, compass directions are all particularly important. And planets. I learn the energetic characteristics of many different places. More, I learn that these energies can be passed on. Not simply by immersion in the place, or a beam from the place, but in essence, in some corporeal form.

It seems that certain homeopathic remedies work in this way, or rather that some may relate to planets and as such offer their energy. For others, there are no commonly accepted offerings, but they may be made. I do not know what relation these teachings have to the everyday reality, but I do know that I feel a certain understanding — it's hard to put a word to it — when I think of various homeopathic remedies. It's almost as if I know which one is for what, but of course I don't, and it's not a subject I have ever studied, or indeed know much about beyond the most basic principles. Now the other world is beginning to intrude into the 'real' world.

1 August 1991 For the first time, a short mention is made of world events. To begin with, I am relieved. It seems that this might be more significant than dealing with the supposed psyches of people I know or encounter, or those who are no longer alive. I am also uncomfortable with a role that aims or presumes to put me in so unwelcome a position in relation to my peers and others. 'Counselling' would never be my ambition. Nor teaching. I'm most suspicious of the motivation, for a start, of those who purport to be counsellors to others, or moral or spiritual teachers. Prophecy, particularly of global events, is considerably easier to understand and accept than most of the processes I have been dealing with. I am half hopeful that this may be the way events will develop. But I notice too a sick feeling in my stomach, and exhaustion.

3 August I merge with T, as has become the pattern. *Then, I am not raised up but seem to go forward in some way. As if I am in the future, not looking at it. Then I am lifted vertically. To the same place I looked forward from. Realise that the direction I am looking is in fact north, not east as I previously thought. (It would be east from where my physical body is facing, but I've left that in merging with T.) I wait for what will come. Two* *facts, about the future for other people, come to me. I am sober. I ask if I am to be a medium or clairvoyant. Yes, is the answer. Am I to channel another being, some other entity who will pass on this information? No, I am not to channel another intelligence, or master. I have a more direct relation to what I am to teach.*

Increasingly, I ponder the relationship between my meditation world and the everyday world. When people I know come to me in meditation, I find, sometimes, that remedies come into my mind. I do not know if they are real remedies, homeopathic or some alternative, perhaps herbal, remedies which already exist, or if they are planetary essences from this other world.

Some instructions are altogether concrete — but opaque. One says: go and see Brenda. Brenda, who's Brenda? I don't know anyone called Brenda. My information is no clearer. I can't glean anything further, so I put it to one side. Perhaps 'Brenda' will materialise, perhaps not. Then, again and again I meet the future in the planetary void. The place between the galaxies. Facing the emptiness. From there, the Christ and the Lord Buddha show me a mountain peak, barely discernible, where I am to work. But Wales comes first.

Saturday, 10 August Saturdays are always 'changeover days' for rented accommodation in the English countryside. We have rented a converted barn close to the Pembrokeshire coast in south Wales, for a week. Angus and Cecilia Dunbar with their three children, dear friends, have taken a cottage close by. For some years now, my children and I have enjoyed their warmth and generosity, spending regular weekends with them at their home outside a small town, and a week in the English countryside during the summer break.

This year, rather than stay with them as we have done in the past, I have found a separate place to rent so that various guests can stay with us too. We are very much looking forward to seeing them, though, and spending time together. Eating gritty sandwiches on the beach, or Angus's splendid barbecues at night, have become traditions for us all. Will it work this year? The children, I know, will easily slot together. Tom, whose liking for the Dunbars is unreserved, will also have a much favoured cousin to keep him company. They are a few years older than the rest. So, I have no anxiety on that score. But what of myself?

Life has been very quiet for me the last couple of months. Is it choice or necessity? I do not know. My head is full of the other world. I am supremely sensitive. To smell and sound alike. My sight, of course, is altered; I see energy, but that, usually, only when I choose. Sometimes, I seem exhausted, often distant from the day-to-day. But not towards the children. If effort is necessary to muster my strength for them, I make it. My attention is always theirs.

I put my condition down to my meditation. It never crosses my mind that a physical cause could be implicated — I have checked this out with Jeanette. Now I worry, how will I handle the noise of all the children combined? And how will I be with Cecilia and Angus? To talk of what's happening to me would be impossible. Neither Angus, a lawyer, nor his immensely professional wife, would surely find it plausible, or tolerable — would they?

The cottage, or barn, is close to the Pembrokeshire Coast National Park. According to the guidebook, it is recognised as one of Europe's finest stretches of coastal natural beauty, with mile after mile of spectacular sea cliffs, beaches, headlands and coves. Well, that may be, but the weather interceded. A favourite uncle of mine, visiting from South Africa with his partner, stays with us the first night and then leaves, amazed that anyone can endure such grey and wet weather.

I am grateful that the barn is newly converted — it's clean and well equipped. The surroundings are undistinguished.

There is no view. It is a desultory farmyard in a dip, with an enormous clay pit filled with murky water, which the children like the look of hugely, in a ploughed field above the cottage. An overgrown path leading to the beach through the fields is on the other side.

We are luckier than the Dunbars. Their cottage is a failure. Even their inimitable optimism cannot conceal that. It's filthy and filled with ancient furniture I do not want to touch when I visit. It bears no relation to the rosy picture that was painted before their arrival. They have been there a week already, with other friends, and obviously look on our arrival, into clean, newly converted accommodation, with appreciation.

I want to transplant the entire family into our barn. But I cannot. Standing in the kitchen with the children running shouting through the house, my whole body seems to dissolve. I hear the noise not as if it's outside, but each laugh, each cry, every sound cuts my consciousness as if it were a knife. I'm horrified. I don't know what to do. It is not as if I can grit my teeth and endure the situation, I simply cannot stay with it. I long for peace. I have to have quiet. And I cannot explain the need adequately. In the silence of my meditation, I find my only refuge and, amazingly, the saga continues as if there were no interruption, only some end point to achieve.

So. We spend the days on the beach in the drizzle, that sometimes turns to rain, and a wild, wilful wind. One afternoon, the children find a boat and sail it on the clay pit. No life jackets and only makeshift oars. Another afternoon, it is the Dunbar children's nanny's birthday and the little ones collect wild flowers to decorate a birthday cake for her. Cecilia surprises me, as in so many things, with her knowledge of the flowers they pick from the hedgerow during the long, damp walk up the cliffs from the beach.

Throughout, I am deeply embarrassed, unable to show the hospitality I feel their proper due to my friends, and unable to explain the problem either. I cannot communicate the reality in which I am living. I suspect my behaviour makes little sense. If they notice (they must surely?) they are too well mannered to comment. My former sister-in-law comes for a couple of days, but I think she is too wrapped up in her own domestic issues to notice me much. Then the week is over and only the long, draining drive back to face. I hope this process comes to an end soon. The children have enjoyed the week, though — pity they didn't find the boat earlier, is their chief lament.

Chapter Eleven

Blood

The summer continues. It's late August and my daughter wants to go to pony camp. Not the African pony club camp I went to, with wild gallops across the semi-scrub, dust blocking my throat, nose and in my eyes. Hot, magic nights, with the bush sounds louder even than the excited whispers of thirty teenage girls, 'Does he?' 'Did she?' 'I didn't, I swear I didn't.' Reputations made and lost, amongst the nail varnish and grooming kit.

At six, in London, my daughter's aspirations are quite different. It's not the tweedy county English Pony Club she's after either. No, her heart is set on pony camp at Wormwood Scrubs, inner London, in the shadow of the famous prison, the brainchild of Sister Mary Joy, an ordained member of I know not which order.

Mary Joy (no sister, please) is building a riding school to serve the local population on ground I never knew existed, premises no-one else surely would have judged suitable and with what funds I do not know. A series of old sheds are filled with a dozen rescued — so they seem to me — animals, and hordes of city children, few of whom have probably done more than sit on a seaside donkey or eye a police horse nervously. Now Mary Joy, in tatty jodhpurs and sweatshirt, is having a pony camp.

25 August 1991 I leave my precious daughter, with her rucksack filled with name-taped articles and sleeping bag at the 'yard', as it's grandly called. A couple of dozen small girls and boys are sleeping side by side (inch by inch) in a barn, on a plastic ground sheet. I am not sure if there are two lavatories, or just one. No point in asking. I hope she washes her hands before she eats. That's as much as I can ask. What a fussy vegetarian will eat, is another matter. At least I've signed on to help with a couple of lunches, so perhaps I'll see.

What I see when I return the next day is pure pleasure. She's in the clothes I left her wearing (of course), no trace of a hairbrush having contacted her hair, or water her face. But a smile so wide it fills me with joy. It's really good — the other mums I work with, dishing up hot dogs onto paper plates, agree. All our children are having too good a time to notice us, beyond my daughter wanting to assure me it is 'brilliant'.

Later, I collect a picture of her in an aerobic pose on the back of a fat black pony, looking supremely confident and poised. At the time, I thank Sister Mary Joy for giving such pleasure, and I'm pleased to have two or three easy days myself, knowing my child is in such ecstasy.

My sleep is broken. Once, twice I wake gasping, with a certain salty tang in my mouth. The third time, I am awake in an instant, carrying the dream with me from sleep to waking. In my mind's eye, my mouth, my throat, are full, a cough spluttering from my lips. My body is frozen. Terror. No, not simply terror, my hands are tied behind my back. The place is a flat horseshoe-shaped piece of ground amongst bare red mountains. A fire burns in the centre of the space. There are many men, women and children present.

It is a scene I have watched before. I know what will happen to me, yet I am powerless to resist. I do not see the moment when the priest/executioner cuts my throat, nor do I stay long enough in the dream to watch them throwing my body over

120

the cliff, though I know that is what will happen. But I wake with the knowledge of the blood that fills my mouth as my throat is slit from ear to ear. A sacrifice. I consider this thread in the construction of myself.

There is blood in my meditation too. But other incidents first. Another location. A pool, in a deep hollow. It seems to be some sort of prophetic place, an oracle perhaps. What I am to do is written in the pool. Counsel, teach, write. The pattern of my meditation sessions now seems to be that I enter the other world and proceed to merge with T's presence. Then my image, I, am taken to a place on a golden orb, from where I travel to the pool. Days, events, pass, and I do not know any more of the pool's significance, or role.

31 August *Then, V takes me to the dark pool with the words written on it. Now I understand what I must do is go into the pool. So I do. Down, down into the water, it becomes a passage way of green luminous liquid, with huge rocks on either side, to the ocean floor. I stand on the ocean floor with V. This is Neptune's realm. It beckons. Intuition is Neptune's province, I must use it.*

I recall being above the ocean with T. The sea of human feeling and human life. Now, I am as deep below as it is possible to go. This is the floor. The place of understanding. What happens way below the surface. I am to use my ability to be in this place. I am clairvoyant. But I am not to use it to tell futures. I am to see into the hearts of others and beyond for the benefit of those who ask. I will use it for no other purpose. I am to use it wisely. It is the gift of my childhood, honed and amplified. I am to use it to connect others to this other realm. To their own intuition, I take that to mean.

In the following sessions, I learn that the clarity of the water indicates the quality of my sight. Emotions more than anything can affect my vision. Anxieties about my personal happiness, or path, undermine my sight. It is as if I am asked to trust in God, and the goodness of God, only, to guide me. The Wrathful Deity is particularly helpful in cutting through obstacles on this path. Again and again, my constant prayer is to be able to do the work of the Unknown, of God. The Christ and Buddha images support me. Now they stand beside me at the pool, encouraging me to enter the water when I hesitate. Far ahead sometimes I glimpse the mountain peak.

Information comes to me in the sparkling, incandescent depths and pictures of others. I see Jeanette Joliff, with a client. They are talking, I understand the homeopathic remedy that is appropriate. Tell Jeanette, my source urges.

Later, I see Jeanette with two clients, a mother and a son. I see some of the energy of all three, and understand that Jeanette is overlooking an important factor with the boy. I am told what he needs. Again, tell Jeanette, my source urges. I stop short.

I have no desire to involve anyone else in following the dictates of my meditation. I do not regard them as absolute truth. I have noticed that sometimes I ask the same question repeatedly — perhaps in my anxiety — and receive different answers. Then it seems to me possible that on occasion the 'facts' I am told may come not to be the case, just as sometimes they may be altogether true. However, I am unable to distinguish what of my input is certain truth, what may be true and what may not be fact. Or even what may come to be true in the future. Nor do I understand the criteria for making those decisions.

Jeanette has expressed supreme confidence in the process that is engulfing me, though. I remember only too well her role in helping it to start. She also urged me always to take the first answer to a question, didn't she? But tell her how to do her job? Worse, how to do her job regarding people whom she may not be able to identify in any way. No, I can't call her to pass that on. However, I am due to see her in a week or so, so I may raise the possibility of receiving this sort of message and see what her reaction is.

Also, I am given an instruction to go and see Sai Baba — I have heard the name, but know little else, and frankly am rather daunted at the thought of doing any more. I have already agreed, in meditation anyway, that I will go and see Orgyen Rinpoche.

Then I find my mouth is full of blood, in the other world. The Christ and Buddha are sympathetic. The session continues. Next time, the blood flow is stronger: blood is gushing from my throat. The Buddha is very sympathetic, the Christ figure less so, he urges me to be *'realistic'*. But what is that? I want to know am I cutting my own throat in some way, by my actions, or what? But no answer.

5 September 1991, later that night The blood is still flowing, only now I hold a small razor in my hand. Christ holds me, and tells me gently that I am cutting my own throat. How? I ask. By self-doubt, he answers. Take yourself to the pool and start as soon as possible. But Christ warns me that if I go into the pool wounded, the blood will attract sharks. So he puts some sort of bandage on it.

I dive clumsily into the water. It's murky, full of algae. Forget order. I ask God for help. (why didn't I do that before?) Light pours into me. V is there, holding me too. I rise above the water, then sink back under again. I am healing, but the water is still green with algae.

The issue isn't ended. Trust, I work on trust. However hard I work to trust, there are still traces of blood. Now the blood is dried. My teeth are outlined in dried blood. Why the blood? I ask the Christ despairingly.

And the notion of a sacrifice comes to my mind. I have been a sacrifice — in many ways. Using my clairvoyance has brought me physical pain and abuse in Egypt, and long ago in Great Britain. I have also been an actual sacrifice in Tibet, and South America . . . Then Christ and Buddha take me to the pool. Counsel, teach, write. The words are spelt out on the surface in incandescence and underlined. All three words are underlined. I wade in the water, and sink under the sparkles. I see myself. The blood in my mouth has cleared. Pearly beautiful teeth. It was not just my cutting my throat, but the memory of my throat being cut. It does not happen again.

12 September 'Have you had any messages for me?' Jeanette asks, quick as a flash, when I raise the possibility. 'You must tell me.' So I describe the first woman and then the mother and son. She thinks for a moment or two, then writes, slowly, in her notes. 'You have to keep a record of anything like that, just write it down and call me straight away.'

'Do you really know who they are? Are they really descriptions of clients you've seen?'

'Of course.'

'That's incredible.' I'm silent for a moment. 'What about the remedies? I don't know anything about remedies — how can I be sure I'm repeating the right thing to you?'

'Don't worry, just do your best. Some of them I'll know perfectly well and sometimes you might get remedies that haven't been proved yet, but don't worry. That's the main thing. What you are getting is all right. Just go on.'

I don't ask what is happening to me any more. We collude in not talking about it. I no longer feel the desire to put words to what is happening. Physically, Jeanette says she's working on my strength.

'It's not surprising you feel washed out after what you've been going through, and it hasn't finished yet. Most people couldn't have coped, I wouldn't have been surprised if you'd have had a nervous breakdown. You're doing really well, just trust and go on.'

Chapter Twelve

Majorca

I agreed to go and see Orgyen Rinpoche and I am sticking to my word. The other world insists. V also said that I would be recognised. While I accept completely what I am told in my inner world, I feel most strongly that in translating inner events to my actions in the outer world, I have a choice. As I am clear that I am not about to become a Buddhist, or a follower of Orgyen Rinpoche, surely going to Spain to see him seems unnecessary? But what is necessary? I want to follow the world I have found inside me. There are other imperatives too. To earn a living. What am I to do in the real world?

I am reminded of a story I used to read my children called *What a Mess*. 'What a mess' is an Afghan puppy who does not know what sort of creature he is, in other words, what he is. He does not identify with his mother and instead goes from group to group attempting to identify himself with other creatures. Each encounter is more chaotic than the last. Visually, the result is — a mess. Eventually, age makes an Afghan hound out of him and the question is answered. A contemporary version of the ugly duckling who turned into a swan. Well, I've no desire to be an Afghan hound, and delusions of becoming a metaphorical 'swan' make me very wary indeed. It's evident that I am not the same as my competent, excellent mother; and to complete the analogy, going to see gurus feels suspiciously as if I am wandering from place to place looking for myself.

Why don't I stop? In Jeannette's words, why not simply trust, and let it unfold? Well, perhaps that is what I am doing. I'm not sure if going to see Orgyen Rinpoche is something I want to do, or should do, listening to what I have been told.

The arrangements are easy. I call Teddy, whose number is in the Orgyen Rinpoche group's newsletter. 'Fantastic, you're coming too! Are you going to share a room or are you in the dorm?'

'Well, I don't know about that. I don't have the details. I'm not sure about it.' I'm backtracking.

'You need to call France. You make a reservation through them and you can pay in Majorca when you get there. Really all you have to say is that you're coming and you want a bed in a dormitory, or a shared room.'

Silence, while I digest this unpleasant nugget. 'Is that the only kind of accommodation?'

'Well you can always camp. I don't think I will, but there're always people camping — it's great. But I've got my wife and her sister staying just down the mountain, so I've decided to go for a room. There's nothing to stop you camping, though. There'll be loads of people to help, I'll give you a hand.'

The last time I camped was pony camp at thirteen. That was on a camp bed in a huge tent. I think this might be rather different and more than twenty-five years have passed. The details arrive and confirm. Dormitory accommodation, shared bedroom, or permission to pitch a tent, but no facilities for providing camping gear. Communal washing arrangements. I'll have to camp if I go. Maybe I should go for three days, not four.

Peter, of Peter and Dora are great campers. Perhaps I could ask their advice, maybe even borrow a tent, if it doesn't seem too mad.

'Easy as falling off a log,' Peter tells me.

'Will you be all right?' Dora asks. 'Not everybody likes camping.' I admit I've never felt the need for it in my adult life. But then the need not to sleep in a dormitory or share a room with strangers is strong at the moment.

That night, I dream I cross the road to watch a group of construction workers who have retreated from the site where they have been working to stand on the other side of a high hoarding. It's not clear why they have retreated. Is it an industrial dispute? An impending event? Suddenly, there is a massive eruption well behind the hoardings, at the centre of some large complex. Particles of ice are blown way up into the sky and sprayed across a wide area.

'She's blown,' someone says. Now there is water spurting into the sky, along with the ice. Then, with the special vision of dreams, I see a dark, secret place, deep below a lofty building, part of the complex — as if protected by it. A spring has come alive again. The spring has been frozen for many years, and the whole area into which water has been flowing for years has been frozen. Now, somehow, the ice over the top of the spring has been blown open and the spring is alive again. The dream wakes me. It is the middle of the night. I have to meditate. Home.

The flight to Palma is easy. I'm carrying a borrowed rucksack, a tiny one-person tent and ground sheet, also borrowed. It's all hideously heavy, and I'm not prepared for rain. 'Take a local bus, or share a taxi, from Palma,' say the instructions. 'Go to Lorenta, where you will have to take a taxi, first left, third right by a bakery and five kilometres up the hill ask the taxi driver for Casa Nanucchi. If he doesn't know, say it used to belong to the Rigone family and now it's been renovated.'

Palma airport is bathed in brilliant sun. It's years since I have been to the Mediterranean. I had forgotten the particular blue of this sky. Freed from families with school-age children, the airport is relatively civilised. I am not anxious to take a taxi on my own to the Retreat, as it's called. I'd like to find someone else who's going, but how? If not, I'll opt for the bus. Given that I have no Spanish, a local bus might be a little tricky to negotiate, but probably perfectly possible. No sign of the local buses. Nor has an arrow in the sky pointed at anyone going to Orgyen Rinpoche's Retreat.

Outside the airport are two dual carriageways, a vast car park, several uniformed gentlemen gesticulating at the traffic and a partly grass-covered island with two or three stunted palm trees separating the roads. Then I notice an ill-assorted little group with a variety of bags standing on the traffic island. That's them I think, and simultaneously begin to weave my way across the first road.

I'm right, a schoolteacher from Madrid, a couple from Palma, and an architect from France, all of whom know one another from previous retreats. Yes, of course I can join them, there'll be room in the taxi if we squeeze.

We squash together like sardines in the old saloon that sets off into the interior. Lorenta is on the other side of the island, in the hills above the west coast. The reconvening group take no notice of their surroundings, but enter into a lengthy discourse in Spanish. Apparently they're discussing community (Orgyen Rinpoche's community) politics. I'm happy enough to look out of the window. Some of the ground appears cultivated. There are vines growing, scattered one- or two-storey dwellings, nothing very elaborate, the odd donkey.

Then we pass a large glass blowing foundry and shop and begin to wind into the hills, where the vegetation is thicker. The Majorcans kindly point out a site on our left as 'archaeological', but famous for what I'm not clear. We pass through a small hill village and soon another which looks more lively. The road is tree lined now, tall straight trees, like gum trees. But I'm not really taking in the scenery because I'm worrying. About the tent. About camping.

129

The site of the Retreat is rather lovely: a set of converted farm buildings, with a swimming pool I notice happily, set in the hills above the sea. Unfortunately there's no view, but the building where we register looks simple, clean and cool in the blazing heat.

'Well, find a place for your tent,' the young Frenchman who signs me in says graciously.

'Where do you suggest?' I ask, having seen no sign of tents, or anything that might represent a place to pitch a tent on this rocky hillside.

'I think some people they found somewhere behind the Casa, you must see.'

The others have disappeared, so bowed under my rucksack, with its bedroll dangling, I make my way around the side of the building. Yes, there are a few tents on the hillside, between the boulders and scrubby bushes, but there isn't a piece of half-way level ground to be seen. Or a person for that matter. What to do?

'Meekle, hi Meekle'.

I turn. Teddy, Tibetan bag on his shoulder and objects (all significant I have learnt) around his neck bouncing, is calling as he half-walks, half-runs towards me. I am delighted to see him.

'Where do you want to be?' he asks.

'Not a clue, got any ideas?'

Together, we pace the hillside. The only question is whether I want to sleep at about 35 degrees on several boulders and some resolute looking tufts of mountain grass, or more like 45 degrees but on just a couple of boulders? I opt for 35 degrees, as Teddy assures me he can cut some tall grass from lower down the hillside and lay it to smooth out the ground for me. I take the tiny tent in its neat package out of my rucksack, undo the drawstring and try hard to remember what Peter told me. Actually, we had a trial run, in their immaculate Chelsea garden. The emerald lawn yielded simply to the little metal tent pegs. Somehow, it dawns on me, I don't think this stony hillside will do the same.

Eventually it's done. But I couldn't have done it without Teddy. He does, while I watch. Helplessly grateful. The ground is like iron. Only completely irregular and undulating. Good as his word, Teddy takes his large pocket knife and cuts an armful of straw-like grass to put under my ground sheet. Then I crawl in. It's like an oven. The underlying rocks seem to have multiplied, and I was definitely wrong in estimating 35 degrees — 65 seems more like it. As for my thin bedroll — it's almost an irrelevance.

'Thanks Teddy, that's great.'

'Good, glad that's out of the way. Ready for a swim. Just bring your gear — there are changing rooms down there.'

A number of half-finished changing rooms, I'm pleased to discover. Most of my co-attendees change around the edges of the pool. Not one elderly lady, though. Aged about seventy I guess, tall, slim and upright, she swims in what looks to me like old-fashioned long underwear. Which it might well be, as after a swim and then a sunbathe, she replaces a long skirt and long-sleeved blouse over the still damp garments. Choice or necessity? I wonder soberly. I don't consider this Retreat cheap, though my accommodation costs are very small, and I'm only staying four days, not the full fourteen.

Dinner provides my first view of the guru. My temper is excellent, partly because the food is rather good. 'Rinpoche always brings one or two of the girls who look after him in France, to organise the kitchen,' my neighbour tells me. Rinpoche is sitting slightly separately at a table with the others. To me, he looks a typical middle-aged oriental man in black track-suit bottoms and nondescript short-sleeved shirt. I am rather intrigued by his companions, though: a young couple, twenties I guess, and an immensely elegantly dressed man, around fifty, who is visiting the buffet to replenish Rinpoche's plate.

131

I'm a little tired — of travel and chatter — so I disappear after dinner. My tent comes into its own. I aim simply to enjoy the immediacy of the warm night and the mountain noises, but the urge to go to the other world insists, so I give way.

I enter through the usual mystical route. It's as if it is a code that is burnt on my consciousness. Will there be a day when I no longer remember this procedure? I wonder, prostrating myself at the place where the Christ and the Buddha energies come together to meet me. Again, as is this new norm, there are no teachings for me, but information. There are a few random pieces for or about people I know, yet again the statement that I can help Sara and she will come to me.

Then the source turns to Orgyen Rinpoche. There is a stream of information concerning what I can only call the male and female aspects of him. The source talks of his makeup and of his family situation. Not simply the wife and children I'm told he has, but the checks and balances resulting from his parents and grandparents too. Then I'm told to tell him what has been said.

I am not happy about that. My trust in this process is absolute. This hybrid reality enclosing me is the deepest truth I know. It is as true as the fact that I have laboured and given birth twice. It is as inescapable and inevitable as the passing of my children from infancy to adulthood. But it is, I recognise, profoundly only my reality. I have no desire to impose it on anyone else at all and feel no right to do so. What of obligation, though? No, I recoil in horror; to consider myself obliged to pass on my so-called wisdom, would be madness. Surely the only circumstances to pass on what is given to me is when someone asks to know?

Even T and V in my meditation have spoken of counselling or teaching 'those who come'. But how could anyone ask for information, if they didn't already know I held it? I am playing with this conundrum, listening to the noise of the crickets in the dark and the crunch of the dried grass beneath me, when I fall asleep.

I expect to be among the first at breakfast, which is held outside in the courtyard, but I am not. There are a pile of freshly baked loaves, coffee, tea and a large open jar of honey on each table. Looks good. A few wasps buzzing around, I notice, seating myself on a bench at one of the trestles, and keeping a wary eye cocked. The bread and honey are delicious. So delicious I am troubled before long by a persistent pair of insects. Finally, seeing the futility of dodging, I let the wasps settle on my plate. When both are immersed in a long dribble of honey, I bring the base of my mug down on them. Squash. An instant's silence from my neighbours.

'What did you do that for?' 'They've just as much right to live as you.' 'They're sentient beings.'

Teachings, a lecture with prayers which I sit out, pursuing my own devotions, follow breakfast. There is an immense comfort in sitting with others devoted to the spirit, in whatever form. I opt to sit on a chair, not cross-legged, and am interested to see the elegant fellow I recognise from dinner doing the same. At lunch, he manoeuvres himself beside me at the buffet and starts to chat. Evan Hornick, architect from New York, now living in Rome with his family. Evan's followed Orgyen Rinpoche's work for some years, he tells me, and offers Rinpoche general help too.

'What sort of help?' I query.

'Oh practical, financial, legal, that sort.'

We swim or rest until the end of the afternoon, when the teachings reconvene. The Rinpoche's words are oddly familiar. I let my mind wander. What am I doing here? The image of a young monk dead in the snow presents itself. I stiffen. The image is from the past lives I saw with Anna. More than once I saw myself as a holy man or woman in an Eastern setting. I have taken that heritage for granted. Curiously, my other world has somehow taught me not to return to my past lives, but to incorporate them and go on. I have a sense that I am not simply picking up my past but incorporating something else, some other new reality too. Yes, I am my past. That seems a truism. My genesis is wider than the limited realities of my past, all my pasts. Only the dimension, the definition of the way in which this is true, I cannot explain. Suffice to say, I accept these Buddhist teachings as known to me because I have known them in the past. I do not wish to re-learn them; not that doubting, or accepting, or even teaching them, should the opportunity arise, is the issue. But something else.

Evan Hornick comes to sit next to me at dinner. He tells me he has followed spiritual interests for twenty-five years, first with other masters before finding Orgyen six or seven years ago. He tells me about his life, his Quaker parents in Massachusetts, his coming to Europe and the influences on him. And he asks about mine. I take a gamble. I tell, a little, about what I've been doing and what has happened to me in recent months. If there is anywhere to talk about my experiences this must be it.

'You've got a voice that speaks to you?' He's incredulous. 'What's he say, this voice of yours?'

'Oh,' I'm vague, 'many things. For me, it's felt as if I'm learning a great deal. Like I said, I've spent hours in meditation most days, for months now. What it means I haven't a clue, I've been trying to find that out, it's partly why I'm here. But recently I started to be given information about people.'

'Oh, what about me, what does your little voice say about me?'

'Nothing,' I smile. 'That makes it sound awful, as if I'm receiving personal information about other people. It sounds like a ghastly science fiction plot, or some terrible way of getting power over people. It's not like that. It's different. But I can't quite explain how. Except that anything I'm given is for the benefit of the person it's about, it's almost as if I'm irrelevant.

'And I haven't a clue whether it's nonsense, true, or partly true. Also, I don't go on remembering it. I can't quite explain, it's something to do with not filing it in the way you do if you learn something that you want to remember.'

'So who've you got information on?'

'Actually, last night there was a lot of stuff on your Rinpoche.'

He's absolutely astounded. Then he grins, 'Well, go tell him, see what he makes of it.' Evan laughs. I smile too. Rinpoche has a reputation for plain speech and not tolerating fools.

'No, I couldn't. What right have I to go up to him and say "I want to tell you something about yourself!" I don't want to tell him anything. I'm not making any claims for my inform-ation, or looking for recognition, but I don't know why I am getting it.'

'Well, why don't you tell him you've got it, and wait and see if he asks to hear it? I'll tell him you have something to say to him, if you like, and we can see what happens. Anyway, he usually sees people at some stage on these retreats.'

Next morning, it's announced at breakfast that anyone who wishes a private audience with Rinpoche is to go to him on the balcony above the casa. I find the outside staircase that leads to the roof of the main building. There are two or three others before me. The young man I saw sitting at dinner with Rinpoche is taking names in a notebook. He takes mine and gives me a time. I've an hour to wait.

It's another balmy, bright day. I head down the dirt track towards the pool, but stop just before the final curve in the road that leads to it. At this point, the road is directly above the pool. A young man is standing at the deep end, naked, arms raised above his head. He pauses and then falls forward into the slightly dull water. He surfaces, swims a few strokes to the edge, pulls himself out and repeats the action with almost meditative calm. I watch. The same performance, like an art being perfected, takes place twice more. The most irregular part of the action is the bouncing of his penis — up, down, side, centre, other side. I decide to give the pool a miss for now.

The allotted time sees me waiting on the casa roof, while Rinpoche, seated in a folding chair, finishes his conversation with the person in front of me. The view is beautiful. The scene is not so much spectacular as unspoilt. At this height, the sea is visible: a deep blue, twinkling expanse. Lower down the hillside, lines of gnarled olive trees take up their positions and wind towards the water. A few houses are dotted here and there, original farmhouses I suspect, not modern developments. A donkey's bray cuts across the morning, followed by the scrape of a chair on concrete. Rinpoche is finishing his consultation. Henri, the young man, indicates it's my turn.

Rinpoche is facing into the breeze, wearing a black felt hat. I thank him for his time and introduce myself. He listens gravely, not looking at me. I lose my nerve. I can't say to this man I've come to tell him about himself, would he like to hear me?

Instead, I start, 'I have been having some rather unusual experiences, for many months now, and I'm here because I'm trying to understand them. I wondered if you could throw any light on the situation.'

'Please, what . . . ' He's clearly not one for wasting words. So I explain, fairly briefly, about stopping work and starting to meditate and a little about the form or shape of the meditation.

When I finish, he surprises me. He turns and looks at me, steadily, for longer than is comfortable, then says, 'You give me healing.' Whoa, I think, what's going on?

'I'm sorry,' I say, 'if I haven't explained clearly, I've been doing meditation, not healing. I don't know anything about healing.'

'You give me healing,' he repeats, as if I hadn't spoken.

'No, you don't understand, I really don't know anything about healing. I'm sorry, but that really is something I haven't a clue about.' I'm beginning to suspect this could be some sort of weird come-on. The way he's looking at me, I would not be entirely surprised.

'Can you tell me about myself?' He certainly has the ability to surprise me.

'I've been told a number of things about you.' It suddenly occurs to me that they're written in my note book, and I have been too preoccupied to bring it with me. But Rinpoche won't hear of my returning to fetch it. So, taking a large gulp, I begin to speak. A curious thing happens. As I speak, more and more words seem to come tumbling out. I'm hardly conscious of the sense of what I'm saying, just that I am speaking. He's studying me intently.

When I finish speaking, he says, 'Thank you,' that's all. 'Now you give me healing, you can,' he emphasises the word, 'do that. You give me healing.'

This time I think OK, if he's so sure I can, I'll try. So I pick up his hands, and press each hand, upright, palm against palm, and consciously, offer. My heart chakra starts to vibrate, as I have become accustomed to in the meditation. It's as if my entire chest is vibrating, not frantically, just steadily. Eventually, I stop and drop his hands.

'Thank you,' says Rinpoche. Then he calls Henri, 'We will go and swim now, I will see people after lunch. You like to swim?' he says turning to me, 'Come, I like to swim.' In which way we proceed to the swimming pool together.

I disappear to change and when I emerge, Rinpoche's stout body, clad in a nifty, continental-style bathing suit, is sitting on another folding chair, with Evan and a number of others around him. I hesitate, ready to slink into the background. He gesticulates to a chair beside him for me. I cringe. Evan smiles and raises his eyebrows, knowingly. I am covered in confusion, am I being set up for some awful pass after all?

'My leg,' says Rinpoche, 'it is not good,' pointing at his calf. 'You give it some healing,' and he smiles.

Is this for real? I'm thoroughly uncomfortable. 'Well,' I say, 'let me just feel if I can feel anything.'

Gently, I feel his calf, the way I've felt my children's limbs for years. While a curious group looks on. There's a click, someone is recording the moment on camera. I don't think I feel anything. Does he, I wonder? Then Rinpoche stands up, thanks me and walks to the edge of the pool. Within instants, he's at the centre of a noisy crowd lunging this way and that in the water.

Evan asks, 'So what happened then?' pulling his chair next to mine.

'He did seem quite taken with me, but I'm not sure why.'

'Michal, listen. Orgyen Rinpoche is no lightweight. He's immensely respected both in the Buddhist community and as an international authority. If this guy responded to you by asking for healing, it's very serious indeed.'

'Oh I don't know, Evan. It's very difficult to know what he thinks — especially for someone who's an outsider, like me. I don't necessarily think that the fact that he asked me for healing is significant.'

'You're crazy. Everyone here is totally amazed. A man like Orgyen wouldn't let any student touch him, let alone ask someone out of the blue for healing. You have to see that it's fantastically unusual. You don't know what a sensation you caused.'

'Really, you think it's something I should take serious notice of?'

'At last! Absolutely. And you never told me you knew anything about healing!'

'Well, I don't.'

'Oh come on — everybody saw Orgyen ask you for healing.'

'Yes, he did, but I didn't know what to do. It was just that he thought I did.'

'No, this is crazy. You say he asked you for healing but you didn't know what to do.'

'He seemed to think that I could do it, despite my saying I didn't know anything about it.'

'Michal, Orgyen Rinpoche told you that you were a healer! This is absolutely incredible. Please, will you give me healing? Will you do exactly what you did for Orgyen Rinpoche? If it's good enough for him, it's certainly good enough for me.'

'Oh come on. This is silly. I told him I don't know anything about healing. All I could do was tell him some things that came in my meditation.'

'Forget it. You obviously don't realise what you can do. You told him what your little voice said to you?'

'Yes, just some things about him. It was odd. I seemed just to speak. There was a lot about his family and ancestors, a lot that I didn't understand. Anyway, he asked me to tell him what I could, so I did.'

'Please can I come to you and will you give me healing, and tell me whatever you can about myself, just like you told Orgyen Rinpoche?' He's obviously not joking. I'm not sure what to reply.

'OK, next time you're in London,' I say, half-joking.

At lunch, Orgyen insists I sit at his table, at supper the same. After the late afternoon's teachings, he orders a film show of his recent trip to Tibet. When the show is ready, he summons me from the back of the hall to sit beside him and proceeds to give me a running commentary on the pictures. I am embarrassed and uncomfortable. But I know now, it's not some kind of come-on. He's entirely genuine.

The following day, my last day, is very similar. I will not be sorry to leave, although in many senses I am impressed by

Rinpoche. I've seen how he is teaching morality in his own way, and believe Evan when he says Rinpoche's first students when he came to Europe were drug takers and drop outs whose lives have been significantly transformed by Orgyen's teachings.

Just before lunch, Rosemary, as I discover the girl who sits with Henri is called — she lives in Rinpoche's home community — asks if I can help with the community dog. The dog has travelled with them by road from France. A sweet-faced mongrel bitch. She has diarrhoea and has stopped eating. A sensible strategy, I think, and am about to say helping dogs is something else I can't do, when I think, why not? I remember the package of homeopathic pills I have brought with me, in case of emergency. One sort that's good for fever and one for food poisoning. Why not try the dog on a pill for food poisoning? By dinner, she is eating again and my reputation evidently exceeds all bounds.

That evening, Henri tells me he will be giving Rinpoche a massage and please will I attend. Why? I ask immediately. To give him healing, or just to be present is the answer. I start to mutter a series of protests, but give up. Henri appears to be a competent masseur. I decline to offer any further healing, but it does not seem to cause any offence. Rinpoche is dismayed to learn I am leaving when the retreat has hardly begun. I apologise and we agree to write.

Taking the tent down is much easier than putting it up. I will be immensely grateful for a bed now. The journey back to London is uneventful. I am glad to be home, but I'm not prepared for what happens next.

Chapter Thirteen

Work

September 1991 Home a week from Majorca, I have just finished painting 'He fell'. An elaborate picture of an event in my inner world. There's an edge in my activities now. How long can I continue without earning? I know I cannot go back to my old life, but where will I go? A circular comes from the College of Psychic Studies. I scan it and put it aside. I don't want to see or hear anyone else. An afterimage strikes me of the name in the top right-hand corner. I pull the pink sheet back, and look at it: Brenda Marshall, the chairperson. I was told to '*see Brenda*' some weeks ago. Is she the Brenda? Seems worth a try. I call. I have to become a member to make an appointment to see her. So I do, and fix to come the next available date, which is not for another month or so.

The pressure from my inner world continues. I am shown how to place my hands in healing. The skill is used to give one of my brothers healing, in meditation, at a specific chakra. I am warned he has a physical problem and requires treatment. But, in the everyday world he appears enormously fit and well, as ever. (Years later a medical problem surfaces, seated at that place in his body.) Others come, still in meditation, for healing. Then, I think I'm being instructed to say what comes as it comes, rather than simply writing it down in my notebook from memory afterwards.

To the deep. It is dark — still, night water. Incandescence shines on the surface, my image glitters. I do not mind the darkness. I am not afraid. Light comes. Glorious sunlight filters through the water. I kneel and ask for the help of the Divine, of God, of the Unknown. I am asked to speak out loud, to repeat what is said to me aloud, and to speak myself out aloud. Speak into a tape recorder perhaps?

Meanwhile, this break has been nine months. My meditation keeps telling me I am ready for work. Work will come. 'Spiritual counselling', or 'teaching', V and T say, but I hardly know what they mean. The phone rings.

'Michal, I hope you don't think I'm completely batty, but I wonder whether I could come an see you as a client — I'm going through some horrible stuff at the moment and it feels so deep and familiar I was wondering if it had anything to do with a previous life? Do you think you could help?'

'Sara, why do you think I might be able to help?'

'Well, partly because of what you've told me about your own experience and then other things you've said. I know you know a great deal — though you don't think you do — but I think you really know about Buddhism. Your experiences are completely different from anyone else's I've ever heard of — and I know you don't think of it as Buddhism and it might not be. I know you'll deny it, but I think you're a very high reincarnation, or something similar.'

Her speech is faster and faster, words tumbling out. 'And although you don't know the names for what you know, you have loads of knowledge of all sorts of practices. You actually see Tara, the female figure you talk about. And I think you're really closely linked with Vajakilaya. All that cutting through. You've described to me specific Vajakilaya practice, I looked it up, it's exactly like the text books say — you even use some of the same words, but you've never done any study. And how he looks. You describe the right number of arms and legs and everything.' Her voice is quivering. 'And the medicine Buddha. You don't seem to realise how exceptional it all is.' Then more slowly, as if drawing breath, 'I am not exactly sure why or how, but I'm sure you can help me.'

'Let me think about it. May I call you back in a few days?'

'Please. But, I'd really like to see you. I don't want to put pressure on you, and I expect I'll just make you cross by saying it, but I think you're an incarnation of Yshe Tsogyel, you remember, we talked about her — there are so many parallels, I think *terma* are being revealed to you — hidden teachings. I could go on and on. Remember you told me about the Undead? Well, that's exactly like Chod practice, going to the charnel grounds, offering yourself up and allowing yourself to be devoured, out of compassion. I'm sorry if I'm going on, but its so extraordinary.'

I replace the phone and sit down heavily. I can't dispute what Sara's saying, but I certainly don't accept it either. It's the words that come to me that I am following. My source in meditation has been telling me that Sara will come to me and that I am to help her. But how?

That night, I ask. After asking for the Christ and the Buddha's help, I go to the deep and put the questions. The answers are very specific. I am told exactly what to do and the nature of the problem. Next morning, I ask again. My source is dismissive. Why am I not doing what I was told? Still I hesitate. It feels as if I have no knowledge, no skills, no special abilities to offer. I have a list of instructions written in a notebook. What to do? Another day passes. I surrender.

I call Sara, 'Sara, yes, there are two or three past lives which have a particular bearing on your present situation. I think it would be useful for you to go through them.'

'Oh, thank you very much.'

'Sara, no guarantees. All I can say is that I had been told you would be calling sooner or later. I'll do my best to pass on what's been given to me.'

Before Sara arrives, I have a strong sense that I should light a candle. I think I'll humour it, just for fun. Then I find myself arranging three candles on the low wickerwork table in my sitting room. The afternoon sun is streaming through the floor-to-ceiling, west-facing windows. A geranium, still in flower, stands in a yellow pot on the gas fire hearth and catches the light. A jumble of shells, plant containers, odds and ends are tucked underneath the table my Aunt Edith left to me.

The room is soft, yellow and pink, but eclectic too. Something old, something new, something borrowed — not much is blue. Except the linings of the curtains are made from the old blue-green-grey curtains that used to hang in my parents' sitting room when I was growing up. In the recess on either side of the fireplace, are the nineteenth-century black and white church prints that have followed me from place to place these last twenty years. The room fits me, I feel comfortable here.

'It's lovely to see you, this room is gorgeous,' enthuses Sara as she comes in. 'Where do you want me to sit?'

'Oh anywhere, I don't mind.' She sits down on the sofa. I pick up a box of matches and bend to light the candles before sitting down beside her.

'Aren't they pretty?' she says, seeing the candles, one of which is stuck in an old shell. 'Why three?'

I am about to say, 'Just for fun,' or something similar, when another string of words pass my lips, 'One for the son of man, one for the spirit of God, one for . . . '

I don't hear what I say I am so astonished. Who is the son of man? Am I talking about the Christ? The words sound like words from my meditation. How am I saying them?

Sara doesn't seem to notice. 'Do you want me to sit, or lie down?'

144

Now it is as if another note has entered altogether. She no longer needs to persuade me to see her. The need to disclaim knowledge has left. All I am aware of is that she has asked and that I must give.

'Best to take your shoes off and lie where you are,' I say, moving the wicker table a little back. I kneel beside Sara and automatically raise my hands to the prayer position. Then the words of the prayer I use before meditation fill my consciousness, 'Dear God, guide me, teach me to follow . . . ' as I empty myself of desire other than the wish to do God's will. A profound sense of stillness descends on me. Simultaneously of ordinariness. It's as if there is nothing special in the situation. The fact that Sara is a friend is somehow irrelevant. I haven't asked her anything about the situation that has brought her to see me. It's not relevant and I am not curious. I know what I have to do.

I pull a chair up beside the couch and for a moment I am aware of an incongruity — sitting in the analyst's position beside a therapist. It is fleeting, this process could not be further from psychoanalysis. Reading the instructions in my notebook, I ask Sara to breathe, just a simple process of shallow breathing from the top of her lungs, to relax and follow whatever comes up. She is anxious, but I know the process will unfold. Soon she engages with the breath and I am aware a different world is taking over.

'It's like meditation,' Sara murmurs. 'I'm not sure where this is.'

'Don't try and analyse,' I say, 'Just look around and see where you are. Don't think about it, however strange it may seem, don't think about anything, just say whatever comes. Try and describe what you see.'

Sara's breathing is light and easy. Her voice sounds as if from a long way away. 'I am standing on flagged paving stones in a large building. It's a bit dark and shadowy. The ceiling's very high. It smells a little dank, musty I think, it's cold. I'm walking near some carved solid wooden benches — are they pews? There are more elaborate wooden carvings on the wall in front of me. And there's a doorway with a heavy velvet curtain behind me. I think this could be a vestry in a church. It feels as if there are lots of comings and goings. I think there are priests or monks whispering, or something like that going on.

'I think,' she pauses, 'we're in medieval times. I'm a man. Perhaps wearing a cloak, possibly I'm armed.' She hesitates, then continues more confidently, 'I think I am around people of power, but I am not sure if I'm a secular person, or some sort of religious authority. No, perhaps I'm both?'

Listening to her, I am altogether focused on where she is. It's as if I see the scene, almost without Sara's words. Although I obviously have no experience of conducting a past life regression, or even been interested in trying, it's as if I know exactly what to do and have complete command of the situation. Yet I am simply following the instructions passed on in my meditation and written in my notebook.

'It feels very real. I feel very anxious. It's really familiar, that sense of anxiety. There's a horrible feeling in my gut. I'm bad. I feel bad in my gut. What am I doing here? I think this is a horrible plot and I'm playing some ghastly part. This is real cloak-and-dagger stuff.' She hesitates. I know part of her doesn't want to go on.

'Look at what's going on,' I encourage. 'Try and understand it, explain it.'

'I'm in the wrong,' she blurts out. 'I'm behaving badly, I'm involved in some sort of treachery, perhaps betraying confidences. I've been engaged in playing one side off against the other in some political and religious intrigue.' Her voice has risen, there's a note of agitation.

It's time for me to speak. 'You're caught up in a world of intrigue. It's a familiar dilemma for you: the interrelation of church and state. You're snared in the politics of the situation. Whatever you do, it's not possible to get it right if you try to wear both religious and secular hats at the same time, because there is a fundamental incompatibility in mixing religion and politics.' I don't know where what I'm saying is coming from, but I have no doubt about it.

Sara has hurried to pick up the story again. 'The image of the church vestry is getting sharper, I can hear rustling — is it coming from the doorway, has someone parted the curtain? I'm afraid, very afraid.'

I feel her distancing herself from the situation, doubting it, 'Just stay with the images, Sara, don't doubt what you see. It doesn't matter whether or not it really happened. The point is to see them as a metaphor and understand what they mean. Remember that images come to open your understanding and to help penetrate the deeper layers of your mind. Don't get caught up in considerations of the truth or falsehood of the situation, try and let the meaning come to you.'

'I feel mean and guilty. I feel dirty in my soul. What I'm doing in the church isn't right. There's someone else there. I can't see anyone, but I know someone's there, I'm afraid. There's a terrible pain in my throat,' she's gasping now, 'I'm choking, I can't breathe. Now someone's stuck a dagger in me, I can feel the blade passing through my flesh. I'm afraid, but I'm also watching myself now. I'm falling down, I'm struggling, I can see myself trying to call out. I can see it all, but I'm also strangely detached. Now I'm making the most hideous noise,' Sara issues a terrible, harsh, guttural cry. It's like nothing I have ever heard before. I know it is her death cry.

'Don't worry,' I say, 'it's all right, you are dying now, just let go, let it all go and continue on past your death. Go on with your journey and tell me what you see.'

'I'm leaving my body and the church behind. It's as though I'm floating or dismembered.' Her voice is lighter, in a higher, 147 keener octave. 'I'm surrounded by a lilac or lavender coloured light. The light is rather dull. Is that because I've had such a shady life? I feel tremendous shame and regret. I really long to purify myself. I feel as if there is a great presence of light and forgiveness, I feel awed and humbled. It's as if I'm forgiven. Does that mean I can forgive myself? Perhaps they're one and the same thing.'

'Rest, be at peace, forgiveness is yours,' again I am speaking without planning the words, but I know they are correct.

Together, Sara and I explore two further lives. Not in quite the same detail, but each culminating in a violent death. In one she is the aggressor, in another the victim. Both involve her throat being cut and questions of honour. Then it's enough. Still following my instructions, I massage the extremities of her body lightly, talking to her all the time, until she is fully present and her body has relaxed.

Then, and only then, do I ask her to say what brought her to me this afternoon.

Sara explains that there are problems in the Buddhist organisation of which she is a trustee. She has an active management role, which in effect now means speaking out against certain actions, which she believes to be wrong, by the man employed as a co-ordinator. It is an extremely uncomfortable situation, with an atmosphere of political intrigue, backbiting and manipulation which is quite at odds with the spiritual purposes of the group.

It has made Sara feel deeply inadequate, and question whether she has the right to speak out. Is she 'good enough' to do so? Or is it a case of 'people in glass houses shouldn't throw stones'? But quite why she should feel that hasn't been clear. At the same time, as an experienced psychotherapist, her assessment of the actions of the co-ordinator and the group around him has been quite clear and very disturbing. The entire situation seems to produce deep distress in her.

Much deeper than she can understand. Eventually talking it over with her trusted girlfriend, Heather, who has no Buddhist connections, she decided to call me.

I link the images from her past life visions with the current situation, and point out how she has power in this life within a spiritual organisation, and the challenge is to use it wisely and well, to follow what she feels to be right and appropriate. Also, how the issue of using her voice has run through her life. I remind her how she gave up a promising career as a classical singer in unclear circumstances. How now, again, the issue is about speaking out, using her throat, which she has seen repeatedly being cut. Privately, I have constantly been surprised by the way I see Sara as accepting the domination of her Buddhist spiritual teacher, losing herself, so it seems to me, but I do not say that. Sara seems stunned, but somehow enthusiastic, as she gets up to leave.

'Michal that was utterly wonderful, I can't thank you enough. May I come again?'

'Yes, in fact there is a little more we have to do.'

'Really, that's wonderful. And I must pay you too, what would you like?'

I had not thought of charging and the question stumps me. But we agree and she's gone. Curiously, I don't think about what has happened. Incredibly, it seems, somehow, nothing special. A week later, a long letter comes from Sara.

Dear Michal,

I am writing because I have been so amazed by the extraordinary impact of the session with you. I want to give you some feedback.

I suppose up until this point, all my life I have had a sense of inner badness or 'existential guilt'. It's a feeling that I have done something wrong, but I don't know quite what it was. I remember the feeling since childhood of never being quite at ease with myself. Therapy has never really been able to fix it, nor have years of spiritual study, meditation and retreats. My session with you, though, seems to be revolutionising my understanding, or sense of self. In fact, it feels as if a complete personal revolution has just begun, and will continue.

Somehow, I have gained a consciousness of a previously hidden darker side, which means I am no longer driven by an unknown fear. You helped me face and accept aspects of myself and to forgive myself, so I can move on. Incredibly, the fear of facing this unknown inner badness has gone, because I have done it and survived — there is nothing to defend against any more (until the next discovery!). I cannot believe how quickly it has happened.

What is also extraordinary in the process is that at the same time as facing my darkness, you simultaneously helped me connect with a tremendous feeling of light within. I have had a great sense of well-being these last few days. I'm not sure, but I think this might be termed 'co-emergant wisdom' in Buddhism. I suppose in psychoanalysis we call it integrating splits in the psyche.

I want to thank you for helping me to gain an altogether different insight into myself than my psychoanalytic therapy and practice. It feels a much deeper, more profound, different sort of insight. I don't know how you can still dispute your power. I hope you won't mind, but last night I went to a supper party where a lama who is a very well-known scholar was the guest of honour. I asked him what it would mean if someone was spontaneously having visions of the kind that you are. In particular I mentioned Vajakilaya and the medicine Buddha. He said it would mean that you are a very accomplished spiritual being who has attained a very high level of realisation in a previous life. Which is what I thought. I hope it convinces you.

With love, Sara

Then the phone starts to ring. First it is Hans, Sara's partner, who wants to come and see me. So do Margery, a former psychiatric social worker, and Julian, a probation officer. All have heard of me through Sara. I give the same answer. They are welcome to come and I will pass on what is given to me — assuming that I am given something to pass on. They come, and come again. As do others: Sam who is a carpenter; Mary, a psychotherapist in training; Tom, another designer; Eve, a retailer; Elizabeth, who lives on a private income; Cally, a student; Nicholas, a successful entrepreneur; Claire, an art therapist; Liz, a musician; Margaret, an administrator; Evelyn, a Jungian analyst, and more.

Before each comes, I sit in meditation, and ask what I am to say and do. I tape record the answers, allowing myself to speak the words as they come. I am told the outlines of the problem and certain points I am to make, or what I am to do. What remedies, if any, to offer. Smell is important too, I learn. Never use incense, don't wear perfume. But, I am also told a little about essential oils. There are a few which on different occasions I am to burn, and later another use for one or two emerges.

In most cases, I'm instructed to give healing. I am told to look at the energy for myself and say what I see. That seems to me a relatively unimportant part of my instructions. I consider myself a conduit, nothing more. My notions of receiving and passing on information, or help, are mechanistic. The idea of seeing anyone without having 'checked' the night before what to do or say is quite unimaginable. Nor does it cross my mind that there might be an aspect of the interaction that is not encompassed by the words, or even actions.

Each session is different. It is as if when a client sits in front of me another being takes my place. My uncertainties, personal insecurities, wants, likes, dislikes and needs disappear. There is only the person before me and a universe of light.

Surprisingly, I find my power of sight clear and strong. Chakras show in differing colours; light or darkness indicate weaknesses and strengths, injury and illness where it is actually in the physical body, or coming close to it. I ask about illnesses since childhood, as often scars in one form or another also show.

Physical weak spots, or troubles of an emotional or physical sort, are clear. The emotional links take me by surprise. Sometimes I see a figure at a particular chakra, or a configuration of some sort. These are telling a story which has a bearing on the individual concerned. Almost always, close relationships, parents, family, lovers, are shown. All this I am able to say. It surprises me, momentarily, when I think about it with my ordinary mind. When I do it, it is simply what I do. When it is done, it leaves my mind and is no more.

I follow the guidance and the framework of my meditation notes. The use of remedies gives me a problem. Telephoning the chemist, or thumbing through a *materia medica*, I check which are 'real' homeopathic remedies and which are not. If not, I make them and offer them without a special qualm, because I know they are no more than sugar pills infused with energy. But, if 'real', I do not know what to do. I am not qualified in any way to prescribe or dispense 'medicine'. My meditation does not seem to regard it as a problem. I do.

Homeopathic remedies are not considered potent by the medical establishment. Liberal medical thought would probably have that they may sometimes be useful, but cannot be harmful, since they are dilutions of matter, often beyond the point where science can find any trace of the original substance in the dilution. Most doctors simply disregard them though. They are freely sold in chemists. There are, I believe, no official restrictions on their sale and use. Still, I call Jeanette and ask her. I describe the conditions of the individuals concerned and outline what it is the meditation says I am to offer.

'That's right,' she says, 'just do as you are told. Don't worry.' I call her once, twice more, with similar questions. Then she, and the meditation, insist that I am simply to follow my intuition. Nonetheless, I prefer remedies I make myself.

I do not understand what I am doing. I simply do it. Healing perplexes me, a little. In offering it, I place my hands at the points to which I am directed. I feel little myself, except a curious detachment and a sort of elation. I am aware of my body vibrating slightly and a surprising certainty. Sara and Heather, both of whom now come regularly as clients (I have to limit how often people come in some cases, where they want weekly healing because it feels so good) treat me differently from the companion of their heath rambles. But gently. Our social contact stops, but, as if they realise I do not understand the feeling my healing inspires, both try at different times to tell me.

'I've had healing before,' says Sara, 'and you feel warmth from the healer's hands — it's very nice. But you seem to be coming from somewhere quite different. You touch very lightly, it's hardly as if you touch at all, and it feels cool, or much cooler, but that's not quite the right word, because it isn't about temperature.

'It's otherworldly, it gives me the feeling that I have been totally filled with light, a sparkly light that comes through you or from you.'

Heather says, 'It makes my heart feel wide open, it brings a sort of really deep peace.' Both agree that often afterwards they go home and sleep. That is so common an experience — with people sometimes drifting off under my hands — that I take to warning clients to expect it.

My feedback from others is similar. Julian, the probation officer, is fighting depression. He craves healing. So does Claire, an art therapist. Her partner is a psychoanalyst and the relationship is troubled. In her unhappiness and tension, healing appears, to begin with, as a panacea.

153

'It's an amazing, pure feeling,' she says after our first session. 'It is the first time since my childhood that I've felt so easy. It's as if all the tension has gone, as if everything has been just taken away.'

I am slightly concerned at these responses, for a complicated reason. Although I am adamant that I am not a substitute for medical help, and urge all my clients who feel they have physical problems (or if I see established medical conditions) to see their doctors, sometimes I find myself dealing with physical problems. A successful theatre producer comes to see me, doubled over a walking stick. At forty-nine, he has reached a difficult place in life and cannot go forward. We talk. He is facing his personal, emotional pain so bravely; stoically too, with no sense that life could offer any other options. Which it always can. Then I give him healing, and watch his foot move in an involuntary arc, while my hands are on his upper body. His condition improves.

But in most cases I do not offer healing as a specific treatment for a particular ailment. Healing is simply part of what I do, which I think of as spiritual counselling. It is helping people to resolve and further their relationship with the spirit, which inevitably involves dealing with their emotional and practical lives. I see my role — as far as I understand it — as helping others to make their own choices, find their own paths, uncover the light within themselves, and so further their evolution, becoming ever more responsible for themselves.

Healing them in the sense of taking their worries away, in some magic process, seems a deviation. Though I concede to myself it may be useful, even necessary, on occasion. Meanwhile, my meditation seems to say that I am not a 'healer', as is usually understood, but that I am sometimes to give healing. So I do, without too much further thought. A line in my meditation alerts me to other possibilities, but I am too busy to consider it much. It talks of the chakras, and healing and

154

what I can do *practically. But, it is what you say and what you give off — your vibration — that is of the truest importance.*

The same problem, but in a slightly different form, occurs with remedies. One client suffers from a persistent bladder infection, which years of antibiotics have failed to clear. Concentrating on her fear, on her attitude towards her sexuality, and giving her a homeopathic remedy, it is quickly cleared. She is overjoyed and insists (for years to come) on consulting me for any physical ailment, certain that I will be able to prescribe.

In another case, Les, a local government worker and active trade unionist, is troubled by a terrible skin rash. I advise medical help. Nothing works. A month or more passes; a homeopath has failed her, as have other expensive alternative consultations. Finally, since a course of remedies has presented itself to me, I tell her what they are, but also that she must check with her own qualified practitioner, and ask him to prescribe them if he feels they are appropriate. 'He says they're harmless,' she says, calling to report, 'and they won't help, but if I want to take them, he's given me a prescription.' She does and the cure is rapid. Which allows us to continue our work, to the point where I feel she is happy to leave me, having reached a new level of understanding within herself.

More people come. Different clients choose to come in different patterns. I am anxious not to create dependants. A few come once and not again, or not for some months or even years. Some come regularly for a short or longer while. Others who come often at first, I then suggest come every few months. Later, I start a healing and meditation group in the evening.

Sometimes the effects are dramatic. I am instructed to wash one particular client's feet with water containing an essential oil. She calls me later in the week, her voice quivering, 'Michal, my legs have come out in boils, or something like that, great big pimples.' She is obviously very upset, but fortunately not angry at me.

'That must be quite frightening, Elaine,' I reply, almost frightened myself, 'have the boils burst?' What I would suggest if she says yes, I don't know, but it seems the right sort of question to ask.

'No, but I think they will. It's very dramatic.' Now she sounds less concerned than I feel, 'It's all the impurities coming out isn't it?' In fact she sounds excited! It's not the kind of statement I feel comfortable with, but there is nothing I can say or do. I intend to check with my meditation and there is obviously no way to go but forward.

When next she comes, I am told to repeat the process. Poor Elaine suffers with boils discharging on her legs for several weeks, until they heal finally and disappear completely. She is delighted. What I notice is that her sense of well-being over the months we are working together alters dramatically; she is able to take major steps to sort out the practicalities of her life, which up to that point she has been seriously neglecting and leaving to others, while pursuing a supposedly spiritual path.

While all this is developing, I find time to keep my appointment at the College of Psychic Studies. It's a grand, stucco-fronted building, with a pillared entrance in South Kensington, no doubt richly endowed in the late nineteenth-century enthusiasm for communicating with the dead.

The receptionist shows me to the lift. Mrs Marshall's room is way up at the top of the building, not a receiving room, not even a main bedroom. Some lesser mortal's province. It amuses me. The woman who faces me across a large desk is tiny, impeccably neat, traditionally dressed and more than sixty, I guess. She's courteous and thoughtful. I repeat why I have come — because my meditation told me to, and how I have, rightly or wrongly, identified her as the Brenda in question. She listens. Then she suggests there are two people who work at the college, a man and a woman, whom I might like to meet. One she describes as an inspirational speaker, the other more like a medium. She gives me their names, and offers to help in the future if she can. Then we part.

That night, when I merge with T, I report the two names. See them both, I am told. Both matter. Which is exactly what happens. One, in particular, becomes an important friend in the next few years.

By December, there are too many clients for me to cling to instructions from my meditation before seeing each one. I cannot meditate twice a day. Some days I cannot manage once. Miraculously, it seems I can speak out myself. I can look, see, listen to an inner voice and talk. I can follow instructions and act simultaneously. Written instructions are not necessary. It's a revelation and a joy.

I have to be careful about becoming tired, though. My physical energy, in years gone by boundless, is fragile. I do not see clients every day. Some days simply rising, taking my daughter to school, preparing our meals, collecting her and doing all that follows with a child after 3.00pm, is as much as I can do. I put it down to the work. But, in meditation I seem to receive nothing but encouragement. The place I find myself there has changed too. The depths no longer call me. Instead, I stand at the foot of the mountain I glimpsed before, a radiant golden mountain, and ask for God's help. It is always offered. I'm working. It is what I wanted. My joy is immense. If only I was not so tired, and Christmas to face.

January 1992 Now I meet the Christ and the Lord Buddha at the top of the radiant mountain. Angels surround us. The air and light are exquisite. The clarity is unlike anything on earth. I address God directly and he seems to speak in reply. I continue to receive information about people who come to me and those in my life. General instructions too — it seems I must go and see Sai Baba, of whom I know nothing, at Easter.

Then there are passages about myself that I cannot comprehend (but that's nothing new). I am told, *'Beloved, you are not human. Release the human condition. Admit and acknowledge and give up your human form.'* In the same session, *'I recognise you are human and will do all I can to fulfil your human needs. But I know too that you are only partially human.'* I feel very much human, and awareness of my human needs never leaves me.

My basement, one room, is empty. It was my brother David's base while he worked abroad as a management consultant. I wonder, am I to work there? I take the plunge, I'm glad to release my sitting room from the stream of clients. And I buy a massage table, specially adapted for healing. My clients change and increase. An even greater diversity of people come, including some who are well known, creative people and rock musicians too. I work. I am happy.

Chapter Fourteen

Sai Baba

February 1992 'No, I'm sorry, but he will not be there. It's too hot, he will be in the hills. Baba always goes to the hills when it gets too hot. Why don't you come later?' The Indian lady's voice is placid and soft, with a characteristic, attractive lilt.

Mine, in reply is despairing, 'It's just not possible. I'm coming with my daughter, in her school holiday and there's only a very tight window of time when I can come. Are you sure there's no chance he'll be in Bangalore?'

'Oh, very sure. You see, in Bangalore in April it can be very warm. He's never there at that time. Baba will be in Kodai-kanal, the Nilgrin hills, you see it's cool there.'

What perplexes me is that my source in meditation is quite adamant that I'm to go and see Baba at Easter. *'You will acquire energy and information that you need.'* The very end of March or start of April is the only time I can go, to fit in with school holidays and the children's arrangements. My son doesn't want to come. My daughter does. I check out cheap tickets. Making a package holiday in Goa the focus of the trip, and planning a short expedition to Bangalore, it's financially possible and will serve two purposes. I will follow the instructions and go to Bangalore, even if Sai Baba's not there, and we will have the pleasure of a week on the Indian ocean. I'm tired. White sands and sea in a relatively unspoilt place appeal. Nearly two months to go, though.

I continue to meditate regularly, when I can. It's like returning to a childhood home.

At the top of the radiant mountain, I enter an enormous source of light and integrate so that I cannot see myself any longer. You are me now, as I am you.

What you see for your clients is not always true in a literal sense. You do not yet understand the figurative well enough, that will come. What you are shown is true in a spiritual sense, like a metaphor. You know what there is to know. You are only remembering it. Or reflecting it. Slowly, I am polishing you, then all will be reflected on your surface and you need only look at yourself to know what is before you.

We leave England early Saturday, 27 March. In my diary, I write,

A long, long journey. To Delhi — delayed by an hour — to Bombay, arriving in early hours of the morning. Transferring to the domestic airport, read *Midsummer Night's Dream* with Ellie at 5.00am, waiting for a flight to Bangalore. Arrive mid-morning.

Blinking in the bright sunlight on the steps of the aeroplane, I am amazed at how different Bangalore is from Bombay. Red hibiscus nodding in the heat line the short walk into the low airport building. It could be Harare, Bulawayo, Cape Town, Pretoria or a dozen other small African destinations of my childhood. The airport seems a small patch on a flat plain, with no sign of industrial development or slums at its edges. Collecting our bags consists of no more than picking them up from the spot they're deposited by the baggage handlers and walking out into the teeming parking lot.

Auto rickshaws, taxis, bicycles, hawkers vie for space. Some men are wearing garlands, there's a sense of carnival in the air.

A tall, middle-aged taxi driver swoops down on us and I give him the name of our hotel as we settle in the back of his old Ambassador — the colonial-style automobile that holds sway in India.

'Is it always like this,' I ask our driver, 'so busy, so much going on?'

'No,' he laughs, 'today is special day. Sai Baba, he's come back.'

'What do you mean, he's come back here?'

'No, not here, he's gone to Whitefields.'

'I don't understand. Sai Baba is not in Bangalore?'

'No, no he does not stay in Bangalore, but early this morning he came back here and now he has gone down to Whitefields to the ashram.'

'Goodness.' I am amazed. 'Were you expecting him?'

'No, no. Normally at this time of the year he is in the hills, but we don't know why, today he came back. Now everyone is very happy. You know he is a great saint here.'

'Are you a Sai Baba follower?'

'Yes, of course, and my family.'

'Have you seen him?'

'Of course. I have been with my wife and my children, many times.'

'Have you seen him do anything extraordinary, make gold rings appear, or heal anyone in front of you?'

'No, but my mother, she has. Once when she was with Baba, she saw him heal a man who could not walk, and he was able to walk afterwards. But there are many people who have seen him when he makes miracles.'

'So I understand. What about virbouti?' The ash, I've learnt, that's supposed to come from his hands. 'Have you seen it?'

'Oh yes.'

'Are you going to see him again?'

'Yes, but I don't know when. It is very busy you know, you must wait a long time to see Sai Baba.'

'I was thinking of going to seen him. Would we have to wait a very long time?'

'Now it will not be too bad, because no-one was expecting him. People will start to go to Whitefields, but there will not be so many.'

'How far is it to Whitefields?'

'Oh not far, I'll take you, do you want to go this afternoon, or tomorrow?'

We discuss time and price — my daughter's needs are more immediate, a swimming pool — so we arrange to go tomorrow, early morning. Then I settle back, admiring our route, which easily justifies Bangalore's title as 'garden city' of India. Acres and acres of park land are threaded through the town.

Our hotel is colonial and comfortable, Ellie heads straight for the swimming pool. I read in the shade, while she plays with a new Indian friend in the water. *Sai Baba Avatar*, according to the cover, is a book about a god-man, detailing the personal experiences of many of those who have benefited from him, and attempting to explain Sai Baba, his path and the spiritual truths that the author sees him as manifesting.

Out-of-body experiences seem common. There are several stories relayed where Sai Baba manifests to followers in times of need all around the world. Manifesting precious objects also seems a common feat. Then there are stories of his healing powers and the sacred ash that comes from him. I gather that he teaches love, truth, right living, non-violence and peace, while playing an obviously superior, guru role to his followers.

There's said to be strict discipline at his centre, with men and women separated and only married couples sleeping together. Service to the community, or the world more generally, is highly rated. I know Sai Baba's organisation is in the process of building one of the largest hospitals in south east Asia, from donations. It seems no money is asked for in audiences or prayer meetings. But donations are welcome, though it's said that Baba has been known to turn funds away if he is unhappy about the source.

Finally, while born a Hindu, it seems that Sai Baba urges that all religions are equal, from the same source, and that all have an inner Divinity. Much of that seems uncontroversial and laudable to me. But I'm looking forward to seeing the man. According to my diary, what happens is as follows.

Monday, 7.00am We leave to go and see Sai Baba, almost an hour's drive. The morning is beautiful. Arrive at Whitefields. Drive through village, held up at railway crossing in a stream of traffic, all going to the same place — Baba, for morning Darshan. Walk into a huge compound, after being hassled by the usual vendors. Cream walls enclosing area, monkeys scampering along the tops. Low buildings painted shades of pale blue, cream and a rusty pink.

Shoes off — huge area of sandals on the ground (put ours in my bag). Ushered across compound to join a square that was being formed — rows of women. Sitting in the growing heat. Eventually, by lottery, the rows are called forward to sit in shaded area. We are about the fourth row to be called. Waiting again. Chattering of monkeys. Conversation with neighbours, mostly Indian, some foreigners.

Baba comes from behind a wall at the edge of the compound, along an alley way in the crowd. His appearance is not special. He throws flower petals, accepts letters, and quite quickly is gone. It's over.

When I shut my eyes and looked at Baba's retreating figure, there was some impression of a 'haze' around him — some sort of energy field I suppose — but most significant I saw two 'energy' beings in outline at his shoulders. Like Indian gods or spirits, comparatively small, each no taller than his head. It's possible there was a third, on his left, but I'm not sure. They were male.

That afternoon, we go on an adventure in an auto rickshaw. 'No museums,' Ellie warns, so we go to the old market area, and wander down the thronging, tiny alley ways. There's a faint smell in the air, invoking memories of Morocco, Marrakesh: the labyrinthine souk in the early Seventies, lamb or goat broiling over the fire; a warren of small alley ways, goods piled high at every turn. Then the image of Agadir follows, and the forest, the king's forest, surrounding his palace. Quiet, dense and undisturbed in the weeks we spent there in 1972, long before Morocco became a fashionable tourist destination.

We camped with a group of Americans and cooked on the open fire at night. That smell. Then Jim, the leader of the gang — an easy rider with the gear and a mellow mood to match — held court, passing the roach, as he called the thin marijuana cigarettes he rolled, around the circle. While I slipped away to the quiet of our partially hidden tent, and wrote my diary, or thought by the lantern light till my smiling lover, later husband, joined me. Sweetly, we turned the lantern down, not out, unaware of the shadows which danced on the canvas as the mellow man and the rest paused to watch. 'Too much, far out.' Or so I later learnt.

That took the place of university when I left, no longer able, physically, to read: the lines slid on the page, letters danced. The medics cited 'emotional reasons,' deepening my confusion and despair. Psychoanalysis was their prescription. More than twenty years later, after surgery, I read the handbook of the *Vestibular Rehabilitation Society* of Portland Oregon, and discover that reading difficulties — in particular moving print, or lines of print — may be an early symptom of an inner ear disorder, a vestibular disorder, or even, occasionally, evidence of an acoustic neuroma, a tumour on the balance nerve.

Motion sickness is also identified as a possible symptom. All my life, and increasingly the ten years before discovery of the tumour, I suffered from motion sickness. Loud environments may be uncomfortable or sickening, the booklet continues. Symptoms worsened by high altitude. Fatigue, everyday tasks are exhausting . . . But I didn't know any of that, in Morocco, in Bangalore, in all the years before the tumour was found. Nor do I learn it in Los Angeles. Not till later.

We go to see Sai Baba once more. It is our last morning in Bangalore. According to our taxi driver, it is Sai Baba's last day too — apparently he has decided to move on. Afterwards, my diary records,

> It's very crowded. Many, many more people than before, flags, music playing. A group sings as we wait. Take our place in line and are fortunate to be second line called into the shade. We settle directly beside an aisle. A middle-aged women in a white sari with ash on her forehead sits beside me. The three of us chat. Singing starts, then Baba comes.
>
> This time I look at him at a distance, then close my eyes, and energy starts 'bumping' through me. Anxious not to alarm Ellie, so open eyes and turn to her. Sensation continues. It seems that whenever I allow it, there is an energy reaction through my body. Check for the energy 'figures'. They are there, above his shoulders. As I watch, with what seems like malicious glee they each direct a diagonal stream — as if they were urinating — over Baba's chest, over his heart. So what I see is two silver streams coming from the two 'figures' now slightly in front of Baba.
>
> At some point, I also become conscious of his heart chakra. I see it as very large, outlined in thick red with a white centre. I see the third eye too, and some sort of magnetic or energy field around him.

165

He comes very close to us and I have a good opportunity to look at him. I look at his feet, and notice, as I did the day we first saw him, how very long his tunic is. It would be quite impossible to walk in a normal way in a garment like that. Underneath his caftan, he appears to wear trousers of the same fabric, again quite long. The fabric is shiny. Silk? He stops in front of us. Passes, catches my eye. Holds my gaze for a few seconds and then turns away.

A few minutes later, when he is a little distance away standing in a clear space before a throne-like chair, I see his back and the two 'beings' are again at his shoulders. Under my gaze, they seem to explode, like lights. As I see the explosions, I feel my body jerk — the usual energy jerks. Could the 'beings' be angry with me?

Sai Baba sits in the chair and the crowd begin to sing, religious songs — songs of praise? — while he moves his right hand in fluid strokes, as if orchestrating the music. It seems to me horribly close to Sai worship. It feels wrong to me, also powerful, but not threatening.

Then it's over. Goa welcomes us. Soon we sit on the sand, the bubbling Indian ocean washes our feet and there is almost no-one else in sight, except a couple of vendor women and their shy children.

Chapter Fifteen

Clients

Some days now, I see as many as five clients. But I never work each weekday. I cannot, I need to rest. While I work, my energy is boundless — I seem suffused and enervated by a quality all its own. Material reality is almost irrelevant. My work is changing, though. What I do is different from when first I began, and no doubt it will continue changing. I am more confident. I trust my words and actions to be appropriate, without constant questioning. I still juggle, of course, with thoughts about responsibility, determinism, love, truth, but that's another matter.

I regard the work as what I do today, accepting that what comes tomorrow may be quite different. My own knowledge — perhaps my access to knowledge — is growing. And humility. The more I know, the more I realise I don't know.

The people who come to see me are very varied. Several of Tsering Rinpoche's London-based senior students come. And many members of his sangha, or community. Most come, or want to come, repeatedly. Given that they are all devoted to the well-being of others, and the sense of purpose (even superiority) that sometimes seems to imbue, I am a little surprised at the pain I frequently see. Many seem to me strikingly disempowered, with little sense of personal worth, though devoted to their practice and beliefs. It's easy to see how some have been greatly helped by their spiritual allegiance, but also that others are not, or not now. The sangha, however, is a powerful one, and Tsering Rinpoche considerably esteemed as a teacher.

Later, Sara, deeply concerned about her guru, tells me she has sent to an eminent lama, a master of divinations (clairvoyant rites), to ask him to do a divination on whether it would be beneficial for Tsering Rinpoche's work for him to come and see me. Apparently the answer is positive. Not that he comes!

I see another Buddhist teacher, a venerable old man, as a client. Conversation is not particularly easy. Language poses a problem, though he seems quite prepared to allow his translator to be present and to use him. It seems to me, the teacher's particular grasp of his own structure makes understanding — or perhaps accepting — what I have to say very difficult. The implications for his work and allegiances would be considerable. Our conceptual frameworks are so different. But some points seem to be taken.

I give him hands-on healing. I feel that this offers the greatest subtlety and opportunity in the situation. His body shows the signs of all I saw while talking to him. A deprived environment and upbringing have played havoc with his physical being, but there are other impediments. I think his suffering must be very great. Then the translator asks if I will see him, so I do.

Yet I find talking about my work impossible outside sessions. The children and I spend the weekend with the Dunbars. Cecilia questions me about what I am doing and I find tears rising in my eyes. I cannot say. It fills me with terror. I cannot imagine confiding in Suzie, or even Anna, 'I am working as a healer, or what you might call a psychic.' My former colleagues' imagined scorn is easy to assume.

Truth to tell, I can't handle the idea myself. I simply see clients because they come. I do not want to accept responsibility in the ordinary sense for what I say and do. But I recognise that I have to. What I say, or do, is simply because it comes to me. I think of it as what is 'given' to me. However, I know that even if I do not feel it is my choice, whether to express it is my choice. I cannot abdicate responsibility. At the same time, I try to exercise some discrimination over exactly what I say. This is a tricky exercise, raising all sorts of other questions; how do I know what could be the consequences — good or bad — of what I say? In the end I give up. I trust. It seems to work.

I am rarely asked to be directive, only to outline possibilities. The emphasis seems always on individual responsibility and empowerment to that end. Truth plays a wonderful part. Similarly, I insist that clients know that it's their choice whether to accept what I say — I do not claim to be speaking the one and only truth. Nor do I see myself as a substitute for therapy, that has its place. Just another voice, an inner voice.

Then, when clients leave, I give myself again to my son and daughter. Afterwards, there is little left, but a stillness. I know I need somewhere to claim my existence as an individual, as a woman. The early summer sun reminds me of another June, in the south of France. Standing in the sea, entwined with my tall husband, only the wide sky, the water and ourselves in existence. A perfect moment. Frankly, for now, there seems too much else to do. Isn't that a common problem for single working mothers? I ask myself, reluctant to believe, or admit, that my situation could be any different. But clearly it is. How to make sense of this reality, where I know everything, but nothing? Where I hardly believe the abilities I seem to have, for which I cannot and do not want to claim recognition, except within each session and each client's response.

Tuesday, 7 July School has ended for my daughter, my son's term ends on Saturday. Childcare and holidays pose the usual nightmare. I juggle clients according to the children's time-tables. Today, my daughter is out to play for the day; better still, she is being collected — I do not like driving.

My first client is a man in his mid-forties. He is an entre-peneur, juggling the financial problems of an emerging company and fighting the need to accept a cash injection from a firm of venture capitalists, who want control in return. This is the third time I have seen him. He came having heard about me at a party. He is not quite comfortable with the rationale for coming — which suits me fine. Our sessions are stimulating and highly engaging.

I began with no input from him, simply 'seeing' what was happening to his 'energy' and interpreting his state of being from there. I saw his allegiance to some other moral frame-work, driven by principle, his desire to contribute in some way, not simply to make money; and his practical problems at home and at work. I identified three people in different places in relation to his heart and we talked about those; saw a physical problem with his left knee; and spoke of the ways in which he was limiting his own intuition and creativity. I wondered at how easy it is to 'see' him. I have learnt that not everyone is equally easy to read.

It is really bad today, the business is close to collapse. Family problems are gathering too. I have been teaching him to meditate, as a route for him to work with his own energy and contact himself in a different and creative way. Robert, my client, says he is aware, in meditation, of major changes in the base chakra. The base chakra is the lowest chakra on the trunk and relates, as I understand it, literally to one's base on earth. Looking at him, I see the same. He understands the changes in his base as related to his attitude towards changes he is facing at work, and simultaneously in his family life.

There are issues he hasn't wanted to face, now he must. I feel today's session is crucial on both these fronts. We talk.

He mentions that he has been to church twice since our last session, for the music. Then I give him specific dietary instructions and healing. As always, my hands move as the voice or voices I hear from within instruct. Afterwards, Robert does not want to move from my healing couch. I cover him with a blanket for a few minutes more of quiet.

The next client is a teenager, the son of a well-known media personality. Making sense of the adult world is never easy, especially now, and in his circumstances, with his gifts and disadvantages. Then lunch. I have to eat. The phone rings constantly. Clients know that between 1.00 and 2.00pm I am usually available. Eventually, I have to use the ansaphone, but am reluctant to do so because it means a string of calls to make in the evening, which is family time. Two more clients to see.

Victoria Willmington-Smythe has been recommended to me by a friend of hers. (Almost everyone who comes has been sent by someone in this way.) In her mid-twenties, she puts her handbag down with a confident air. She starts to tell me a tale of work difficulties. Sometimes I let clients start that way, usually I prefer not to.

'Victoria, I think it would be more helpful if I were to tell you what I can see about you and then we can talk about it.' As usual, I add the request, 'You may not feel that what I say is correct, but I ask only that you think about it before dismissing it. Perhaps, if you can, put it on one side and wait and see if it makes a little more sense at another time.'

I look away, I never like to look at clients when I am talking about them, but focus instead on the three candles I keep burning on a shelf on one side of the room.

'I am going to start by looking at what I can see in the energy around you. The first most noticeable thing is the darkness around you. It's as if the space around you, particularly around your head, is very dark. Perhaps it's best described as polluted, or dirty. This is the sort of pattern I associate with drug-taking. I suspect that you are taking heavy rather than soft drugs, although there is no such thing as a harmless drug. All drugs alter your perception, the way you see and therefore the way you relate to reality.

'I am not making a judgment here, but what I am saying to you is that if you are trying to cope with reality, the clearer your vision, in every sense, the more effectively you will be able to assess and understand the situation. At the same time, in my terms, drugs make it impossible for you to hear what I can only call the highest set of instructions you are receiving. Or put another way, to be receptive to the finest energy at your disposal, which you can think of as metaphors for doing and being the best that you are capable of. And I understand that's sometimes very hard to face.

'Sometimes drugs can even seem to support you in certain ways that make other things possible for you. Or to give you insights. I can't and won't make judgments about that. But, it's usually a waste of your money and both of our time to come and see me and to take drugs at the same time. If you want to stop it is possible, though I suspect it won't be easy. Sooner or later it's what I think you are going to want to do. Forgive me if I'm wrong, but I think it may be right to call you an addict — and you'll need specialist help to give it up. I'm not qualified for that.'

Her face has darkened as I've spoken. 'It's just social, from time to time. I used to have a problem, but I don't really now.' Her lips close firmly. I know she does not, cannot, hear what I am saying. I am sorry.

'Well, you must decide what to do with what I say. I can only tell you how things appear to me. Ultimately you choose, you decide, it's your life. If I can't help you by telling you what I see, how do you feel I can help you?'

'I came because I heard that you're a psychic and can help with all sorts of things. I wanted to talk to you about a problem about starting a business with a girlfriend of mine. Her father was going to put up the money, but there are some problems now. Can you see what's going to happen?'

The story is spurious. It is no more than the myth of an interior decorating business. I believe the real issues relate to her addiction, and behind that to her family, their personal and financial relations. The way they love.

I try again gently to turn the issues back to those that I consider to be underpinning her position. 'Have you thought about your situation with your own family?'

'Oh yes, well that's not really relevant. I think it's Emma's father who's causing the problem here. She definitely said that he was going to put up the money. What I want to know is if you think it'd be a good idea if I tried to pressure him, there are some things I could do.'

There is little I can say. Have I been too clumsy in using the opportunity of her visit? Have I spoken too bluntly? Not heard what was said to me? I know not to question anyone's appearance on my doorstep.

We talk in circles, the time passes quickly. She rises to leave. 'Oh, I realised just before I got here that I left my cheque book behind. Shall I send you a cheque?'

What can I say? She never sends a cheque. I suspect it's not right for me to see people like Victoria, not good use of my time, but I am not sure how to refuse, or if I have the right to refuse. I am learning. A couple of months later, I heard that Victoria had taken a drug overdose and been sent by her family to a very strict clinic, a condition for their continuing financial support.

I am glad to see my last client of the afternoon, a young, immensely energetic management consultant in her mid-thirties. It is the second time I have seen her. She is fascinated by my psychic input. In our first session, I outlined everything I could see around her and about her. Today, she has come back with a list of questions spawned by our session. She is superbly elegant in her black designer suit and white silk shirt, but tortured too. Do I recognise my former self? Her questions are precise and to the point. She wants to contact her inner authentic self, she wants worship, meaning and love in her life. She is conducting this search with her head, frozen heart safely tucked away. I know the problem.

When the afternoon is over, I am happy to collect my beloved daughter and bumble in the kitchen together. Tomorrow, I see only two clients, an Anglican monk turned prospective therapist and a television personality. Then it's the Science Museum — where my daughter says they have a great new rocket launch pad section.

July passes quickly. It's a great pleasure to have my son home from boarding school. Then it is August and I am on my own for two weeks. India, again.

Chapter Sixteen

Himalayas

August 1992 I had not wanted to see the Dalai Lama particularly, when the invitation came. But something of India called. At the same time, Philip O'Casey, who issued the invitation, is a real India buff, veteran of prolonged stays over several years, and an intimate of the Dalai Lama's inner circle. This was an invitation to come as a guest of the Dalai Lama, to a special ceremony where few Westerners would be present. How could I refuse?

It will mean a flight to Dehli, then another flight to the old British hill station, Simla, followed by a road journey up into the Himalayas, to a restricted area which borders Tibet. There, at Kalpa, the Dalai Lama will address those Tibetans who have been able to make their way over the mountains to see him, for whom the ceremony is especially arranged. Apparently, Kalachakra means the Wheel of Time, and it deals with time on the inner and outer levels. The ceremony is a complicated three-part ritual, regarded, I am told, as a powerful tool for the realisation and preservation of world peace.

Saturday, 1 August A night-flight from Heathrow to Dehli. The food on Air India is wonderful. Arriving in Dehli, it is a pleasure to be travelling with Philip — he has no problem finding us a taxi to go to the Hotel Imperial, an old colonial-style establishment, where the turbaned commissar takes *175* charge of my few belongings. The corridors are vast, the ceilings lofty. I love my bathroom: well-worn white marble. I sink into the huge bath and then sleep for a few hours. I spend the afternoon at the slightly muddy swimming pool, in the company of a number of Indian families. Lying with a book, or just lying in the sun, is bliss.

Towards the end of the afternoon, Philip appears, he wants to tempt me out to see the city, which he knows well. I am reluctant, the rest is so welcome, but we have to make contact with the Tibetan travel organisation who are arranging the Westerners' accommodation at Kalpa, where the gathering is being held. We are to stay in tents. It will be very comfortable, Philip assures me, he knows this organisation. We haven't even brought sleeping bags, as everything is to be provided on site.

Two blocks from the hotel, we pass — a foot or two away — the coils of a tall browny-grey cobra, hooded head raised to the thin notes of the snake charmer's pipe. No-one seems interested. It is a far cry from the beautiful serpent of my meditation.

Early next morning, we leave for the airport, and arrive to a slightly puzzling scene: it's very quiet. Picking up our bags where the taxi drops us, we walk across the road towards the terminal building. It has a deserted air. There are no other taxis, no porters, almost no-one to be seen. The terminal doors are locked, there is no-one inside. As we stand, baffled, a very old man approaches, 'No flights today,' he smiles, and dips his head respectfully, 'everyone on strike.' He holds out his hand in supplication. I offer a small coin. Dealing with beggars, or knowing when to tip is an aspect of India I have not mastered.

'You wait here with the bags,' says Philip. 'I'm going to find someone to talk to.'

A few minutes later, he returns with a young man. We can wait till tomorrow, or we can do the journey by road, he explains. My heart sinks. I find road travel so difficult. But

Philip is enthusiastic, going by taxi will save us money, the cost of our air tickets will be refunded. The young man is a taxi driver. We are to go with him while he returns to his home, collects what he needs, including the relevant documents, and tells his family he will be away for two days, one to drive us to Simla, one to come back. The car is, of course, an old Ambassador. The body is black, the roof yellow, the age of the vehicle difficult to say, in excess of twenty years is my guess. Suspension, lacking.

We set off at 10.00am, and drive north, all day. We stop for lunch at an old converted fort. Philip and the driver judge the restaurant there our best bet. It is situated up a flight of stairs, at the end of a bougainvillaea-lined walkway. I am almost dizzy with heat. We are the only Westerners inside the restaurant, where the curtains are drawn and a man moves slowly between the tables in the semi-dark. The food comes on metal plates. It's good. While the men drink the strong local beer, I stick with bottled water, as ever.

After lunch, we continue across the great plain towards the Himalayas. Gum trees, scrub land, some fields, more trees line the road, which is narrow and potholed. Too narrow for two cars to pass. The heat is stifling, all the windows are open. I am battling with car sickness. In the end, I put my head down and lie on the back seat. Finally, we reach the mountains at the edge of the plain, and start to climb. The road bends and twists. My nausea becomes unbearable. The driver is trying to make good time. I ask him to stop, while I leave the car and retch violently. Philip is concerned, but quite unaffected; after years in the subcontinent, he judges this a relatively luxurious journey.

At nightfall, we reach the former hill station, Simla. Despite the turmoil in my body, I recognise it as unbelievably beautiful. The driver carries my bags up the hill — no vehicles allowed

— to a hotel with a spectacular view across the valley from the reception area. I walk up the internal stairs to my room.

Opening the door, the room is neither small nor large, with undistinguished furnishings, a mixture of dark wood and faded red plush. The curtains are drawn across a seemingly large window. I walk over and open them. The sight astounds me. It is a fairy tale aspect. The window is almost at the level of the wispy clouds floating in the sky. It is as if this building literally hangs in the sky. Below the window, the earth falls away, dropping vertically to the snaking silver river glinting far below, and beyond that, dark, coniferous woods spread out over the hills and valleys that ring this place. A place of magic.

By the time I reach reception in the morning, Philip is deep in negotiations with a local taxi driver. The deal is done, and we are led down the hill to a white mini van, the standard local transport. I think it could be a Japanese model. Better suspension than the old Ambassador, I hope. No such luck. It is the most basic of vehicles, driven along the tiny roads at great speed.

Very soon, I am too sick to admire the spectacular scenery we are passing through. Extraordinary mountain passes, dark valleys, hidden clearings almost escape my notice as I try to concentrate somewhere beyond my body's nausea. From time to time, we stop to allow me to pour my sickness out in a dry stream.

Towards the middle of the afternoon, travelling beside a wild river, along the floor of a narrow valley lined by high mud and rock sides, we reach a border post that marks the start of the government designated restricted area. The politics of the area pass me by. Who are the indigenous people here? What do they do? To whom do they offer allegiance? Why the political restrictions?

A small group of vehicles are waiting — a couple of jeeps, a few shambolic lorries, another white mini van. I open the door, but remain in the front of the vehicle, in my place, in a sick haze, while Philip and the driver take our passports and papers in to the guards. Apparently progress beyond this point is not allowed without the proper permissions, which we have been given as foreigners visiting for the purpose of hearing the Dalai Lama.

Half an hour later, we are on our way again, crossing a great river by a small stone bridge. The driver is worried by the hour. The light will begin to fade soon, and there have been reports of landslides or mud slides in the area. The landscape is rougher now. No sign of any dwellings, gnarled trees, scattered boulders, steep slopes and coarse grass part the smallest of ways to allow the ever-narrowing road to pass.

As if on cue, we turn a sharp curve and come to a sudden stop behind a sagging lorry. There's a mud slide ahead — the road is blocked. The driver goes to investigate. We wait, fortunately not too long. A group of men return and climb over the sides into the open back of the weighed down lorry. The road has been cleared. Dark begins to fall as we continue climbing.

There is enough light to be amazed by the scene which greets us shortly afterwards. It is as if all the colours of the earth have been poured out and mixed in a bubbling mass of activity. Brown predominates, along with movement. It is a flat place, at an altitude of about 2,000 feet amongst the peaks, altogether filled and alive with a throng of people and a mass of stalls. This is Kalpa, more a general area than a specific place. Anxious to return, our driver is eager to leave. A deal is struck, he will collect us at the same place in eight days.

I step out of the van, into the street, feeling no different to my luggage, to be jostled immediately in the throng. Many are wearing what I discover is the Tibetan national costume. Women in long slim dresses, covered from throat to ankle, with knee-length aprons, often striped, tied around their waists. And jewellery — silver, turquoise, coral and stones I do not recognise. Almost all the women are wearing finery of some sort in honour of the occasion, Philip tells me. The men wear bulky coats, which seem to be tied at the waist, and flat hats of different designs. I am astonished at the number of monks, in their red brown robes, some with yellow ochre drapes.

Again, Philip's expertise is invaluable. He steers me towards an alleyway built at a slightly higher level. Here there are concrete rows of what I take to be small shops, rather than the mass of the bazaar, and the odd electric light bulb strung up on a wire illuminates a small area in the descending gloom.

Philip leaves me in charge of the luggage, sitting outside a makeshift office — something to do with the ceremony we have come to attend — and disappears to investigate, for what seems like ages, then reappears triumphant. The site of the Kalachakra is above us. We are to follow a road leading up into the mountain, where we will find the camp site for Westerners, above which an amphitheatre has been constructed for the ceremony itself. So, on up the road in the dark. Tibetans or locals, I do not know the difference, pass us in both directions as we trudge slowly upwards.

Mr Tinnley Gari is a wonderful surprise. He is the Tibetan maestro organiser, and owner, of the camp. A neat array of circular tents (with decent ground sheets as is later proven) and a large, outdoor dining area, are illuminated by the electric light emanating from an open-faced cook tent. I choose a tent close to the cook tent, uphill (upwind I trust) from the two Western style lavatories, in adjoining tents like medieval booths. How they work on this isolated hillside I cannot imagine. There is a shower too, I am told proudly. Well, a tent you can stand up in, with wooden slats on the floor. You take a bucket of hot water from the cook tent to the 'shower', and, having taken off your clothes, pour the contents over yourself.

Supper — rice and something vegetarian — I hardly notice, at one of the outside tables, before I fall asleep, despite the smell of the sleeping bag I select from the pile offered and the hardness of the ground. My last thought: what if it rains?

I wake early to brilliant sunlight and struggle to dress. Outside, breakfast is starting. Philip is sitting at a table under a tall pine tree. With him are a slightly familiar looking man and an exceptionally beautiful young woman. I join them. 'Cindy and Richard,' says Philip, before returning to a conversation about past Kalachakras he and Richard Gere have shared. Another thirty or so Westerners are expected: some trekkers passing through, a few to join us at the Kalachakra ceremony.

Having arrived in the daylight yesterday, Richard and Cindy have had a chance to explore the layout already, and they pass on the basics. I hear the programme. The Dalai Lama will give four days of teachings, as an introduction to the event. Then a day of rest and dancing, followed by two days of specific preparation for the Kalachakra. Finally, the day of what is called the Kalachakra initiation itself, when there will be blessings and prayers along with the display of the sand mandala — a symbolic picture, representing the pure world, which the monks will have been constructing with coloured sand for the previous two weeks. The ceremony has tantric, astrological and other esoteric significance, and is said to be the basis of all Buddhist cosmology. I am curious.

We walk up the mountain road to the site of the ceremony. It is a large stadium, on a slope, constructed in concrete, with a raised dais at one end covered by a number of magnificent tarpaulins, backing onto a wood and glass structure. In the centre is a very grand throne, looking out over the stadium and across to the neighbouring mountain sides and peaks with their blanket of clouds. A number of stone, holding walls contain the areas to the sides of the dais, and support the far end of the stadium, where a separate small village seems to be established. Two or three thousand people are expected, maybe even more.

A Western contingent is present, perhaps a couple of hundred people sitting together in a semi-orderly patch to the left of the dais. The centre ground immediately below the throne is taken by rows of hundreds of monks, nuns too — presumably in their allotted ranks — and then numerous Tibetans and local hill tribes people fill the rest of the ground.

His Holiness arrives on time with his retinue. I have found a space in the Westerners' patch, along with Philip and friends of his. Richard and Cindy are sitting cross-legged on the dais, to the left of the throne, with three or four other 'chosen' Westerners. To an outsider, it is an extraordinary cross between a large, important, authentic oriental religious festival, attended by local people in traditional dress, and a crazy encampment of a small number of Westerners, ranging from hippies and media hounds with all their camera and video gear, to would-be Tibetan ladies (women in imitation traditional costume).

I have barely settled myself when Philip's attention is caught by one of the smart, navy blue blazered attendants of His Holiness's retinue. No danger of traditional costume here. He's gesticulating that we should leave our places and come with him. I am happy where I am, and keen not to follow Philip to join the attendant, whom he seems to know. However, according to Philip, it would be rude to refuse an instruction, or invitation. So we battle through the straining crowd to join the navy blue blazer. It seems we are expected to sit with Richard and Cindy at the great man's feet. I am seriously reluctant, for a number of reasons, none of which wash with Philip.

A pattern is established. Some mornings, I join the group of monks who meditate and pray with the Dalai Lama in the wooden structure behind the dais. For an hour, from seven to eight, I sit at the back of the room, and watch or meditate, relaxed and peaceful. Then we are served a breakfast snack — Tibetan tea, a weak concoction of milk and cardamom, and hard, grey bread. As well as the monks and attendants, up to half a dozen other Westerners are usually present, often including Richard. Then back to camp for breakfast proper, followed by the morning session at the stadium.

We sit, on a red carpet, in two rows to His Holiness's left. An American 'student' — a very devout man I am told — and Richard first, then a Tibetan monk with a tall head-dress, Philip, Cindy, me, a French woman journalist who is wearing Tibetan garb, an elderly grey-haired woman likewise clad, and one or two others.

It is awe inspiring to look down on the hundreds upon hundreds gazing up at the Dalai Lama. I feel uncomfortable occupying such a privileged position before so many devoted followers. I am no more than an interested observer. For me, this is an unusual holiday, or research trip. Not a pilgrimage, as it clearly is for these devout people who worship their man-god, their spiritual and temporal leader. I feel like a Western imperialist sitting above the locals.

The process is slow. His holiness speaks in Tibetan, which is translated into the local dialect, and then into English. I find the teachings oddly familiar and pleasing, interesting culturally and historically too, but somehow not enough to hold me, or counter my disquiet. In the intervals, I sneak into the wooden structure, or once, not to be repeated, to the monks' lavatory to which Cindy directs me — offering a large wadge of tissues simultaneously.

Although I don't attend all the sessions, those held in the morning offer an opportunity. Then, I switch on, so to speak. My inner knowing comes alive, and my ability to see also. I see lines of energy, as I think of them, or threads, between various of those present. It appears to me, too, that the Dalai Lama's heart chakra is wide open — he is working from that place at the moment. The sight is impressive.

A couple of days later, concentrating on the Dalai Lama, I suspect he is becoming ill. I see it growing in him. Should I say something? Surely it would be very presumptuous? These people must know far better than I do. But lunch offers a perfect opportunity. Some of us on the dais are asked to lunch each day with the Dalai Lama's retinue. It is first and foremost a delicious occasion. The meal takes place in a series of small rooms, little more than storerooms, in the encampment at the bottom of the stadium. There is a wide variety of meat dishes, rice, vegetables, fine noodles and fruit. 'Tibetan aristocrats' food,' as Philip informs me, 'not peasants' food.'

Here I meet Dr Choedak, the Dalai Lama's own doctor, a mild, impressive man, who escaped after twenty years of torture at the hands of the Chinese. Apparently he and three others alone of the hundred who were imprisoned together survived. His English is broken, but one of the team's several interpreters is also eating with us. I learn that to keep alive, Dr Choedak used to eat undigested grains from the manure of the horses the Chinese rode. Then, when he finally escaped to India, he wrote down whatever he could remember of Tibetan medicine.

I ask Dr Choedak about Tibetan medicine. His answers refer to Tibetan plants and herbs. Do the same flora exist elsewhere? Or can similar effects be achieved in other places with other plants? Is the relationship between the flora and the inhabitants of a particular place specific to that place and those individuals? What about minerals and medicine, or astrology and medicine? Does he have knowledge of planetary resonances? The last are subjects on which I have had teachings in my meditation and practice.

I gain some answers, but primary healthcare is a major concern for most Tibetans in their devastated country, or in exile. What of the interrelationship between teachings, meditative practices and well-being? Yes, it exists, concedes Dr Choedak, the one is able to influence the other.

I ask about the Dalai Lama's health at the moment. Dr Choedak is immediately interested — why am I asking? I explain, briefly. He appears fascinated and prompts me to go on. He asks if I have any suggestions for dealing with the situation. After a pause, I say I could offer him a homeopathic remedy or a remedy of my own making, containing nothing but energy in a sugar base. Immediately, Dr Choedak wants the remedies, which I promise to deliver later. Then, with typical inscrutable courtesy, he thanks me. Whether the information is useful, or even interesting, I do not know. Or whether the Dalai Lama took the remedies. However, the illness does appear in a mild form two days later, but he continues to teach and it passes.

The fourth day is the day of dances, monks doing ritual dances, Tibetans filling the stadium with folk dances, and that night the Westerners' party. Another camp has been set up next to ours, though the forest and its boulders form a complete screen so that we cannot even see their tent tops; the sounds of drunken revelry extend far into the night. A group of Italians who have arrived are causing problems at our own camp. Mr Tinnlay Gari is not pleased.

Then it starts to rain, and Mr Gari's problems are compounded. As are ours. The tents are waterproof, but the ground becomes a sea of mud. A large tarpaulin goes up over the dining tables, but everything is damp. Two Germans arrive. Men dressed in black with shaved heads. A professional clown and his boyfriend, a writer. The clown has come to petition the Dalai Lama. Cindy seems particularly taken with him. She sits next to him at dinner and talks animatedly while tucking into the tinned tuna fish she has brought to supplement our vegetarian fare. I feel wet and miserable. I do not belong here. No way of leaving until the taxi arrives from Simla. There is talk of landslides blocking the road.

I wake in the night. I wake constantly. After the first night, sleeping on the ground has become a real problem. It is difficult to believe that I have become so 'soft', or so old, that I can no longer manage without a mattress. But tonight I need to pee. Problem. I do not wish simply to slip outside and relieve myself amongst the tents, for obvious hygiene reasons, but the lavatories are some minutes away down the slope. The howling sound of wild dogs echoing across the valley and the ghostly shadows among the trees, when I look out of the tent, make me unwilling to wander away from the site into the dark, though the light of the moon is bright.

There is no option. I make my way across the uneven ground, stumbling over the rocks and loose bark down the hill, leaving the tents behind, towards the three small booths that comprise our sanitary arrangements. The cries of the dog pack sound closer, then further away. The sound seems to resonate between the sides of the mountains. There is no sign of any other life, only endless rows of ragged fir trees dissect the rock face in the eerie light.

Rapidly finishing, I start on my way back and slip on a small branch. The noise rebounds through the valley, magnified. As if they hear, the dog pack seem to turn with a wild howling sound that swells in my direction like a wave threatening to break over me. Terrified, I stagger blindly back towards the tents. The yelps and howls seem closer each instant, till shaking, my heart in my mouth, I collapse into my tent. Cheated, the sound of the dog pack turns, or recedes. Surely, they could not have been following me?

By the last day, Richard is quite ill. He says he is always ill at the Kalachakra: it is a positive, not a negative effect. The sound is enough to make me ill — monks blow huge ceremonial trumpets. Deep drums beat. My hearing seems very sensitive.

The collected assembly is jubilant. We all file through the small wood and glass room where the sand mandala is on display. Different colours of sand form a series of intricate and beautiful patterns, so precise that each grain occupies an allotted position on a huge board. The picture symbolises the world in its pure state. To each who passes round the tables, the monks hand out a long-life pill and a red protection cord. Then it is over. The monks carry the sand mandala down to the river way below at the bottom of the valley and pour the sand into the rushing water. The crowd mills prior to dispersing. We wait for our taxi.

I am relieved to be leaving, but apprehensive of the journey — with good cause, it soon appears. Philip and Anne, a friend of his, sit in the back chatting, reliving highlights of the ceremony. In the front, beside the driver, I am sick beyond my wildest dreams. Soon it is almost too difficult to concentrate on the moment; my strategy, all of life dissolves in agonising nausea. 'Take aspirin, or travel sickness pills,' advises Anne sensibly, but I have none.

It is late in the evening when we reach Simla again. I manage to tell Philip that I cannot face a taxi ride back to Delhi, I will have to fly. Worried, Philip offers good naturedly to return by plane too, and to make the arrangements. Sleep swallows me up.

The drive to the airport is almost bearable because it is relatively short, winding around the valley. Clouds are gathering. The driver predicts a monsoon. If it reaches the airport before we are able to take off, we will be grounded.

Cindy and Richard are at the small airfield, waiting too. The winds are wild. We climb into a small light plane. Richard looks as sick as I have felt. Fortunately there are enough seats for everyone. Sometimes, I am told, there are not, and then somebody has to share, or to stand.

The little plane heads off down the valley, stopping at remote airstrips on the way. The second time, we leave the plane to walk on the yellow grass of the field where we have just landed. The sky is steel grey and almost vibrates with the coming rain. Richard walks to the boundary and lies on the ground, sick and silent.

I welcome our return to Delhi. A day's pause.

A lama asks for my input, so I give it. Again, I am struck by the disparity between the teacher's high position and his personal pain.

Heathrow, at last. I am weak.

Chapter Seventeen

Sensitive

October 1992 'So you think being so car sick was nothing to worry about, Jeanette?'

'Oh no, you're very sensitive, much more so than ordinary people, and roads like that at those altitudes would have all made it worse. Luckily it cleared up very quickly.'

'I get so tired. It even seems to me as if I am looking different, my face is thinner, I think.'

'Are you eating? Just look at you, I'm sure you're not eating properly — really, potatoes, things like that, that'll fill you up.'

'You're wrong, actually. I eat pretty good meals, and there's nothing the matter with my appetite. In fact I'd say I'm hungrier now than I've ever been.'

'Well, don't let the work get to you. You know you just give, it's the way you are, and people will take and take if you let them. You be careful not to give so much that you're exhausted.'

'I don't think that's a problem, though I could be wrong. Actually, work's the only time I feel really great, energy-wise. It does give me a fantastic high, it's wonderful.' Giving is receiving — but what about the rest?

She smiles, 'I know how it is. Maybe there is one other thing you could do. Have you heard of Peter Blake?'

'No.'

'He's a kinesiologist, and when I was pregnant with my youngest I had a terrible time, I was so ill, and nobody could suggest anything that helped. Anyway, I tried him, and he found there was just one mineral I was short, so I took it and everything cleared up completely in a week. Why don't you give him a ring? He's in Berkshire. Tell him I said to call him — that way he'll fit you in. He's very busy.'

'I'm not sure I know what kinesiology is, but if you think this chap might help, I'll certainly give him a call.'

'Yes, I do. Give it a try. Kinesiology is muscle resistance. They measure the body's muscle reaction to all sorts of things. You just lie on the couch and raise an arm and he puts pressure against it. You'll be amazed how you get different reactions according to what he has rested on your chest. If it's something that agrees with your body, you'll find your arm is really strong, and if it's something that disagrees with you, you go all weak. I never thought it would work, but it does. Go and see for yourself.'

Peter Blake has a huge sheep dog. It nuzzles me in the waiting room. That's a point against him. Dogs should not be allowed in waiting rooms, and worse still, the dog follows me into the consulting room.

'You don't mind Tiny, do you?' says Mr Blake. That's minus another 200 points . . .

I lie down on his couch, which is beautifully positioned. Autumn trees are framed in each of the room's three windows. He raises my arm.

'We just have to check for a baseline,' he says, pushing against my hand. I resist as instructed. Then the testing proper starts. He puts a series of substances, one by one, each in a little glass jar, on my chest. To my astonishment, the strength in my arm fluctuates. Certain substances seem to give me power, while others definitely weaken me.

'Hmm, borderline wheat, 'he says, 'but milk's all right,' and so it goes on, until my arm gives up resisting.

He's finished. I slide off the couch and put my shoes back on. Meanwhile, he's preparing two bags of slugs, or so it seems, for me. Large dark capsules, and even larger lighter brown ones. Apparently they are mineral and vitamin supplements, intended to perform specific functions in a certain digestive chain reaction. Maybe it's pseudo science, or I don't follow his argument well enough, or my grasp of the theory is incomplete.

The slugs don't seem to do much for me. Is my attitude involved? I'm prejudiced towards a varied diet, rather than reliance on nutritional supplements. Though I take the point, what is a healthy varied diet? And does our additive-loaded food really provide adequate nourishment?

Work is continuing stronger and stronger. I can do it. People come, we talk, sometimes I offer healing, they leave, the session leaves my head. Simple as that. My meditation continues. Sometimes a couple of times a week, sometimes more, sometimes less. I am tape recording my sessions now, and roughly transcribing the tapes into my diary afterwards. Frequently my voice seems dreamy and detached when I speak the words said to me. I think I understand less than ever. God, what is God?

'I am here, beloved, why do you doubt me? I am the voice inside you. You do not have an adequate concept of me, you do not understand about me yet. Wait, the silver thread will come.'

My inner world urges me to begin to talk to small groups. I have already started weekly evening meditation and healing groups. I did not know what the first session would be. I started with Wordsworth's 'Ode to Immortality':

> Our soul is but a sleep and a forgetting
> The soul that rises with us, our life's star
> hath elsewhere its setting,
> And cometh from afar,
> Not in entire forgetfulness

> And not in utter nakedness
> But trailing clouds of glory do we come
> From God who is our home.

The fifteen or so squeezed in my room are silent. Then another force takes over and I feel I am holding all those present. Lots of people want to come.

Now, it seems I am being prompted to talk, *'Talk. I will tell you what to say, before you are to say it. It will not be a channelled talk, but you will speak from inspiration, as you always do. I will prepare you and you will know a little in advance what you are to speak on, but that is all. There is no need for you to worry, and no need at all for you to prepare.'* The idea scares me stiff, in a way even talking at the Institute of Directors never did. This time I turn to Browning:

> Truth is within ourselves.
> There is an inmost centre in us all,
> Where the Truth abides in fullness; and to know
> Rather consists in opening out a way
> Whence the imprisoned splendour may escape
> Than in effecting entry for a light supposed to be without.

I hold the talk, the room is full. I speak without knowing what I will say. One word follows the other, unplanned, till spoken. Sara urges me to tape record it. 'No, it's really not a big deal, its not worth taping,' I insist, unwilling to accord the talk such status. She takes notes. Later, I realise how comprehensive and sure-footed my speech was. At the time, I am glad it's over, and unwilling to repeat the exercise. Who am I to tell people how to live?

Sometimes, I think the God who speaks to me is no more than an aspect of my functioning — though I couldn't qualify precisely what I mean by that. At others, the words that come suggest another entity entirely, '*I do not speak to you of S and R because you already know these concepts and you use other words which make more sense to those around you. It is for you to work with the bricks that are already on earth. You are not to draw down foreign notions, they are not relevant at this time. You will put your knowledge in everyday words, as far as possible.*

Then there will be other things said to you and you will translate them. Do not worry that no knowledge is given to you in speech. All that you need is given to you in your action. You are supplied from all the highest sources . . . build the bridge between the earthly and the heavenly, now. Work well.'

21 November 1992 *Lord Christ and Lord Buddha take me not to the radiant mountain, but into space. We go first to a planet, P, then further, on to another, O. O is the holder of the images. I see the images. Images of all time, like a library, upon a library. Like a raindrop. Now I am there, reaching out my hands for the books. The spell for everlasting life. The Midas spell, and its antidote. All is held at O.*

Later, I turn to God, who speaks to me, 'Come forth, do not integrate with the Light now. Stay and let the Light pass through you. You must learn to retain your form with the Light passing through you. You must live on earth for a while yet, and for this purpose you must let the Light pass through you.'

Then I encounter three energy beings of a different sort. My voice on the tape recorder is eerie and quite 'other' when I speak their voices. It feels benevolent, but somewhat mysterious.

31 December *Lord Buddha is a long way away. Lord Christ is there, the landscape seems to be falling away. Lord Christ carries me to the sacred mountain, saying 'You have much to learn now, a new chapter is opening.'*

I ask for God's help, and am taken not to the Light, but in a north westerly direction, where a new force, or forces, seem to enter me, 'We are here from God, of God, as we are a part of the universe and part of you. You are part of us. We will draw you to us . . . We wish to show you the pure dimension that you inherit from us.'

I travel with them to a land of pure light, a space of nothing except light, and within the light a series of planets, all of which I know of and have learnt. Discussion follows of the planets, and what comes afterwards, then a statement that particularly surprises me, *'Being is simply a reflection of God's eye.'* Writing it afterwards, I hesitate, but my voice — eerie as it is speaking in the energies' tones — is clear: God's eye, *'That is all that being is. However, it is also an opportunity to evolve beyond energy into the ultimate, infinite form that integrates with the universe.'*

The energies continue to speak of the future, and of the importance of Justice and Light, *'All the wisdom that appears to accrue from books is to no regard whatsoever if the principles of Justice and Light have not been learnt.'*

My meditation that night is a long one. During its course, and afterwards, I note that my face, particularly my nose, itches furiously. The following night again, as I am on holiday, I meditate, and it lasts a long while, including the sentence, *'Our body is changing. You are engaged in the process of transformation. As you become lighter and lighter, the nature of your substance changes. The process will continue as it has started.'*

The process of my spiritual, mystical transformation, or some other process? I do not understand, but then there is so much I do not understand.

Meanwhile, my youngest brother, David, is getting married. There is a party afterwards, on Saturday night, at her parents' home in Hampshire. I drive with my daughter in the winter dark. The lanes become tunnels, direction disappears and I do not know left from right, forward from back. We seem to follow a dark winding route to nowhere. By luck, we round yet another corner and I recognise the place. A lawn, already filled with lines of parked vehicles, appears and we join them. The extension to the old downland farmhouse is ablaze with lights, and chatter reaches out into the cold evening air.

A huge throng swallows us up as the hall opens into a marquee erected for this evening. I shiver. The gas heaters that blow in the corners seem sadly inadequate. No-one else appears to notice. Noise comes from all directions. It descends on me. Why do I find the occasion so oppressive? It's as if there are too many people, too close, too loud, too cold. I'm shivering uncontrollably now. I can't join the throng, smart young people from both sides of the Atlantic and a good mix of their elders. Its a great gathering. I stay on the outskirts.

Dinner is announced. Perhaps it will be warmer, but no, the marquee we enter is further from the main house and even colder. We are seated at a table with old friends, how joyous it should be. Course follows course, the clatter of cutlery and voices assailing my senses. Then the music starts. It is unbearable. Nausea rises. I am freezing cold, my head aches, what is it? Migraine? Sensitivity? The old chestnut, transformation?

Hurrying back to the car, anything to escape the music, my body wretches miserably, rocked by waves of nausea and agony. Then the darkness and the stillness soothe my nerves, till a certain peace returns. Peace, but apart.

Not my days. People crowd to see me. Sara is reaching a crisis. She has continued to have monthly sessions with me, sometimes to deal with her own issues, and sometimes those she encounters with her clients. We have found that if she gives me the name of a client, or sometimes simply focuses on a client, I am able to tune into the person concerned and speak about them.

This crisis is her own, however. Affairs at the Buddhist centre have continued to be difficult. Increasingly, Sara finds herself standing not only against the co-ordinator, but also the Guru's handling of affairs. Worse, his handling of 'students'. I know the problem at first hand, having been consulted by two women who have felt capitulated into sexual relations with gurus. In both cases, my personal deduction was that they were abused.

Now Sara, solicitous for years about her Guru's personal well-being, cannot escape the conclusion that in several instances he has behaved in what she takes to be an inappropriate way with women students. As a specialist in sexual abuse where the abuser is usually a family member or close friend of the family, she is horrified to see the parallel here, with the Guru as the perpetrator, and his students the child victims. She tries to discuss the situation with him. He refuses, alleging her inadequate understanding, or ignorance is the real problem.

Eventually, in deep distress but utter conviction, she writes to the Dalai Lama, outlining the case, and resigns from the Buddhist organisation of which she has been a trustee. Her letter is never acknowledged. However, she feels greatly relieved and begins to see the organisation in the light of a cult. Simultaneously, Sara's new home, a pretty house in a sunny street with a good garden, is ready.

A film star, a household name, calls, but I cannot see her because my diary is full. She cannot, or will not, wait and she will not join the waiting list for a cancellation. Plenty of others will. Their bravery so often inspires me. 'It must be dreadful for you, everyone bringing their "stuff" to you,' one man says to me. Nothing could be further from the truth. I feel privileged to do the job I do. And astounded by my client's gratitude. Amazed at the shower of cards, letters and flowers that Christmas brings.

March 1993 My meditation stops. It happens gradually. My time and inclination to turn to my personal meditation is less and less. It feels as if the Light — or some other dimension — is with me constantly. Perhaps, to be more precise, part of me?

In February, God had spoken to me, saying, '*You will always be mine, whatever the way in which you are working, for your allegiance is to me overall. Although particular manifestations will draw you at particular times, I am the field in which you work. You will need all your strength. Do not ignore your earthly powers, past or present. This is the point of integration. You must become the person whom you can be. You understand too well this other dimension — hold back from it. Surrender yourself, beloved, it is you, as you are it.*'

The Three Energies come to me. I do not know then that it is the ending of my meditation, in this form. I think it is just another change. '*We bid you farewell. You have to go for now, but we are pleased to make contact with you and will stay close to you.*'

Then God speaks again, '*Beloved, now it is time for you to go. I have high expectations of you, as do others who are with you. Persevere. Remember you are a voice for us on earth.*'

Then it is over. Only I do not know it. While I hear the words that are said to me, I don't try to understand what they mean. I draw comfort from them; simultaneously it's my habit simply to accept them, and let the next thing happen, if I can. Nothing changes. The other world is alive in me. I act from my own instincts. I am teaching others to enter their own versions of the domain — at those times I meditate, but I have no need of words to speak to God. It is different. And I hardly notice what has happened.

An Easter holiday with the children. The three of us share a room, and stay up late watching telly. In the day, we go swimming together, wander and talk.

Then it's summer, so quickly I have not had a chance to raise my head, dogged as I am by fatigue, work, joy and love. We are going to Devon, with the Dunbars again. Grass slopes from our cottage back garden down to another row of cottages, and beyond that to a picture book river where sailboats glide by, and the chug of motor boats hardly disturbs the ducks paddling beside the banks.

My bedroom is at the rear of our cottage. The summer is warm. I open the windows wide, lie on my bed and absorb the view. The gentle scene revives me, slowly. What am I to do? It cannot be right to be so tired. Perhaps it's time to look further afield than Jeanette for help. We spend a day at a beautiful bay. But the beach is made of pebbles. I can hardly walk on them without my shoes. No-one else seems to have the same problem.

'Jeanette, I wish I could share your certainty that all this is OK, but I can't. It can't be right to be so tired. Either the work is wrong, or I'm wrong for the work, or something else. I think it's unlikely that the work is wrong, because, bluntly so many people want it, and as far as I can tell it's doing good. I have to think something else is the matter.'

'I know, but it's all right, you just have to be patient. There is something else I'm working on it, though. You won't like this, but it's nothing to worry about. It's the menopause. I know it's early, but it was just like that for me, and for my mother. I think it's hitting you very hard, what with everything that's been going on.'

'Oh no, I have absolutely no signs of that. There's nothing at all wrong with my cycle. I can't accept I'm tired and all the rest because the menopause has started.'

'Please trust me — just give it another month and we'll see what we can do.'

I want to say no, but frankly I don't know who else to turn to. My experiences as a medical correspondent for BBC television taught me how few and far between good doctors are, and anyway, what would I say? 'I'm very tired, I got really car sick in the Himalayas, I think I look worse than I did five years ago, and by the way I work as an intuitive, and I do healing too. And I'm a single mother.' I can imagine the reaction I would get.

Also, I remember how helpful Jeanette has been over the years, clearing up my irritable bowel syndrome, dealing with my daughter's small ailments and my son's scary battle with glandular fever. The doctors were really not much use then. It was Jeanette's remedies that brought his temperature down, and Jeanette who helped him regain his energy afterwards when all they could say was 'there's nothing we can do'. Surely it's safe to assume that she knows what she is doing? Anyway, I decide to give it one last try.

That night is the end. I take Jeanette's remedies on going to bed, and seven hours of torture follows. I am drenched in hot sweats, electric shocks run up and down my spine. Shivers, palpitations. I call her, 'Jeanette, this is not OK.'

'It is, just give it time.'

No. I hurry to Harley Street, where I know of a gynaecologist, Dr Marie Turner. I want the data on this.

Dr Turner pats her grey bun. 'No, I can't see any evidence for the notion that you are menopausal. You are, after all, only forty-one, everything looks absolutely normal to me. We will send the blood tests off of course, but I am almost one hundred per cent sure that they'll be perfectly all right.

'The symptoms are a problem. Obviously, I don't know anything about your work, though I have to say I'm very sympathetic to healing work.

'Homeopathic remedies can bring on symptoms, but it's only temporary. I do know a little about that, and I'm sure that's what happened to you the other night. It's the principle of treating like with like. So, if the lady who was treating you felt you had menopausal symptoms, she might give you a little bit of menopause, so to speak, which will stimulate the body's own reactions. But it's all over, there's nothing for you to worry about.

'What I think would be best is for you to go and have a chat with someone who understands homeopathic as well as allopathic medicine, and really sort things out. How does that seem to you?'

'Fine, absolutely perfect. I am relieved to hear what you say about the menopause, I couldn't think it was real. Obviously I'm still concerned about being so tired constantly. And of course since I have been using homeopathic medicine, and I know the hostility in certain circles to it, it would be a great relief to see a proper doctor who was also sympathetic to that route and knowledgeable about it.'

'Yes, of course, it's a pity things are so slow in changing, but you'd be surprised, they are. I'm going to suggest you go and see Robert Pointer at the Casstle Clinic. He is very knowledgeable, as a doctor and a homeopath, and very sympathetic to healing.'

Robert Pointer. We've met socially. He is interested in a wide range of subjects in the self-development sphere, including the intuitive. If I remember correctly, he lectures internationally on the role of the carer and caring for carers. Making an appointment at the Casstle Clinic is easy.

Chapter Eighteen

Doctor, Doctor

12 October 1993 The Casstle clinic is smart. Alternative prosperous, I'd say. Bossy receptionists, protecting their very important employers. Private medicine seems to make a point of opulence. I wait. When finally the door opens, and he calls me in, I remember how 'normal' Dr Robert Pointer seems. Pale blue shirt, nice blue check tie. Blue for healing. Cheery sunshine yellow picture on the wall.

'Michal, nice to see you. Now, what can I do for you, my dear?'

'Thank you for seeing me. I'm here because Marie Turner, the gynaecologist, sent me. Did she call you?'

'Yes, she did. Why don't you tell me the problem?'

I pour my heart out. I explain about Jeanette. That I love my work. I always have a waiting list of people to see me, but I have to be careful how much I do because of the tiredness. Divorce has been dreadful. My children are wonderful.

Yes, I have been to the third world, to India twice last year, and on the last trip I suffered fantastically with car sickness and really didn't feel very good. My face seems thin, I seem thin, though hungry, but my weight has hardly altered. And so on. And I have a tick in my eye now.

I lie on his couch and he prods my stomach, looks in my mouth. We talk. He comes to his conclusion. It is nothing medical. He is pretty sure that the problem is spiritual, perhaps emotional if you prefer to couch it in those terms. Something in my attitude to my past and/or my present is at the root of my trouble.

'Go away, think about it,' he advises. 'Call me again if you think I can help further.' I'm stunned.

I call him back. If it is a spiritual or emotional problem, what on earth can I do about it? I have been through myself with a toothpick, I cannot believe that I'm missing something of this magnitude.

'Well,' he says, 'it really is a question of counselling. It may be that you need someone to help you see the issues in a different light.'

My heart sinks. Can this possibly be true? My whole history spits out in my head, like the drawers of an upturned filing cabinet. Psychoanalysis, the works. I cannot bear this. But, is it pride that makes me feel I cannot benefit from examining my past, my feelings, with another? Why should someone else not be able to offer valuable insights? I am able to offer them to others. Warning lights flicker in my head, but I disregard them. I am no different from anyone else, I tell myself. This is too serious to leave any stone unturned.

In the interests of speed, Dr Pointer offers a telephone session — for him to counsel me — and see where we get to. I accept. It happens. Well, actually little happens. I offer up any weak point I can think of and he makes some observations. They are not particularly acute. I am reminded that the quality of his heart did not particularly strike me when we first met, as it does in some cases. Which gave me no reason to doubt him — certainly not in his professional capacity as a doctor and homeopath. Whether he has insight or not, he certainly does not offer it to me in our 'counselling' session. But I am ever wary of pride. I do not dismiss him (and I pay his bills when they come).

That night, I think it through again. Not only am I tired, and have a tick in my eye, but recently I see a problem when I work with my healing and meditation groups. I meditate on those occasions, with the group. For the last couple of months, I have concentrated the meditations on healing or 'seeing' techniques — not travels in the other world. I have been 'seeing' my right-hand side as increasingly dark. I have been able to clear the dark, but not to keep it clear. If I saw a dark area like that on someone else, I would be sure it indicated a physical problem.

Of course, it might well have its genesis in a mental problem. But, if it was still largely an emotional issue, then I would be likely to see the darkness, and other images, outside the body, or coming into it. In my private sign language, darkness of that sort actually *within* the body indicates an existing physical problem. I would be certain of that, if it was anyone else. I realise diagnosing myself is hopeless. I don't expect to be able to be impartial, to see myself, as I have to be to see others. Why not ask the other world?

I am strangely reluctant. A strong sense tells me that the lessons I have been taught have not been to make me dependent on input from another, higher source outside myself. Somehow they are to make me capable of true action and direction from my own depths, or inspiration. I must face the situations my life poses, they are mine to address.

Yet what about the fact that intuitive or psychic input for others flows so freely from me? I speak as an outside source to them. I have no answer to that conundrum. Yes, intuitive guidance can be for my benefit too, but I cannot and somehow must not try to reach it by appealing to another being. Why? I am not sure. Can I reach it by simply turning to myself, in the everyday? I do not know. But I must try to find the answer to my physical distress, urgently.

I call Robert Pointer again. I tell him that I am sure there is a medical problem. He is indulgent. He assures me I am wrong. He sticks to his belief. 'Its a spiritual or emotional problem, call it what you like,' he admonishes me gently. 'No-one else can deal with it except you. There isn't a pill or a potion to cure it.'

'OK, you may be completely correct. But, to satisfy me, could you do some blood tests, at least eliminate some possibilities, or check some things out practically?'

'If you really want to you can, but it'll cost you an arm and a leg and I don't think you'll find anything.'

'Thank you, I just have to get to the bottom of this.'

I visit the laboratory around the corner from his consulting room carrying a form covered in ticks. It seems as if my blood is going to be tested for everything.

'We'll have the results back in about a week,' the pert receptionist tells me. 'They'll be sent to your doctor.'

I count the days. My anxiety is mounting. My intuition tells me this is physical — and acute. I have a sense of the clock ticking.

'Dr Pointer is away this week,' his receptionist tells me.

'Gosh,' I say, 'can someone else help? I have some blood test results which I believe have been sent to him and I'd like to know what they say.'

'No, there is no-one else to look at his mail. Anyway, he'd have to interpret the results for you himself. He'll be back on Monday, the week after next, if you'd like to call him then.'

Furious, I call the Casstle Clinic administration. I am told that the clinic has no jurisdiction over individual practitioners, they simply hire out their consulting rooms, so no-one else can help. The clinic's image of respectability and authority is a marketing ploy. This is a property company who happen to rent rooms to doctors and other practitioners.

The laboratory has strict rules for procedure. Obviously. Blood test results can only be given to a doctor. If Dr Pointer has made no arrangements for another doctor to cover for him, can I find one to whom they could release the results? That's it. I have a brother who is a doctor. In New York.

I call transatlantic. 'Right, so you've had some blood tests,' says Jeremy, my brother. 'No problem, I'll call the lab, get them, and fax them to you. I can tell you if they say anything dramatic, but you know you'll have to take them to a doctor who can examine you and talk to you on the spot. This doctor seems negligent though, going off with no-one to cover for him.'

Earlier this year, Jeremy was in London. A geneticist, healing, homeopathy and spiritual development are not interests of his. But he did notice a change in my state. Looking at me, he suggested anorexia. That worried me. I am sure my face, my whole body, is different. But my weight has hardly changed for years, and I certainly don't have a problem with appetite. What to eat is more of a problem. Certain foods just don't feel OK — like tomatoes, or potatoes. They bring on head-aches, or unsettle my stomach.

A few hours later, the results come through on my fax machine. Jeremy calls again. 'They're all borderline, M, except for iron, you're a bit anaemic — not seriously. Get some iron into you straight away. And the billirubin is raised, which will make your skin yellow — it can be the result of a genetic condition. Put any pressure on the liver, like being tired, and Gilbert's — that's what it's called — comes into play. I wouldn't be surprised if you've got it. I have.'

'Thanks, it's true my skin is looking pretty sallow.'

'Well, I'd want to know why you're so run down, but you must go and see your own doctor.'

I haven't seen my own doctor, Dr Alexander Beresford, for years. I dread going along with a tale of using homeopathy and doing healing. But it's clearly time to overcome my prejudice. *205*

Dr Beresford is very popular, in some circles. He sits on all sorts of committees, and is generally regarded as having 'influence'.

'The first appointment I can give you with Dr Beresford is on the 12th, 10.30 in the morning.'

'That's nearly ten days time — is there nothing earlier?'

'No, you can see one of the other doctors, but Dr Beresford's very busy.' I imagine it will be better to see him, as the senior doctor in the practice, so I agree to wait. But I'm worried. I have already sharply reduced the number of clients I am seeing each week. Some weeks I've had to cancel altogether. Now I pencil in two more days to see the cases I judge most necessary and cancel all the rest. I have already stopped the evening meetings.

On my last day, I see a psychoanalyst, a psychiatric social worker, an acupuncturist and a management coach. I soar in the sessions. My non-physical strength is stronger and stronger, as my body weakens.

A couple of clients have mentioned seeing a Dr Rose Guan, a Chinese doctor, with considerable success. Apparently she used to work at a famous children's hospital, but now runs a clinic of her own practising Chinese medicine. She might be worth speaking to, I think. Looking back, my trip to Kalpa seemed to be a turning point. I have definitely felt significantly worse since then. Perhaps Dr Pointer had something questioning any trips to third world countries. Perhaps I picked up something in India. In which case, an Eastern doctor might well be more attuned to the possibilities. I arrange to see her in a couple of days. At least I am investigating all the possibilities.

Meanwhile, I join an advanced class with a Chinese 'master', so-called, visiting London from Belgium, teaching the oriental art of Buqui. It's a method of promoting health by moving the *chi*, or energy. I am not convinced it's any good for me, but I hold my scepticism in check.

Standing on the scales, I see I have lost a few pounds in weight, despite my nagging hunger. Given my food intolerances, I'm not surprised. When I lie down to sleep that night, sudden inexplicable tremors, like electric shocks, run up and down my spine, jerking me awake from time to time. Something is definitely very wrong.

Dr Rose Guan is lovely. 'Oh how excellent, you have blood test results. That makes my job very much easier.' She asks me to lie on her couch and takes my pulse in a couple of different ways. Perhaps checking out my organs the way acupuncturists do, I think. Then, with a little smile, she tells me I've had hepatitis, it's affected my liver, and the rest of the body, and I need treatment.

'There is no good treatment in the West,' she tells me, 'but not to worry, I will give you some herbs that will be very effective, it is not difficult to treat.'

Really? My debilitation has a name, and can be treated, just like that? I'm amazed, overjoyed. That simple. Of course I'll take her herbs.

But it's not that simple. They smell ghastly when I brew them as instructed. I gag trying to force the disgusting liquor down my throat. Eventually, I take half the dose, and leave it at that. That night I am very unhappy. The electric shocks down my spine intensify dramatically. I feel as if I could die at any moment. This cannot be right. Later, I learn that the shocks could have been the effect of spinal fluid escaping. Disaster.

I call Dr Guan, who makes time to see me straight away. I explain. She is mystified. I say I dare not take anymore of her concoction, it feels wrong. She shakes her head, it is all she can offer, she's sure its appropriate for the condition. I must persevere. But I won't.

I turn to the other world. Perhaps the only way to reach the answer is in meditation, after all. Access is easy, as ever. I am welcomed warmly. This is my home, delight rises in my soul at the familiar surroundings. But, 'Go on beloved, go on,' is all the help I receive. I do not feel deserted, only strangely reassured. I am being nudged to use my own power in some way, even if I don't understand quite how, or why.

It's a relief to walk into Dr Beresford's consulting room, finally. I am so glad to see him. But where to start? No, I haven't been to the practice myself, just brought my children when necessary. I remind him I've seen him several times with my son. I tell him I've taken homeopathy — his eyebrows shoot up — for various minor complaints, but I really need his help now, and I explain: my fatigue, my symptoms, who I've seen, what's been said to me.

'I must say, I'm disappointed that you didn't come to see me earlier, before all these Chinese doctors, homeopaths, and whatever.' He looks down, disapprovingly. 'You say you're a healer,'

'No,' I interrupt, 'I work as an intuitive, and sometimes that involves offering healing. It's not work I choose, and certainly not something I'd say I understood. But it is what I have been doing for a few years and my clients include therapists, and professional people.' Why do I feel I have to justify what I do?

'Ahh, hmm, and what precisely do you do?' he asks. I stumble and bumble.

'Home problems, emotional problems?' he goes on.

I can see the line he's taking. It's not the way to the solution.

'Perhaps it's some alternative remedy that's causing your symptoms,' he suggests. 'From these blood tests you've shown me, the only thing I can see is that you're a little anaemic. Do you eat red meat? No, I thought not, well do so. That'll solve the problem. Rest, come back and go to the nurse in two weeks time for another blood test. You can telephone for the results.'

That's it. No examination. Nothing. No comment on the 'electric shocks' I am suffering, absolutely no interest in the flicker in my eye — I think my lip may be flickering now too. It's been worse than I could possibly have expected. From the way he is treating me, he certainly does not appear to think anything serious or physical is remotely the matter.

Eat red meat. Since Jeremy told me the blood tests showed anaemia, I have given up my vegetarian diet of several years. But I'm surprised it resulted in iron deficiency. I know a little about nutrition. I've been interested in it for many years. I am pretty sure I was eating a reasonably balanced diet. Perhaps a talk with a nutritionist would be helpful.

Gwen Halber is popular with alternative doctors at the moment. I take notes of everything that passes my lips, and see her at her City clinic. I am not impressed. 'Candida, I think,' she pronounces, 'if it feels right to you.' A yeast infection? Reading the last patient's notes upside down, I see he or she too was diagnosed as suffering from candida. The prescription: only raw food, and a series of other strictures and supplements. I don't buy it.

Another set of blood tests satisfies Dr Beresford that I'm improving. The test show too that I'm not suffering from hepatitis, A, B, or C.

'I feel dreadful,' I say. 'I can't work, I'm utterly exhausted and I don't understand why some foods just don't suit and these electric shock-like feelings at night are quite terrible.'

'Well,' he says, in his slow deliberate manner, 'I could give you a prescription for antidepressants. I suspect you would not be very happy with that. Or I could refer you to see a dietician at the hospital, and they would send you an appointment. It would take a while.'

'Actually, I've been to see a dietician, and I didn't find it very helpful.'

'In that case, I really don't think there is anything else I can say.'

I go to see George. He has moved to Harley Street now. His high-ceiling, first-floor room is very grand. My movements are slow. There's tension in his pensive face. He searches for the words.

'Michal, have you checked it out physically, completely, with the doctors?'

'Of course, but you know I've drawn a total blank.'

George pauses, 'Well, the higher chakras are very strong indeed, but it's very difficult to get the energy to come down into your body.'

'That's exactly what it feels like. I'm tremendous at my job at the moment, but my physical body is leaving the earth. I can't put it any other way.' I feel as if I am dying, but I don't say the words — fear of sounding too dramatic? Fear of admitting it?

'What about seeing another doctor? The best doctor I know is out of London. Would you be prepared to travel to Sussex?'

'Why not?'

Linton is a beautiful small town in a dip in the South Downs. I step off the train optimistically. From all around you can see the hills. Seagulls wheel in the air from the English Channel twenty miles distant. The directions to Dr Hollander's clinic are clear. It's fifteen minutes walk on a cold December afternoon. There are the remnants of snow on the pavement, and white tracts on the surrounding hills.

Dr Hollander is running very late. 5.30pm and the receptionist leaves. Dr Hollander himself comes to fetch me, full of apologies. His kind grey eyes, set in a lined face framed by thick grey hair, study me from behind horn-rimmed glasses. We talk. He looks at my blood under a microscope, examines me, noting, I think, my sharp hip bones and emaciated chest. He feels my neck, with the deep hollows in my collar bones below. He is concerned.

'There is nothing I can find,' he says. 'You know, I think this is emotional. I would like you to have some very good therapy. It is a little unusual, but my wife is an excellent therapist — I can't do better than to suggest you go to her. Lots of rest, too, and cooked food only, as it's much easier on the digestion. Then there are some supplements that will help to build you up.'

I am stunned and say so.

'I'm late for a meeting now. Why don't you go back to London and just think about what I've said? You can call me if you want to talk about it some more.'

Kind as I think Dr Hollander, I am not tempted by therapy with his wife. But I swallow the supplements. Why are supplements so expensive?

Still, the other world is no help. I am offered love, support, but no answers if I ask. The effort of connecting and entering the domain is almost too much. But there is a voice ticking in my head, like the voice I hear when I see clients, like the voice that feeds my voice when I stare into a candle, or away from the face of the person in front of me, and talk. *'Time is running out the voice says, hurry, hurry.'* And I feel death beckoning. Who to go to?

I cannot face more of Beresford's disdain. Yet. We've spoken, again. My symptoms have been noted. He's offered nothing further. Surely I can find someone who will uncover the problem?

I call Jeremy in New York. 'I'm not getting anywhere with my doctor,' I explain. 'He doesn't think I'm ill. Not physically anyway. Do you know of anyone I can go and see privately?'

'It's always so difficult. You don't have any idea what could be the matter?'

'Well one suggestion has been that it's something I contracted in India. It seems that my liver is involved, marginally anyway.'

'Well, you need someone general to start with. I'm going to speak to an old Cambridge colleague of mine, Michael Southern, 211 he's a blood specialist. I think he's at the Hammersmith at the moment. Either he or I will call you back, when we've spoken.'

I have lunch with a broadcaster friend from the old days. His daughter has been very ill for many years. Conventional medicine has failed to solve the problem. Recently, apparently, alternative medicine has helped considerably. 'Yes, we found this extraordinary doctor, called Dr Falliday. She uses homeopathy largely, and I can't speak highly enough of her.'

Worth investigating. I call. Dr Falliday is fully booked for six months. Her receptionist is referring patients to a nearby Dr Dawes. Checking his form, I discover he has had wide experience as a local doctor in the country as well as in London, published a few books and articles and been described in a newspaper article as a leader in his field. Sounds acceptable.

Our consultation is brief and snappy. Like Dr Dawes's coordinating tie and handkerchief. He answers the phone, just after my arrival. 'No, no,' he assures the caller, 'I won't be long.' And he isn't . . .

I take my tights off and he fixes my foot to what he calls a Vega machine. The machine, he explains, simultaneously attaching electrodes to my toes, tests electrical conductivity — the body's reaction to substances. It's quite painless. Then he gives me a series of phials to hold, one at a time, while he monitors the score on the machine. Each phial holds a different substance, he explains. In all this, he does not have much time to take my history, and none to examine me.

Then he pronounces, 'I think you're suffering, or have been suffering, from hepatitis. All that traipsing around India. I know A, B and C have been ruled out, but I want you to have liver toxicity tests at the Sci-lab, to check it out.'

I do as I am told. I've heard of the Sci-lab. It's new, alternative and does a range of tests not available anywhere else. Expensive. Controversial. Money is streaming from my wallet.

Sci-lab is packed. Obviously very popular. The results are ambiguous. 'Yes that's it,' announces Dr Dawes. I want to believe him, how I want to believe a doctor.

'If that really is what it is,' I ask, 'is there a treatment for the symptoms?'

'Of course,' he blusters, 'a tried and tested homeopathic remedy from Germany — have you right as rain again.'

'Dr Dawes, I am very reluctant to use any further homeopathic remedies. I simply feel I've reached the end of their usefulness, isn't there something else?'

'Nonsense, you can't have had this stuff because it's not available in England. The only other thing I can suggest is that you live with it; eventually it'll probably improve, or else it'll get worse and you'll come back to me for my remedy.' He's drumming his fingers on his desk.

'OK,' I sigh, no fight left 'I'd better give it a try.' What else to do?

'Good, here's the form to order it. It'll be sent to you in a week,' and he disappears back to the reception area.

A week to wait. I try an appointment with Master Tan, the Buqui practitioner. He is a great favourite of acupuncturists, and is running a number of courses for them during a three-month stay in England. His English is poor. My work fascinates him. Speaking, I am exhausted. He is kind, if extraordinary. I start to cry. He stands behind me and touches my shoulders and then my neck. I don't know what he is doing.

'Energy here, not right,' he explains, and jerks my neck in a quick movement. It releases with a tremendous crunch. For a moment relief floods through me, tears drown my face. But it's temporary. By the next day, any effects have worn off. Later, when I see the MRI scans I realise Master Tan could have killed me. But he spotted the right place.

Meanwhile, Michael Southern has called. He offered to refer me to a colleague of his, a consultant General Practitioner at one of London's major new hospitals, and I accepted. St Patrick's reminds me of the Science Museum. I can't find the private wing. I feel like Alice down the rabbit hole. Then the door appears, and shortly after that, Dr Wheeler.

'Now, you're Michael Southern's friend? No? It's your brother who's Michael's friend, and you've spoken to him on the phone and he suggested you come and see me. Am I right?'

He's charming and chatty — it's easy to tell him the whole story.

'Intuitive work, my goodness, well we can certainly do with a bit of that,' and 'Oh really, healing, how fascinating, I can't imagine what you do' and 'Homeopathy, of course I don't know anything about that.' He seems genuinely concerned by my symptoms and general debilitation. He examines me, pokes, prods and suggests a liver scan. I shrivel at the thought of yet more expense. I say I'll think about it, and call him. I wonder if Dr Dawes might have the answer, which would make a scan unnecessary.

Dr Dawes' medicine arrives. It's just before Christmas. My daughter has a friend for the day. I prepare the dose on the kitchen table. I am scared. It doesn't feel right. I have to trust someone else. I want to so very badly. *No, no, no,* goes the voice in my head. I propose a compromise to myself: half the dose. It says take four drops morning and evening, in water. I'll take two. So I do.

Then we all get in the car to go to the supermarket. I feel funny. Backing into a parking space it seems to shift its size. Is it the car or the space? Am I too close to the post? No, there seems loads of room. I'm nearly on top of the car on the other side. Is it moving, is it rolling forward on its own? There's a crash. What is it? Why is my car shaking? It's me. I've driven into a post.

I call Dr Dawes. No reply, message service, it's too close to Christmas. That afternoon I go to see George. To talk. 'It's no good George, that medicine has blown my head off,' I say.

He's examined me. 'You're right,' he says.

'George, what do you think is going on? You had Hollander's report.'

'Yes, I must say it surprised me. There's no way you need psychotherapy. That's a joke.' George has even sent clients to me. 'But Hollander's good. I don't know what to think.'

No-one calls back from Dr Dawes' surgery that night, or later.

Christmas is quiet. Being with people exhausts me. Soft colours, silence is what I crave. In the early hours of Christmas morning, I wake to see my bedroom door opening. The street light outside shines faintly through the blue slated blinds at the windows. I see someone standing by the door. A girl with long dark hair, wearing a white night gown.

'Ellie, darling,' I stumble with the words, and the girl disappears, as I collect my senses and remember Ellie is not at home tonight. She is with her father. Perhaps it was nothing. Perhaps the remnants of a dream, muddled with my waking. The following night I wake again. This time she's at the end of my bed, looking at me wistfully. It's not Ellie. This is a teenage girl, older than my daughter. Fear grips. Of course, I should not be afraid: I work with the notion of dead people, the link between life and death, often. But I am terrified. My worlds are colliding. Worse, I know she's afraid and needy. I know that I could help her, and my heart somersaults with horror. I've gone too far. As if sensing my agitation, the girl makes a swift movement and is gone.

Oh God, please let this be my imagination. I do not want my everyday world to become populated by spirits whom I can see, who want of me. And I am not ready to leave my body for the other world yet. A couple of nights pass undisturbed — electric shocks aside. Compassion wins. If she comes again, I will speak to her. On cue she does. This time I wake as she stands at the door, and watch her move into the room, stopping at my bookcase, then coming close to the bed to look at me. She's so timid.

'Can I help, what the matter?' I force myself to say to the silent room. The words are too much. Barely are they uttered when she's gone, and does not return.

The Christmas holiday week is almost over. Tim, a friend, takes my daughter and I away for the weekend to a charming cottage in the country. She drives with him, I take the train, no more car drives for me. It's better out of London. It's as if I feel the lights in the city burning into me now. I cannot enter big stores, the glare from the neon lights is too painful. It hurts my head. Not my eyes, but the crown of my head, somehow.

At the cottage, all I have to do is cook, eat and rest. Tim's amazed at how much I eat. It's as if the food simply passes through my body without a trace. The cottage is next to a riding stable. My daughter beams and disappears to fix a ride. I wonder, longingly, whether I might have enough energy to ride just a little, in a school. A jolly girl bring a solid looking pony for me to a small covered school and I mount unsteadily. Such pleasure in connecting with an animal again. The pony feels sturdy and predictable. Putting my heels to his sides, I think I'll risk a trot. Mistake. The motion throws me in the air, triggering trembling and exhaustion. What's happening?

Back in London. Back to Dr Beresford. I have a sour taste in my mouth too. He has nothing to say. (Later, I see from my diary that in despair I went to see him four or five times that January and February.) I know I have little time left.

Dr Dawes finally responds to my calls, a couple of weeks after Christmas. 'Really, I've never heard of anything like it,' he says, when I tell him of my reaction to his medicine. He rigs me up to the Vega machine again.

'Just hold the medicine.' I hold the bottle of homeopathic drops in question. 'Yes, you're right, 'he says with a chuckle, looking at the machine, 'right off the scale I'd say.'

In other words, his own machine indicates that the medicine he prescribed was not suitable. 'Injections, I think we're going to have to do it with injections,' he announces.

No, we're not. I decline.

I go back to Dr Wheeler. I have the liver scan, which shows no abnormalities at all.

'Well, that's a relief isn't it,' breezes Dr Wheeler. 'You are looking a little better. Whatever it has been, perhaps we can safely say it's passing now. It seems to me that with some good rest you are on the right road. I must admit I was worried about you, but not now. You're all right.' And he draws a line under the case, bills for prompt settlement please.

Nothing left to say. No desire to say it. Try another nutritionist? Find the best, must be a doctor. With a bit of trouble, I get to see Dr Alan Rosen, co-author of the current nutrition bible. He examines me. He's blunt about the thinness around my neck and chest. Back to Sci-lab. Yet more tests. The results show — nothing. He's sorry, but nutritionally I'm basically all right, and he can't help on my food intolerances or other symptoms.

I do not try to disguise my condition from my former clients. Many continue to call, to ask how I am. They offer help on all sides. One tells me of an alternative doctor, an Indian, whom she has just seen, describing him as first class. Another doctor? Why not? He's interested in the work I have been doing. He's culturally sympathetic to it, and has also been working in both America and Europe on combining healing techniques with Western medicine.

'It is your work that is making you ill,' he says, 'but there is no-one I know of who can help you. You will have to go to India. There you may find a holy man who can help. Or you will learn to treat yourself.'

He comes round the desk and stands behind me. I have no sense that he is about to take any action. In an instant, he cricks my neck.

'There, that is better,' he announces, 'you have a great deal of tension in your neck, I have released it.' Like Master Tan, he could have killed me.

There's a chorus building in my head. Again, it's like the instructions, or more correctly 'sense', I receive when I'm working: *Go back to the place you were born. Go back before the time of your birth. Go back, it is the way.* I hear it, then I don't, then I hear it again. There's no need for repetition with clients. I say the words as they come. Is this guidance for me? Still, I hesitate. Is this taking responsibility, is this what it is to follow my own lead?

My medium friends are no help. No-one can 'see' the problem. I have been to Anna. Tarot reading is one of her skills. I am not keen on the use of the tarot, but desperate. She does the cards.

'Oh Michal, lots of men around you, but I can't see what it is.'

I am spending half the day in bed every day now. Dr Beresford has proclaimed 'viral fatigue' to be the problem, and written a certificate to that effect. (Reluctantly, I felt.) No suggestions for treatment. No further investigation.

Sara has taken to cooking for us. Sara and Hans even come to stay at the weekend so I don't have to get up at all.

Hurry, go to the place you were born. Go before the time of your birthday. There you will find the way to go. I know I must follow. Am I being told to go to meet my death? I was born in Cape Town, South Africa, on 19 February, high summer there. I long for the heat. How can I afford a ticket to South Africa?

I tell my family it's what I want to do. They are worried. My brother Jeremy is puzzled. He knows Dr Wheeler by reputation. Above question. Yet my condition is undeniable.

Together, my brothers and my mother wonder if I'm suffering from hypochondria, some nervous state, or even some dark condition brought on by my unorthodox employment. They want to help. 'Can we give you a ticket for your birthday?' they offer.

It's too late to make the arrangements to arrive there in time for my birthday. Surely that won't matter? Is it a mad whim? At a deeper level, I know I must trust the voice. Trust myself, but I am riddled with conflict. If my illness is the result of following the other world, then however much it benefits those who come to see me, as they constantly tell me it does, it's disastrous for me. How can that be? What sense to make of the contradiction?

What else could be wrong with me, my logical mind debates? Why is one side, the right-hand side, the side which usually symbolises practical life, dark? Why am I being told, so urgently, to go back to the place I was born? I don't know. But I know I have to go. I know something physical is desperately wrong, even though everyone else denies it. I know I am facing death.

Chapter Nineteen

Cape Town

Thursday, 24 February 1994 I sit up through the night in the upstairs of the jumbo jet crossing Africa, reading, thinking. My eyes are watering, or is it just one eye? The plane is almost empty. The sun is touching the clouds. There is a silent pink world outside. It reminds me of my other world. The unreality is equal. Presences from the other world slip through my mind, I think of them with affection. They are separate, somehow, from whatever is happening to me, my devotion undiminished. I drift between worlds, half present, half not.

Cape Town is baking hot, gripped by a heat wave. The little airport reminds me of India, or India reminded me of this. Reeve, my aunt, has come to meet me. A formidable lady, a doctor and administrator, I am her elder sister's eldest child, a close connection in a close Jewish family.

'Shelley darling,' she says, once we're safely past the airport confines and heading towards the city on a comfortable freeway, 'what's the matter?'

A pep talk follows, one divorced woman to another, but her heart is tender. She feels for me.

'You have a lovely holiday, the weather is stunning. Everybody is anxious about what will happen with the election. The ANC will win, but we just hope it will be peaceful. Mandela's very impressive. And we can see how you are after a good spell on the beach.'

My dear aunt, who can talk to me, care for me, as if I were a teenager, instead of the mother of a teenager.

It's about ten years since I visited this city. The politics, as much as anything, took away my desire to return. Coming around the foothills of the mountain from the airport, the view I remember from earliest childhood opens before me. The mountain behind, the city in front, the foreshore and then the docks, the sea and the curve of the bay down to the south and the wide blue ocean beyond.

Home, my childhood home. My grandmother standing bent over a walking stick on her balcony, as my father brings me to see her, the Cape winter rain, my dear nanny Leenie, first school, daddy's office, the wild cats in the garden of a house where we once lived, my favourite uncle's laugh, my mother's parents' farm, the house cow's byre, my parents in the billowing sea, and sinking my sturdy feet in the sand, baby volcanoes running through my toes. A thousand memories crowd forward. I can touch them, a reality so immediate, perfect and intoxicating.

Reeve's apartment is on the sea front, a spot she has occupied for thirty years probably, switching apartments only once. It's a narrow space at the foot of a small mountain, Lion's Head, where the rocks fall into the sea. The light glitters. There's a quality in the air unknown in the northern hemisphere.

Four, five days pass. There is nothing I want, except to stand on the rocks with my feet in the icy Atlantic water, and look up at the mountain and beyond. Perhaps this place is the cure. I am stick thin in the new bikini I've had to buy. Strength soaks into my body with the heat. But I know it is not true. There is more to come. *Go and see him. Who? The man who grows the orchids. Go and see him. Go beloved, go.* My sense is that I must go to the hospital, but I am not sure why. Or how.

Reeve and I have supper together, curried fish, a Malay dish my grandmother must have learnt from her Cape coloured servants so many years ago. It's a rare evening in Reeve's hectic social calendar.

'So you still feel that there's something the matter darling, something organic?'

'Oh Reeve, I wish I didn't. I am stronger and better here than I was in London, but only in one way. The doctors were absolutely emphatic, there's nothing the matter with me. But, the last few days I feel as if I'm worse, even though I'm better, if you know what I mean.'

'Well, if that's how you feel, there's nothing easier than for us to have you looked at.' As the past administrator of Groote Schuur hospital, Cape Town's show-piece, world-renowned hospital, that's true.

'Then at least you can settle this once and for all. We still have some of the best people in the world here. If they can't find anything the matter with you, then I'd be confident that it's not organic, and you'll have to decide what to do.'

'Thank you.'

'I think you should see a gynaecologist anyway, because that's easy. But who else?'

'Reeve, who's the man who grows orchids?'

'Oh, Solly Marks. That's a brilliant idea. He's semi-retired now, but he still works at the hospital. '

'Who is he, what is he?'

'Solly was at medical school with me — your mother knows him too, he's a professor of gastro-enterology, world renowned, really first class.'

'What have orchids got to do with it?'

'Oh he just happens to grow orchids, he's mad about them. But he's a wonderful physician and internist. It would make sense, with your food problems, for you to see a gastro-enterologist.'

She gets up from the table and walks to the telephone around the corner. Strains of a chatty conversation float back, 'Lovely, I'll do that . . . thank you so much . . . all the best.'

222

'Solly's away — he left around the 19th — but he'll be back in about a week and he'll call as soon as he is.'

He left around my birthday. If I had come before my birthday I might have seen him sooner. Now, there's a week or so to wait to see the orchid grower.

It's not difficult to pass a week on the beach, and seeing people from my past. It may be a cliché, but the beauty of the Cape catches me unawares. The shaking off of apartheid is bringing a wildness with it that simultaneously frightens and pleases me deeply. Near lawlessness and reconciliation run hand in hand. I realise I am in love, with the place and the unaffected, almost naiveté of the people.

I have a spot on the tiny beach amongst the rocks outside the apartment where I go at the end of the afternoon, when the fiercest heat of the day is over. For a few days, I notice the same hip group of young people settle a little way away from me. They look so well. On the third or fourth day a young man, mid-twenties I guess, approaches as I begin to pick up my things to leave.

'Hi, I've seen you here the last few days, are you visiting?' He squats on the coarse sand beside me, heavily tanned, smiling and bursting with health. 'Cape Town's great isn't it? Where're you from?'

'Here actually, but I live in London, and yes it is wonderful'. He reminds me of my eighteen-year-old son, when he wants something.

He pauses, 'Hey, I don't know what to say, just that you look really cool, and can I take you out for a drink?' He smiles.

I smile back, incredulous, 'Thank you, that's very kind of you, but I'm a lot older than you are.'

'Oh hey, I don't mind,' he interjects quickly, 'that's nothing, that's cool with me, you look fantastic, you can't be that much older.'

'Thank you. I'm flattered. But, I'm here to convalesce, and I'm taking things very quietly, I have to. Thanks all the same.'

'Oh, right,' his face falls, dismayed. 'I'm sorry if I disturbed you.'

'That's OK, don't worry, nice to meet you.'

At night, I sit on the balcony and watch the moon on the water, listening to the sound of the sea on the rocks below as the heat of the day settles. I'm not tempted to meditate. It seems unnecessary.

Solly Marks is back. I'm going to see him this afternoon. Reeve drives me to the hospital. Groote Schuur must be the most beautiful hospital in the world, nestling in the green foothills of Table Mountain. Reeve bustles through the thronging lobby with the air of one entering her domain. Once, indeed it was, her bust is in the hall.

She leaves me with Professor Marks' secretary. A tanned man, sixties I guess, in an open shirt with a cigarette in his mouth, passes the door.

'There he is,' says his secretary. 'I'll tell him you're here.' A few minutes later I'm sitting with the great man, who's extinguished his cigarette. Through the window the city spills down the hill, over his shoulder.

'Your aunt says you think you're sick — why do you think you're sick?'

'Well, maybe I'm wrong, or maybe I've brought it on myself,' and I pour out the story. 'So you see, nobody thinks I'm sick. I've even been offered therapy, or antidepressants, when my sense is that the symptoms are all physical, and that it's getting worse and that actually . . . ' I don't finish, 'I'm sorry if I'm bothering you unnecessarily. If you tell me it's nothing, I'll just have to accept it.' My mood has changed.

As if sensing my despair, he continues in a matter of fact way, 'Well, it doesn't seem to me as if there is anything crazy about you, so, why don't we assume that there is something the matter, and that I'm going to find out what it is? I'll look at every possibility and then at the end we can decide where we are.

'You probably feel like a pincushion, but I'll want you to have some more blood tests. Have you got the results of your last tests on you? Good.' He scans them. 'There are two sorts of billirubin — why don't the Brits separate them?'

Then he lies me down on the couch, pokes and prods, asks me to sit up, breathe in and out. 'Do you have any numbness in your face?'

'No, but the right-hand side feels different, I can't say how, from the left.'

Silence while he looks at me. At last, 'I'm very susceptible to flattery, but why do you keep winking at me?' Obviously he has a sense of humour.

'It's the tic I told you about,' I say, 'it's what I'm told is "just nerves", a sure sign that all this is mental not physical. I've got a slight twitch in my right upper lip sometimes too.'

Then he fills in a form and sends me off for more blood tests.

Half an hour later I'm back with him. 'Let me see, this eye of yours, you say you have a tic in it, and sometimes a little in your lip too?'

'Yes that's right.'

He picks up a piece of cotton wool. 'This won't hurt,' he touches my eye. I don't blink. Footsteps pass along the corridor. He looks aside. 'Japie,' he calls, to the man in the doorway, 'have you got a second?'

A plump chap, also in an open-neck shirt, enters the room. 'Take a look at this,' he touches my eye again. Again I don't blink, 'Do you think this is what I think it is?'

'Yeah man, got to be, no question.'

Solly Marks turns to me, 'Michal, I think we are beginning to find out what the problem is,' his voice is gentler now, almost avuncular. 'I want someone else to have a look at you. 225

You wait here sweetie, while I go and fix it.'

So, there is something physical the matter, or there might be. It's too early to be relieved. After what seems like an age, he's back.

'Look, you sure have picked a helluva time for this. I want you to see a neurologist, but nobody's free because they've got a conference starting tonight. But don't worry, they'll fit you in. I'll get Pam (his secretary) to take you over there and we'll wait to hear what they have to say.'

I've been sitting in a waiting room for what seems like hours when a tall man with rumpled brown hair looks around the door. 'Michal Harvey?' he says enquiringly, I jump up. 'This way please, sorry to keep you waiting.' Alan Bryer sits opposite me over a large desk, shifting papers to find a space for the current file. 'So, you've been seeing Professor Marks because he's an old friend of your aunt's,' he says, a slight edge in his voice. 'Well I have to say this is a very busy day, the department is hosting an international conference, and I don't have any time.'

'I'm sorry, I don't want to put you out, let me come back later,' I say, almost rising from my seat. I feel too fragile to force myself on the situation.

'No, no that's all right,' he says, visibly softening, 'It's just that I'm fantastically busy, but now that you're here, let's go through the story.'

I start. Within minutes, he's tangled, confused and cross. 'I'm sorry,' apologising again, 'I don't know what to tell you, I don't know which bits are relevant and which aren't.'

'OK,' he's resolved, if irritated. 'Tell me everything, just let me get it all down and try to make sense of it.' Slowly, point by point, we work through the history. Busy or not, he is meticulous in taking everything down. He questions me forward and backward, the taste in my mouth, the sickness, any deafness, any changes in my hearing. A host of questions.

Then the physical examination starts. He doesn't just want to prod my body, he wants me to move my limbs for him. I raise a leg, it trembles uncontrollably. We are both silent. He's gentler and gentler putting me through the tests. 'Look to the left, and to the right,' my eye trembles uncontrollably too.

Finally, he asks me to put my dress back on and go though a few tests standing upright. 'Now I want you to walk in a straight line,' he says, 'heel to toe.' Only I can't. 'Put your arms out if it helps your balance, I'll be right in front of you to catch you if you fall.' So debilitated. I wasn't prepared to find myself so far gone.

I sit on his couch as he starts to talk, using a large wall chart to illustrate the points he's making. Acoustic neuroma. The words mean nothing to me. He thinks I have one. He wants me to have a scan to confirm his diagnosis. It'll mean an operation.

It's real, that's all I can think, I'm not crazy. No-one's suggested it has anything to do with my work. I can have an operation and it'll be over. The words Dr Bryer is saying are beginning to sink in now.

It's benign. . . . The operation will mean losing your hearing on one side. The tumour is pressing on the brain. Usually you notice these tumours, because they affect the patient's hearing — yours seems to be different.

I don't hear many other words, then a phrase penetrates, 'Where are you staying?'

'With my aunt, at Rocky Bay.'

'Is she coming to collect you?'

'No, I'll take a bus back, or a cab — I'm quite tired.'

'No, you can't do that,' he says, 'it's not far out of my way. If you don't mind waiting while I tidy up, I'll give you a lift.'

'Gosh, that's very kind, I'm really grateful,'

He drives me home. I lie on my bed, resting, half-dozing. Reeve comes back. I hear her bustling. Annie, who has been her maid for twenty years, close to retirement now, is making supper. We're eating together again tonight.

'Well, how did you and Solly get on? He's an amazing man isn't he?'

'Fine, he was very thorough, very kind, very decent. He sent me to someone else. I saw him this afternoon, a chap called Alan Bryer, a neurologist.'

'I don't know him, but anyone Solly would send you to would be first rate.'

'He was very thorough, and kind too, he gave me a lift home. He says I have something called an acoustic neuroma.'

A moan, like a little bird, escapes Reeve's lips. I look to her face, her eyes are glistening.

Solly and Reeve speak on the phone. Solly arranges for a scan. My favourite uncle is with me, in the late afternoon, waiting for the radiologist's report.

'It might not be Shelley, it could be something else, some little thing,' he says to encourage me.

'No, Boetie,' I reply, 'this is what it is.'

And it is. Not less than four centimetres large, like a peach pressing on my brain, I'm told. It's a Friday. I take the pictures to Alan Bryer. He sees me at home, delaying the conference drinks and dinner. I'm introduced to his small son, who's running round in his pyjamas.

The scans are extraordinary. My brain stem is pushed completely out of place, like a huge ox bow. Alan Bryer is almost excited by the pictures; their clarity defines the tumour, even to my eyes, like a lump of parasitic coral inside my head. 'It has to go,' he says, 'and quick.'

'Is there a surgeon here who can do it?' I ask. 'I doubt it. We have fantastic surgeons here, but you don't often see these things, and you need to be with somebody who's done several. And very important, you need all the newest technology. But I'm going to do some research for you — I'd like to find out what the state of the art is at the moment. As soon as I have a chance, I'll hit the literature, and investigate. Just give me a day or two.'

'Thank you very much, Alan. But please tell me just a little more about the operation. You say it's likely I'll lose my hearing on the right. What other effects, success rate, recurrence, what's caused it?'

'Well,' he pauses, 'as I explained, you'll probably lose the hearing on that side because the tumour is usually on the acoustic nerve; and the way to get to it may be from just behind the ear. It'll affect your balance too, but you should be able to cope with that in time. And,' he pauses again, 'there is a danger of damaging the facial nerve, which can leave you with a facial palsy.'

'What's that?'

'Facial paralysis on one side. We want to do our best to avoid it. In good hands, I think you should be able to have a successful operation, get rid of the tumour and the chances of it recurring are very low indeed. I don't think anyone knows what causes them. But, like I said, I really would like to look at the literature before I say anymore.'

'And what if I don't have the operation?'

'You have to.'

What to tell my children? As low key as possible I think. How to make a tumour on the brain low key? It's operable. I'll be fine afterwards. Those are the main facts. Reeve talks to my mother and brothers on the phone. Grim conversations. I speak to my children. Yes, I'm absolutely fine, luckily the doctors here have found out what the trouble is, it's a little worrying, a tumour on my hearing nerve, but nothing that can't be dealt with. It will mean an operation, but I'll be home as soon as everything is settled here and then we'll sort it out. Lots of love. See you then. Not a day has gone by without my thinking of them. I have spoken to my daughter every couple of days. But I am glad I was on my own these last few days. I need a little more time alone too. This needs to sink in.

In my bedroom at Reeve's, there's a bookshelf. *Christian Science*, the title on the spine of a paperback catches my attention. Not bought by her, I'm sure. Perhaps some other visitor left it. The operation seems — unthinkable. To allow myself to be deafened on one side, and half my face perhaps paralysed. Can it be right? My intuition is silent.

I look up the Christian Science organisation in the telephone book. A number of offices. None near. I call, a lady answers. I explain that I have just been diagnosed with a brain tumour and I am keen to look into the alternatives to surgery. I don't want to talk to anyone, but is there any literature I could read at this point? No, I don't have transport, is there nothing local? Finally she offers one of our members could deliver some booklets to you; he wouldn't have to come in to talk to you. Would that help? That would be wonderful. Mr Steele. I'll expect him around 2.00, tomorrow afternoon.

Next morning, standing in the cool shallows, looking out to sea, then back at the mountain shimmering in the perfect heat, I want to live. The longing hits and overwhelms me. Yes, of course I want to live for my children, for all the other good reasons; but also I want to live for myself, for the sweetness of it. The voice speaks to me: *you must have the operation, have the operation, it will be well.*

William Steele arrives at 2.00pm promptly, the hottest part of the day. I suspect the temperature is around 100F. He stands at Reeve's front door, wearing a tie with his short-sleeved shirt, dripping perspiration.

'Thank you so much,' I say, 'have you come far?'

'Well, I had to come from Wynberg.'

I know it, it's forty-five minutes drive in the heat of the day.

'But you wanted some literature and there was no other way, so it had to be done. I won't keep you. I know you

230

don't want to talk. When you do, please call,' and he turns to leave.

'Please, can't I offer you a drink?' It seems inhuman to send him back into the blazing sun.

He walks into Reeves' cool blue and white sitting room, grateful for the respite. I ask how he comes to represent Christian Science, and just a little about what he does. It seems he believes sickness can be dealt with by belief, prayer and right living. How's that applicable to my circumstances, I wonder? What have I been pursuing? OK, so I haven't got it right, but so wrong?

'What do you do?' he asks. We talk of my work. I explain because I am thinking about it: the unintentional quest for truth, the joy of helping others. Pious words, yet in reality, it seems all there is to do. The issues are tumbling in my head. He's fascinated. Shortly, we part on warm terms. I know I will have the operation.

Next morning, 7.30am, William Steele is on the phone. 'I'm sorry to call so early, I didn't know if you'd be there later. I just wanted to tell you something extraordinary that's happened to me. For many years now, I've had a lump in my throat. It's grown to the size of a duck's egg. Initially, I went to the doctor with it and I was told it was probably a cancer and should be removed.

'Well, of course I did nothing, but I've prayed and done all the other things I believe to be right. Last night, I went to bed, having prayed as usual, and this morning, when I came to shave I saw the lump was gone. That's it, it's disappeared. I wanted you to know.'

I am going back to London today. I have letters of referral. Assorted communications have taken place. My doctor has been told.

'Do you know what he said when I called him up and told him?' my mother asks indignantly over the phone, 'Oh really.' That's all he said, nothing else!'

I assume the operation will be in London, and very soon. Alan Bryer has been as good as his word and filled me in on the latest techniques, how and why they matter.

Chapter Twenty

London

Saturday, 20 March 1994 Back to London. Suddenly, life seems just a wisp I am clinging to. There's an appointment for me to see a professor at a major hospital. 'Difficult, yes, it's difficult,' he says, looking at the scans pinned to a light box on his wall. 'The brain stem involvement is what makes it so difficult. Very unusual.'

He explains that the tumour is pressing on the brain. His analysis of the situation is blunt. Blunter than anything I have heard before. A knock or a fall at this stage could result in paralysis. Within weeks, as the tumour continues to grow, death will result. It's inevitable. Removal is essential.

'Can you operate?' I ask.

'I think I would like to refer you to someone else, who sees rather more of these cases than I do.'

'Can you tell me what's caused it?'

'That I can't.'

'Or do you have any idea how long it has been there?'

'More than ten years, is my guess.' I was told the same in South Africa.

'But what made it grow?'

'Don't know — some do, some don't.'

That afternoon, I am at the Harley Street consulting rooms of the surgeon to whom I have been referred. Why isn't he seeing me at his hospital? I wonder fleetingly. He's blunt too.

Very. With tumours of this size, there is a mortality risk. In other words, he's telling me that I may die during the operation. He runs through the issues. There's a risk of unsteadiness after the operation. The right-hand side hearing will be lost. The facial nerve is a problem. It's not common to show a weakness in the facial nerve beforehand, as I am with the twitch in my eye and lip. The odds of preserving the facial nerve in his hands will not be good. He performs fifteen to twenty-five of these operations a year.

Generally, the facial nerve is saved in fifty per cent of cases. In this case, he would not put the odds that high — he thinks it more than likely that the nerve will be lost. Even if it is preserved, it does not mean that my facial features will be normal afterwards. Complete facial paralysis on that side may follow. Tumours as large or difficultly positioned as mine are rare. I am absolutely terrified.

He sees this as a long operation — it could take him more than twelve hours, perhaps two operations. I notice, in passing, that he doesn't seem positive at the prospect. He doesn't see death occurring within the next few weeks, more like the next few months. The picture seems unremittingly dark.

Then, I understand him to ask if it is financially possible to have the operation abroad. 'Anything,' I mumble in my shocked state. It seems to me that he is saying I might have a chance of a better outcome if I have the operation abroad. (Later I learn he says this was never said. At the time it is certainly my understanding.) We proceed to discuss various European options and a North American whose results have impressed him.

Finally, I get up to leave and thank him. He has been remarkably frank. I have grown accustomed to British doctors who appear to think they know everything. Here's a man admitting I will do better by going elsewhere. Remarkable, I think. I am reeling, with horror and anxiety.

Who to turn to? My family are resourceful. Already, my brothers have been checking the records of various British surgeons. When I leave the Harley Street consultation and tell them, on the phone, what has passed, they react identically. As does my mother. We'll find the best person outside Britain to help you. Don't worry about the cost. We'll take care of all that now.

As a doctor, trained in Britain, working in the USA, Jeremy knows the ropes. His wife has already discovered the excellent Acoustic Neuroma Support Group. Now they turn to Medline — the on-line medical file, scouring tens of papers on acoustic neuroma surgery. Which is how they find Dr Brackmann in Los Angeles. His team perform more than one hundred of these operations in an average year. Numbers, experience, count.

The outside world seems distant now. It's the end of term on Friday, 25 March for my daughter. She's in a school play. I'm so pleased she has that to distract her. Much of the time I'm in bed. My brother David sits beside me, holding my hand. We thumb through a literature pack sent by the support group. Smiling men and women with skew faces. It's not only the action of the two sides of the face that appears to be different, somehow the very shape of the features looks different, as if the two sides belonged to two different people. A woman grins with half her face only, a grotesque leer.

Letters: 'I find that with the disguise of thick glasses and plenty of coloured eye shadow my surgery is hardly noticeable,' writes one survivor encouragingly. 'My dear husband has taken on the task of running our family magnificently.' 'The six months I spent preparing for my surgery was most valuable.' 'My tumour was large, three centimetres, one of the largest my team had ever operated on.' Eye care seems a major issue. I read, but can't understand, what the papers say. If the facial nerve is damaged, it seems there are various options for 'eye care'. What does it mean? Then I understand, if the facial nerve

235

is damaged my eye will not be able to close. I can't absorb what's said. Surely my facial nerve will not be damaged? That can't be asked of me?

The other world seems close by. I feel the presences beside me. It seems I am never alone now. It crosses my mind to wonder whether there could possibly be any relationship between my experience of the other world and the effect of the tumour. Do I experience the other world because I have a tumour pressing on my brain? Can't be. I am certain of the Light. And the gifts it has brought. Have I reached the other world because, in some way, of my tumour? Why did the tumour occur initially? Why has it grown? Questions without answers. *'It will be well, beloved, it will be well.'* Friends and family are amazed at my composure.

Monday, 28 March We leave for Los Angeles, my mother, my daughter and I. My son wants to come too, I think it better for him to stay at home, where he has good support. The operation is scheduled for Thursday, 31 March. My brother Jeremy will meet us in Los Angeles. My former husband will join his daughter there.

Chapter Twenty-One

Intensive Care

Something hard is sticking in me, but I don't know where. I can't see. No, I can, a little. But I can't move. Hands near my face, on my face. Someone is pouring burning liquid down my throat. The pain in my chest is unbearable. I can't get away from it. I'm trying to resist. I have no strength. My limbs won't do, can't do, what I want. Mobilising immense energy, I'm trying to call out, 'Get away, get . . . away.' Simple words only. All I can form. Like a child. A high-pitched, Mickey Mouse voice squeaks from somewhere, saying the words I say.

Someone is talking to me, 'It's all right, it's just medicine, it'll help the nausea.' The words should be comforting, but the hands are hard and unsympathetic.

'Go away. You bad nurse, for me.' Even in my crazed, semi-conscious state, I recognise she's not bad, only bad for me.

Is this the operation? Have I had the operation? Is this intensive care? Will I die? I'm not ready to die. I have to fight. No strength. My body is empty. No way to go except forward. There's a green curtain in front of me. The curtain moves. I hear my brother and my mother's voices, 'Hello Shel,' carefully spoken words.

'You're doing just fine, just fine Michal.' It's the surgeon's booming voice, 'You're very well.'

The hell I am, I won't let that nurse near me.

'Why is she speaking like that?' It's my mother's voice, floating from somewhere else.

'Shock, just shock,' says the surgeon. 'I don't think the vocal cords will be permanently affected.'

I seem to pass in and out of reality. Sometimes the curtain is open, sometimes not. The light seems always to be on — wherever I am conscious of seeing.

Am I standing beside my bed? How can it be? I'm looking down. I am naked. My legs are trembling. Wires, hard edges everywhere. I can't stand. The nurse is supporting me. I'm trying to shout. She's hurting me. Shift changes. 'She's a fighter that one, she's OK,' someone else's voice. Have they changed shifts before? The hard-handed nurse is replaced by another. An oriental girl. She's gentle, I'm grateful.

I wake, and recognise my surroundings straight away. The window with the hazy view of the hills is on my right. It's the little room on the ward where I started. My body, my chest, my groin, my neck, not my head, ache. I daren't move. It's as if I'm wired up in some way. I'll stay out of my body I think, that way I'll be able to handle this.

'Shel, hello, how are you feeling?' A figure leans forward into my line of vision, my mother.

'All right, I think,' I say, and the Mickey Mouse voice pipes again, 'What's happened?'

'You've had the operation darling, it's going to be all right.'

They haven't damaged the facial nerve I think, information flooding back, as there's a commotion at the entrance to the little room and the space at the foot of my bed fills. It's the surgeon, plus sidekicks.

'You're very well, Michal,' he booms, permitting no human link. 'It was a very large tumour, nearly six centimetres big, much bigger even than the MRI showed, but we got it all out. You're fine now. I'll be along tomorrow to see how you are. Meanwhile you try and drink. Bye bye.' Spoken in a stream continuously, till he is almost out of the room with the last words.

The senior houseman remains. He's human. We spoke at length before the operation. 'What's happened?' I ask him, speaking, squeaking the words, almost beneath my breath. He pulls up a chair to sit beside my bed.

'Well,' he says, 'they weren't able to save the facial nerve.' It can't be true. Then I allow the words, and float with them. 'But, Dr Brackmann did a fantastic job and gave you a nerve transplant at the same time. You'll be OK.' He pauses for my reaction.

'What do you say he did? What happened?'

Encouraged, he continues, 'Well the tumour was very big, much bigger than we anticipated, and situated right on the facial nerve. There was just no way he could save it. So, he took a nerve from the ear,' he indicates along the contour of his own ear, 'the greater auricular, which is about the right thickness and a very good match, and he gave you a nerve graft. All you have to do now is wait for it to grow in.'

'How long will that be?'

'Some time after nine months or so we should see it beginning to take effect, assuming all has gone well.'

I can't form the words to ask the questions I want to ask. I'm struggling. He seems to know that. 'Look, try not to worry now. You must rest, drink and get your strength back, so that we can have you walking and out of here. There'll be plenty of time to ask whatever you like, over the next few days, but you just get strong now. You lost a lot of blood on the operating table, but the main thing is that there's nothing left of the tumour and the lab analysis shows that it was definitely benign.' He pats me gently on the shoulder and leaves.

Then I start to explore myself. No question of anyone giving me a mirror and I don't ask. It seems there's a bandage around my head. Something is over my eye: I can see through it, but it feels like a plastic bubble. There's an intravenous drip attached to my right arm. Very unpleasant. I can move my feet, a little, but my body from my chin downwards is stiff with pain. It seems a medley of wires and bandages.

Later, I discover there is a wound in my neck where they 'harvested' — as they so charmingly express it — the nerve running to my ear to put into my face. Then they made a cut just above my pubic hair and scraped below the skin for fat to pad the wound on my head. It is hideous painfully and a bottle is attached to the wound for it to drain. I hardly notice that my right hand, attached to the drip, is limp.

I suck water through a straw. I can't manage a cup. One half of my mouth is quite limp and dead. The liquid burns my insides, till thirst is preferable to more pain; only the promise that the drip will be removed when I can drink sufficiently encourages me to persevere. The first night back on the ward, I drift in a sea of pain and dreams. Strange colours float through my head like an oil slick on a pool of water. I am searching for my children, till fatigue causes me to lie down.

In the dream, I wake surrounded by people. A man beats my head, then stamps on my face savagely, as I try to raise my arms to protect myself, 'Oh please, no, no,' I sob. Jerking back to consciousness, I take hold of myself. Somewhere down the corridor, a man is screaming, a hoarse low sound. I discipline myself.

'You hear that boy?' the nurse comments in the morning, as they take my blood pressure. 'He scream and he scream. They all get nightmares after the operation — you don't get no bad dreams?'

The removal of the drip is a milestone. Maybe I will be able to stand up again.

'You've got to work, to get out of here,' the senior houseman urges me. 'We can't let you go until you can walk a few steps.

You have to do it. Eat and get up. It's the only way.' More like a coach than a medic.

'What about my hand, will that . . . ?'

'Nothing to worry about, should be fine.'

My gullet hurts and the internist wants to give me more drugs. I speak to my friend the houseman. 'I've been refusing sleeping pills and pain killers, but would it be good for me to take some more of that stuff?'

'Oh no, look I'm a surgeon, I'm not keen on drugs — anything you take will have a whole series of effects. You know sometimes you have to, but the less you take the better.'

I have only been back on the ward two days, or is it three? They've removed the catheter and I refuse a bedpan. I want to get up to go the bathroom. I need to be held, every step of the way. I am a rag doll, with no power of independent movement. But volition. I press the bell for the nurse to help me to the lavatory frequently. It seems my body is automatically flushing out all the drugs I've been given. That night I ring and ring. No one answers. A lazy voice speaks to me over the intercom, 'All right, your turn's coming.' I wait, half an hour. My bladder is bursting. I press again. 'Hey we busy,' I'm told, 'you want a bed pan, the nurse she bring you a bed pan.'

'Thank you, but I want to get up and go to the lavatory, it's important for me to move.'

When I think I'll wet the bed, a comfortable lady walks into the little room. 'You sure do wanna pee pee a lot,' she says. 'Nurse she said she took you right when she come on duty.'

'It's the drugs,' I say, struggling to be civil. The nights are long, I depend on the staff.

'Why don't you have a bedpan?' Folding her arms, 'We can give you a catheter, no trouble, you go pee pee whenever you want,' she says, still not moving to help raise me from the bed.

'I must get back on my feet as soon as possible. The only way to do that is to move. But I need you to help me do that.'

THE POOL OF MEMORY

Half standing on my dignity, half-pleading. 'Well, then you jus gotta wait,' she says, moving forward at last to help me from the bed, 'we help you when we got time.'

I see myself in the mirror in the tiny lavatory. Medusa. My hair, stiff with grease, is plaited in thin stands that rear up like serpents around the front of my face. One side of my face is altogether collapsed. The plastic bubble that covers my eye in the day has been removed and the eye taped shut for the night. Horror engulfs me. Standing up, I lean forward, put my hands under the tap, while supported by the wall, and call out, 'I'm ready now, thank you,' a fraction away from tears.

'Now, that better be the last,' the fat woman says, in a warning tone.

I look at her and my spirit rises. Words fill my mouth and leave before I have time to think of what I am saying. 'You have three children, two daughters and a son. It's the youngest whom you truly love, he's the apple of your eye. Well you beware, life is not so easy. The charmed life you think he leads won't last for ever. And your daughter-in-law — disaster doesn't just strike other people.'

I can see myself, spitting out the words furiously, a crazy, thin, half-dressed wreck of a woman, face destroyed, holding onto the bed, unable to stand unsupported. The nurse looks at me in astonishment. She's probably from the Caribbean. She doesn't know what to make of what I've said, 'One more thing,' I go on, 'there's a mark, on your breast — do you have it, or your mother?' She screams, an excited yelp, and opens the top button of her uniform to show me a brown birthmark, 'It's me and my mother, she got one just like this! You a fortune teller?' gabbling out the words.

'No,' I say, 'but something a bit like that, sometimes. Please, I'm tired, can you help me back into bed?'

I can hear strains of the excited hum at the nurses' station on her return. No trouble with the service after that. I have only to press the button and there's someone to help me. I fall asleep, amazed that the gift has not left me. The operation, the removal of the tumour, have not deprived me of the ability to 'see'. Even more surprised that I have used it to frighten someone. It's quite the contrary to anything I have ever done before, or even thought of doing. Later, when I realise the miraculous effect my òutburst has had on the standard of nursing care I am subject to, I am glad. God is good.

In seven days, I am out of hospital. Walking, if you can call it that, with the help of a zimmer frame, a few steps at a time. I am set up in a hotel, with twenty-four-hour telephone access to a doctor and the team who have been looking after me. My mother and my sister-in-law, who's arrived from New York, are in selfless attendance. My daughter, reassured that I will be well now, and her father — who has been a real help — have gone back to England.

I have another operation: making my eye on the damaged side smaller, and placing a wire spring in the eyelid to enable it to open and shut. The eye surgeon is kind. I have my doubts about the procedure, but I'm told it is by far the best option, and who am I to protest at this point?

At the eye surgeon's, I make a friend. A tall, very attractive red-headed woman is paying the receptionist in the eye doctor's waiting room. She's wearing a classy cream-coloured suit and high heels. Will I ever wear high heels again? Closing her purse, she turns and seems to see me in my corner, with my zimmer frame. I turn away. When I look again, the red-head has disappeared. Then the door opens, it's her again. She walks towards me.

'I just want you to know,' she says, speaking in a classic Southern drawl, 'that I've had the same as you,'

'What?' I mumble inarticulately. Mickey Mouse has given a great deal of ground, but the voice I speak with is certainly not my own.

'You've had an acoustic neuroma, haven't you? Well, I had one too.'

'Gosh, but you look tremendous. How long ago did you have your operation?'

'Oh, maybe five years ago, and I did have one or two things done afterwards, but you're going to be fine. I looked just like you after the operation.'

That seems unbelievable. 'But, did you lose your facial nerve too?'

A slight shadow passes, 'No I didn't. That's what's happened to you? But I still can't manage a full smile. I had my eye done, just like you, though. You've had a spring put in, well me too.'

I'm overjoyed at meeting someone who has shared some of this experience. 'Look, forgive me, but is there any chance of us having lunch together?'

She hardly hesitates, 'Sure, that would be real nice, Oh, I'm Debby Anderson.'

Fifteen minutes later, my mother, supporting my arm, as ever, Debby and I are downstairs in the 'soup n' salad' restaurant on the ground floor of the building. Needless to say, walking and holding a tray are more than I can do at the same time. Finally, we're seated at a table. Where to begin? Debby wants to know a little about me. Why am I in Los Angeles for the operation, not London? How big was my tumour? Who was my surgeon? (We've both been 'done' by the same man.) How did I find it? How many children, and what do I do?

I eat slowly, laboriously chewing on my one side, occasionally pausing to suck from a straw, the only way I can drink. It's so nice to hear her speak, that I say very little, and let Debby fill in the answers, or ask more questions, or tell me about herself. She's my age, I learn. Her tumour was found in the middle of her divorce, she has two children, she's an exer-

cise fanatic, which she says has helped her to recover, and

amazingly, she believes she is a nicer person since the tumour. She's a sweet, wonderful woman and I am so pleased to have met her.

Debby seems to have researched all aspects of her treatment. 'I even went into an operating theatre to watch one of these operations. Afterwards,' she tells me, 'I just had to understand exactly what'd happened to me. It changes everything,' she says softly, 'but right now, all you have to do is build up your strength, then you'll see. But, you seem very calm, so peaceful. What is it?'

I laugh, as far as I can, and explain, offhand, that in some way I feel protected — ghastly as this process has been — and I believe in my eventual recovery, somehow.

Later, sitting under one of the massive indoor plants in the foyer waiting for a cab, I quiz her further. (Fortunately, she's deaf in the left ear, and I'm deaf in the right, so sitting side by side, conversation is easy.)

'Debby, what's the cause of these tumours? I keep asking and all the doctors say is that they don't know.'

'Most of the time they just don't know. I guess mine was a little different, because I had this X-ray treatment, radiation, when I was a little child, for my throat — they were trying this new treatment instead of having your tonsils removed. But later on, a lot of the children they tried it out on have had acoustic neuromas. Not all, mind. The doctors here will never admit it, but I think that's probably what caused my tumour.'

'Debby, me too. I had that treatment too.' I look at her in astonishment.

I remember it happening . . .

I am a child again, about six years old. It is a cold and wet Cape winter. There's a kettle boiling on the floor of my bedroom. Daddy comes in and out during the night, he stands over the kettle, there's a funny green line around him, from the night light, I expect. I don't like the smell of what they put in the kettle. My throat really hurts. I can't breathe.

They're taking me to the hospital. I like Dr Moor better than Uncle Jerry. I don't like calling him Uncle Jerry. He makes me feel funny. Daddy takes me to see him lots. He's always looking in my throat. I won't have to take my clothes off at the hospital. I don't even have to stay there. It's a nice drive, past the wildebeests and the zebras on the hill by the hospital. There's the good smell that always comes with the rain.

At the hospital, they put me on a big table in a room by myself and this enormous machine comes right over me. It doesn't hurt, but I don't like it. Dr Moor says it will stop my sore throats, otherwise I have to have my tonsils out. You just lie there while it does this clicking. It's all dark, too. I have to come again next week and the week after for them to do it again. I wish I didn't have to have it.

Chapter Twenty-Two

Afterwards

Sunday, 24 April 1994 We arrive back in London. I am ferried around the airports in a wheelchair. What a luxury — but a necessary one. I am clasping ice to my eye, the result of a last minute surgical 'adjustment' the day we were leaving, as well as being very unsteady on my feet.

During the previous three weeks, I have learnt to walk without my zimmer frame, holding onto someone else, usually my dear mother. The day I walked with faltering steps two blocks down to the sea at Santa Monica, clutching her arm, I felt as if I'd climbed Everest. Slowly I am learning to see in three dimensions again, but at times I lose it completely (and still do three years later). I care for my body, tenderly. The effects of the shock reverberate.

Meditation still does not seem necessary, or desirable, though I turn to the Light often in my mind. I recognise, with no surprise, that it is always with me, in a certain peace in my heart. I feel I am not alone — that is, I am alone, but I am part of the universe, so I am never alone. I am intimately connected to God and the presences I have encountered in the 'other' world, which is also this reality. It is hard to say if I am part of them, or they are part of me. Questions of why, how and what does it mean surface from time to time. I let them be. Easily.

My house is tall. The sight of the stairs reminds me. To go from the kitchen to my bedroom I have to walk up two floors. Will I ever be able to do it alone? It takes two days. (Though three years later I'm still, sometimes, dizzy, and unsteady.) It's great therapy. Meanwhile, the children are delighted to see me, my message book is awash with messages and bowl upon basket of flowers are delivered. Friends and clients are immensely kind and concerned. At last I am able to rest without guilt, without nagging questions about my frame of mind, or what I'm doing. I have been suffering from a brain tumour. It has been removed. I have to rest.

Did the pressure of the tumour give me access to the other world? I cannot know. (Later I try to find out through the acoustic neuroma support group if anyone else has had any sort of 'psychic' experiences prior to the removal of their tumours. I draw a blank.) Now that the tumour has gone, will my feelings or my understanding be altered? Again, I can only wait and see.

Within a couple of weeks, it's clear that I'm not going to be able to enjoy being an invalid. Not only are there practicalities to attend to, but clients call. After an initial horrified response on hearing of the diagnosis and removal of my tumour from those who did not know, they ask 'When can I make an appointment to see you?'. Thursday, 16 June, I see my first client, half-an-hour appointment only.

I open the door and his eyes go to my face. I have warned him. My voice is half an octave higher than normal and slightly slurred, the result of the operation, I explain. We go upstairs to my sitting room.

'Are you OK?' he asks, a little nervously.

'Yes, thank you,' I answer. 'What can I do for you?' Within a minute or two, he has plunged into his own problems, and we concentrate on those till the doorbell rings, and he goes downstairs to open it for the client who is taking his place.

When she leaves, I go to bed for the rest of the day. Persevere, I tell myself, the more you make yourself do, the more your strength will come back.

The following week, I see four clients, each for half an hour. Words continue to come, though I do not heal with my hands. I am learning how to deal with deafness, which I do not publicise. It seems each hour I work means two days in bed. It is impossible to explain the fatigue that lays me low. A brain operation always results in fatigue, a chest or a stomach operation in pain, I am told.

But that's not all. My memory seems to have escaped. It's hard to remember what I have done, or promised to do, at any given moment. Directions, how to travel from one place to another, often present a mystery; even simple words, names, faces, disappear. Fatigue or the slightest stress make it worse. It's not possible, the doctors tell me. Your memory will not have been affected by the removal of the tumour. The site of memory in the brain and the site of the tumour are quite separate.

The Acoustic Neuroma Association newsletter carries an article by Belinda, a former New York television producer, who amongst other symptoms after her operation lost the ability to know the meaning of a red light, didn't know how to cross a road, and shampooed her hair repeatedly, having forgotten she'd already done so. I call her.

'Yes,' she says, 'it's a terrible problem. When I spoke about it at the annual meeting of the Association, there were dozens of people with the problem. I think the doctors are getting a little better at acknowledging it exists, but it's hard to deal with. I don't know why they deny it. Over the five years since my operation, my memory has improved fantastically, though it's still not the same and I have to watch it, especially when I get tired. And don't talk to me about that! I used to go shopping and then I'd be too tired to unpack the bags.'

Driving is difficult, concentration, for any length of time, hard. After quite a short while, it becomes impossible. So I limit the amount I drive. Being tired makes everything worse. It's as if the wires in my brain fuse. I pace myself. Half, sometimes more, of every day I spend in bed. After three weeks, I stop seeing clients. It's too early, too draining, I decide, and turn to healing myself first.

I research the particular problems confronting me, finding for example the Vestibular Rehabilitation Society in Oregon with excellent advice on how to improve my balance. And further confirmation of the possible effects on my memory. From their literature I begin to understand how long I may have been suffering and showing signs of this tumour.

I am waiting for my face to show any improvement. I have been told it will be at least nine months before there will be any sign of whether the nerve graft has taken. Then the question will become: how well has it taken? The possibility that I might never recover any movement in my face sobers me. The operations that then become options do not appeal.

I wait, and pray, silently. Without saying, or even thinking the words, I believe God, the Light, call it what you will, will never desert me. I accept I do not understand the force or principles involved. I accept not knowing. Clichéd as it sounds, I believe in the triumph of goodness, grace and truth. I find peace in the arms of the moment.

By a stroke, I have been changed from one of the more striking looking women of my generation, to one of the strangest looking, face collapsed, distorted on one side. To my brave son, I am simply 'mum', how I look makes no difference, he assures me. My daughter, now an exquisite eleven-year-old, shakes her head and says I am still beautiful. Only when I cut what remains of my hair, which she has always known long, like her own, does she cry.

My looks bring mixed reactions from others. Small children cringe. It hurts me so. Being beautiful, I never thought about the smiles I drew so easily from children. Now they look at me with amazement, fear too. A smile from me, intended to be reassuring, draws my face into an even more hideous, one-sided grimace. I have to work to win their acceptance, and sometimes it is not possible.

There are adults who fail to understand too. I steel myself to go to a party. Some look beyond me, unable to face my transformation. One woman who has offered me nothing but honeyed malice for years, rushes to embrace me. An old friend simply refuses to believe my face will not recover, and tries to draw me into a project to present a television programme. His affirmation is a tonic. Peter Hatchard tells me 'You shine through your face.' There are men who want to draw close to me, reaffirming my faith in myself as a woman. It seems that for some I, not my former beauty, have the power to please. Then there is warmth and support from the most unlikely quarters. The family at my local corner shop treat me almost as one of them, rushing to perform small kindnesses. The unexpected goodwill of bystanders gives me immense pleasure.

January 1995 A slight flicker of movement. Over the last few months, the shape of my face has seemed to improve. Unnoticed by me, still stunned by the drama of the transformation, muscle tone has been starting to return. Now the corner of my mouth flickers. As movement increases, I learn about psychokenisis — movement of the sort I don't want. It seems that while a nerve graft may, miraculously, work, it will not return quite the same movement as before. There's no science yet to connect all the fibres of one nerve to the matching fibres of another — random, sometimes exaggerated and inappropriate movement is inevitable. Still, I am so grateful to be able to show even a glimmer of how I feel with my face. It continues to improve over the year, and years following.   *251*

I see George. Haltingly, he tells me how sorry he is he did not suspect the presence of a tumour. He feels, as a cranial osteopath, he should have. (Some months later George calls and asks if I would be prepared to speak to someone else in whom, having experienced my case, he spotted a similar tumour which has just been removed.) Dr Hollander, to whom George sent me, writes. He has seen an article I wrote for a magazine, on my illness, and wants to say how sorry he is not to have found the tumour, though of course it was a difficult case, and how glad he is that I am now on the road to recovery. His letter restores my faith in him, and reinforces my belief in the few genuinely wonderful doctors I have met.

The nutritional doctor I saw speaks to me too. He says that although I consulted him only about nutrition, his speciality, he is sorry he did not think of the possibility of a tumour. Real carers, not one of the others — from Jeanette Jolliff, my practitioner of many years, to eminent Dr Wheeler — make any attempt to contact me after my story is publicised by an article in the London *Evening Standard* and in a medical column in *The Times* (as well as elsewhere). Of course I am not surprised. But an apology, at least, for their failure would have meant a great deal.

A year, two years pass. I need the time. The healing process will not be hurried. I marvel at living, and when I am able, see a small but steady stream of clients, new and old. I do the best my strength will allow. I don't think about it. I hardly consider what I 'believe', or whether the use of my intuition in this way is a 'legitimate' activity. It seems I can offer help to some people, so I do. I do not seek to understand.

Sessions change. I am rarely willing to see new people regularly, for reasons of strength and inclination. I offer one session, with perhaps a follow-up when they have considered the first. It is a reading of who and where they are, with suggestions of strengths and weakness, blockages to be overcome, talents and abilities to be developed, relationship patterns to be considered. Then I ask the client not to come back for several months. Increasingly, people who find it most valuable have already questioned the spiritual for some time, or are involved in creative work.

After two years, I am beginning to wonder about my future. I see life ahead of me and I do not know what to do with it. I am frustrated by my physical limits, will they lessen? What to do? I am not tempted to turn to meditation to try and find an answer. I know that there, I have already been told — see clients, teach, write. What do I have to teach or write? I am reluctant. I don't question what I was told. I know that in some way the 'other' world and I are indivisible. So, why not do as I was told? Because I feel no desire to do so. Is it fear, weakness, reluctance or something else that holds me back?

While I have to limit the number of clients I see strictly, at the same time a gnawing is beginning to stir within me. What will satisfy that? The changes to my physical reality seem immense. Are they absolute? Belinda in New York, and Debby in Santa Monica, counsel that two years after the operation it is too soon to expect to have returned to normality. Belinda thinks it takes five years to stabilise. I am impatient.

I consider all the options. How to manage my energy? How to live? Even if I wanted to, I realise there is no going back. The changes to my non-physical reality are total. I am different in ways I cannot say. When I try to analyse it, I flounder. It seems I have been profoundly changed. Yes, I have come to accept my role, as a go-between, between worlds. But it is more than that. In myself, somehow, I hold both worlds, combined. In one way, it is as if nothing has happened, and yet everything has happened. Seeing clients is today's work, I always reminded myself. Tomorrow may be different. And so it is. But there is no going back. Who am I? What am I? Even asking the questions seems irrelevant, though. There's a deeper strand. That strand is at peace.

Easter 1996 I drive through Knightsbridge towards Hyde Park Corner, London is grey and grand. I am still pleased to be back in command of a car. I park in a deserted Belgrave Square, deserted because it is Easter Sunday. The richness of Belgravia is still; only the harmony of the Georgian form speaks. I mount the steps of a stately building. As I pass through the revolving doors, I attract few stares. The damage to my face is hardly noticeable, in repose, to a casual observer. God is good. I have come here to be with God, in some sense. This is a spiritualist centre. Why am I here? Because it is Easter. Because I know the reality of rebirth. Because I want the special comfort of being, briefly, with those for whom my other reality, at least some version of it, exists too. I know my notion of 'God', or the forces of the universe, probably does not correspond to the beliefs this organisation holds. But my difference will be allowed, I think. Will the words of prayer, the unexpectedly mild April air, or the vast clouds in the pink-grey sky above this elegant, enormous square, answer the questions I do not formulate?

I follow the signs up the stairs to the grand first floor room where a so-called service is being held. A very thin old woman stands at the door, distributing hymn books. The large room is full — an African man in a wheelchair, several well-heeled looking women, a surprising number of younger people, and rows of elderly men and women. There's a stage a few feet from the floor at the far end. Behind it, light streams through a row of windows, highlighting a stiff triangular arrangement of yellow and white chrysanthemums and lilies, uncomfortable on a plinth.

Another, equally grey-haired but plump and smiling, woman appears to conduct the service. A third matron strikes a chord on the piano and we're off: the first hymn. I have never heard it before. Or a service quite like this one. But my mind drifts. The atmosphere is warm, friendly and eccentric. All too soon it's over. 'There will now be a demonstration by our visiting medium,' announces madam speaker.

A 'demonstration'? I'd like to attend. Down the stairs to the marbelled hall, I open a heavy mahogany door. The man at the end of the room surprises me: he's young, perhaps not thirty-five. Ordinary too. Nice smile. Brown tweed jacket. He takes a small portable telephone from his jacket. 'This is my special means of communication,' he jokes weakly. 'Actually I *am* a hospital manager and I'm on duty, but it's unlikely I'll be called. Shall we start then?' There are about twenty of us in the room, an odd seance. Or 'demonstration', as it's coyly called.

Is it just curiosity that's drawn me here? Or do I want a sign, perhaps a spur? Am I hesitating to listen to my own intuition? Wasn't I told, years ago, what to do? Working for others, it is easy to offer what is given. I don't question whether it comes from another source, or some aspect of myself. I am scrupulous in checking that I am free of any desire, emotion or need when I look at clients. Even then, I am almost never directive, I unfold possibilities, analyse, reveal. Then leave them to make their own choices. But how can I simply follow instructions on what to do with my own life? Instructions received through my own biased self? I am waiting for certainty, or enough certainty. For desire.

We sit in rows, facing the speaker. He walks down the central isle, turning to the right-hand side of the room first. Two messages, then a third, a man I might even have been sterner with if I'd seen him as a client. But then he would not have come to me. 'You can take a holiday for as long as you like, but it'll still be there, you will still have to face what you have to do, after your little — or long — detour. Do you understand me?' 255

'Yes.' Even from across the room, looking at the man, I see an alcoholic, probably a drug user. He's unwashed and attempts to appear contemptuous of his surroundings. But I wonder at his being here, at his wanting to be here.

The medium turns away now. He speaks to a corpulent fellow, sees a dead relative, describes him, apparently accurately. But the message does not come from the dead man.

'You have to look in the churchyard, where you'll find what you need, the next bit of information, where several members of this family are buried. Do you understand?'

Fortune telling? It's different to what I do. The words are a little awkward, the sense disjointed, but then I do not know the issue — probably this medium does not either. Mental command of the matter in hand, in the usual sense, is not how this is done. I should know. But the man who receives the message is deeply affected, he questions details, more comes.

'It's as if you are looking for one thing, but you're going to find another. This farming man is standing in front of a fire, warming himself — you will do the same soon.'

The message seems part metaphor, part fact. I am interested. Another man becomes the focus of the medium's attention. He is embroiled, apparently, in business complications, a piece of paper, a document perhaps, is being sought.

'No point in being hotheaded,' says the medium, 'it'll come to light, eventually.'

It seems to me as if, in part, seeing the dead is a device, a way of leading into, identifying, aspects of the individual's character, or situation. Which of course is what I have been doing when I work. Dead people rarely (not never) appear to me.

I almost miss the medium's gaze.

'Is there someone who had trouble with his throat?' he's asking me, 'with speaking, not with any mental ability, but a mechanical thing?'

Perhaps my Uncle Kenneth, I think, who died about three years ago. He was crippled and his ability to talk was badly affected. My meditation spoke of him, I recall, even warned me of his impending death, and urged me to reach out to him. Simultaneously, I am amazed at the medium focusing on me. I have never had a message relayed to me by someone else in this way. After all that has happened, all I have been told, and more, as a giver of messages myself, I am still in some small part a sceptic. Can this man really have something to say to me? My hesitation lasts too long, confusion, I do not want the medium to turn away,

'Yes,' I say, 'perhaps.'

'He is telling you to speak out, you must speak out now.'

His gaze is warm and sweet. A river flowing from the sacred peak to the sea far below. We meet on the banks. Way beyond the medium's tweed jacket, polished brown shoes or unexpected young face.

'Please,' he repeats, 'speak out.'

I almost hold my breath to say, in a whisper first, that grows, *'I have known the other side, the unused side of the brain, like the darker side of the moon. Or perhaps I have travelled beyond the brain. Into space, to another domain, one without location on the four co-ordinates. Known nothing and everything, of myself and others too. Learnt to experience and love God and man in all guises; stroked death's face, then turned back to life by way of the surgeon's knife: to place myself at the service of the forces I seek constantly to accept and understand, in my heart.'*

The words well within me. Do I listen to them? Can I say them out loud? I don't know. But I know it's true — I know I must begin to speak out.

Later, I sit at my desk, toying with a pen, I am starting to try to write the story of my journey. Do I have anything to say? Will anyone want to read what I write?

Chapter Twenty-Three

Joy

'Speak out.' Is there no other way? Could, would, the cloister beckon in another age? I brush the question aside.

I start to see a few more clients. Some come in groups, for what we call, loosely, meditation — journeys into the interior — healing and instruction. A group of psychotherapists, anxious to understand the spiritual dimension better, come for a number of sessions. I organise a dozen or so clients who have been coming to see me regularly since I started working, into two groups. The aim is to develop their own intuitive skills, as well as working on self-development, by healing and inspiration. Others, new and old clients, come individually.

Henry is a new client. In his forties, he has done considerable spiritual work. For years he has worked towards enlightenment, following a spiritual leader, turning away from earthly attainments. He has aspired to develop peace in himself and work for what he understands to be the benefit of mankind. For some time, he even lived in a community with similar aims. That way of living seemed to come to an impasse. Now he is groping towards a different lifestyle, unsure of quite how to proceed, only that he needs both to hold onto and develop the core of his spirituality, at the same time as making his way in the world. Over the past few years, he has been developing a business as an international trader, while trying to stick to

his deeply held spiritual beliefs.

At our first meeting, I study his energy and tell him what I can see. A spirit image joins us. Spirits don't often show themselves to me. I describe him, he's wearing small, round spectacles. 'It's my father,' Henry says. Henry's father, who's no longer alive, illustrates certain aspects of Henry's upbringing and relationship pattern. How his father related to his mother, and her to him, and how Henry relates to others in various circumstances now. It's clear too that Henry's attitude towards achievement has been affected in quite specific ways by his father's approach to related issues.

While Henry has considered some of these insights, what astounds him and gives them particular force, and inclines him to accept the rest of what I say, is that they come from me, a stranger with no experience of him. One preference that has stayed with me from the very beginning is that when clients first come to see me, I do not like to speak to them apart from the briefest preliminaries. Instead, I proceed and tell them what I 'see' before we talk. (And I enjoy telephone sessions because I don't risk being distracted by the client's physical presence, and can concentrate solely on the information I am receiving intuitively.)

I suggest new ways for Henry to think about the tight spiritual principles — for example, a strict meditation ritual, focus on enlightenment and rigid dietary constraints — that he has been trying to live by. Compassionate action goes without saying in my book, but I emphasise the importance of developing a well functioning, powerful, authentic self. Not so as to throw external power around, but to use it to be effective. To be able to choose, and act on your choices.

Henry is steeped in his understanding of the need to give up his ego, as expressed in Eastern thought. Like so many, he equates that with not putting himself forward, losing desire, working only for the eventual benefit of others. For me, the links between becoming ego-less in this sense, and being a sacrifice, or impotent and unable to act, are close for those who live outside a religious community (or even inside?). It's a very complex subject and we skim the surface. What is effective and appropriate action in the age and world we occupy? What does it necessitate? How to understand the relation between self and others? How to differentiate between and act effectively, considering the needs of yourself and others?

This opens another subject: to be able to act for and in the now, the present; to consider an action in the context of this life, both in terms of immediate gratification and effects and the long-term consequences. Not largely, or even solely, with a view to eventual enlightenment, or worse, for a better next life. I hold that it is the present, this life, this moment, that matters above all.

As the session closes, because he has heard of the work I have done in the past, Henry asks for remedies. I consider his request. It is clear what would help him, but I am not sure I wish to play this role again. Eventually I compromise. I suggest a homeopathic remedy that I believe will help at this point, and recommend the dosage. Then I leave it to him to decide what to do with my recommendation. Finally, I tell him to go away for at least three months, before he comes to talk again.

Meanwhile, taking courage in both hands, I organise a small talk at the local community centre. I write to a few clients, saying that I will be giving an intuitive, or channelled, talk; I don't know what it will be about, but tell them where and when. As the day approaches, my anxiety escalates. Leaving the house that afternoon, the lock on my front door jams. There's no way back in. It's as if someone knew that if I could, I would turn back. Five minutes' walk to the Tabernacle Community Centre. The only room available is tiny, crammed full of chairs and tables, and baking hot.

I leave the first three or four people who arrive to organise the space while I run to Mario, the locksmith down the road, to help with my front door. I leave my key with Mario and hurry back to the Tabernacle, sit down and prepare to talk. I have not thought of a subject, or let myself think about points I might want to incorporate in a talk, or any of the normal things you would do before giving a speech or lecture. I focus on three candles brought for the purpose and open my mouth. What will I say?

Words flow[1]. I am amazed. It is a talk about God. Or the principle called God, that exists within each of us. God is the uncovering of the Light within us, though at the same time an external God-force exists too. We are all divine. It is a warning against the guru or priest as the sublime holder of knowledge, the sole giver of enlightenment, or the institution, or even social order, that keeps the individual distant from God, from appreciating their own divinity. And of the responsibilities of being God for each and every one of us. (The locksmith knocks half way through, to return my key. The job's done. With an amazed look, he beats a hasty retreat from the stifling little room, candles ablaze, and my monotone.)

The audience response is very positive. A few have brought friends whom I have never met. One or two are therapists, with specific questions. I am hugely pleased that they find it interesting.

Afterwards, my heart sings. Energy and exaltation pulse through me. I paint the mantelpiece in my kitchen and a dingy looking blind, working off my high. But I don't plan to do it again. The words I have said underline why I don't want to sit in front of an audience and tell people how to live. I don't want to promote myself as an authority of some sort. I explain all this at one of the meditation and discussion group's sessions. They want me to give more talks. Sara, for example,

---

1. The text of this talk is available from 10 Bamborough Gardens, London W12 8QN.

has been asking me to do so for years. They are all dear to me. We have been through so much together.

Then someone makes a suggestion, 'What if we ask you to speak?'

'What do you mean?'

'What if we organise it all, invite the audience and are responsible for it all. We'd invite you to speak because we'd like to hear you. Would you do it then?'

How can I refuse? Why would I want to refuse?

They give themselves a name, the Circle Discussion Group, and set out to organise the next talk. Not only will they send out invitations, but they will put their names and a few lines about themselves on each one: Bonnie Cracknell, a mental health occupational therapist. She has worked for the National Health Service for fourteen years. Rupert Cracknell, an art therapist with over twenty years experience with the National Health Service. Chris Fallon, a script writer and director in film and television. He also teaches Ki Development and Ki Aikido. Neil Spencer, a writer and journalist who specialises in music, popular culture and astrology. Ruthie Smith, a psychotherapist and lecturer in mental health and therapy, and a jazz musician. Rosalynd Ward, a researcher and script reader (later drama producer) working mainly in radio. Kolinka Zinovieff, an aromatherapist and cranio-sacral therapist who runs a business selling essential oils. They are joined by a member of another group I have been working with for some years, James Hood, a professional musician and composer who describes his records as esoteric music.

My physical health continues to improve. Rest, rest, rest remains essential and while my nature protests, sheer necessity always wins. My eye remains an issue. Experts in London and Los Angeles are adamant that the wire, or spring, in place in the eyelid must stay. Their dire warnings ring in my ears. I feel differently. Dare I say I think they're wrong? Not another confrontation with medical authority, I groan inwardly. I even have a logical case for looking further. However eminent the medical views I already have, they come from those with a vested interest, or those with little hands on experience of the spring and my particular situation. A doctor in London accuses me of 'being emotional' when, explaining why I want to explore further, I point out that I would have died had I listened to the authorities before my tumour was discovered.

Fortunately, this time I am not alone. My own doctor (a new doctor!) supports me because I have good logical grounds for at least investigating another option. I find an eye specialist in New York with an extensive track record dealing with Bells palsy and problems of my sort, who says what I feel. A second opinion on Park Avenue supports the same view. I go ahead and have the spring removed. The pain or irritation I have felt around my eye for the last two-and-a-half years disappears. As an added bonus, my appearance is further improved. Will it last, or some other problem occur?

Three months are up, Henry is back for his session. It's different from the first one, but then they are all different. He's bursting to talk.

'I thought a lot about the things you said last time and in many respects it was very awakening. I think perhaps I'd been doing certain things that weren't particularly healthy.' He hasn't lost the language of his spiritual training.

For my part, I struggle with speaking clearly, as an inner force within me, which expresses itself in a slightly convoluted way, seems to want to take over. In some sessions I follow it completely, in others I try to present a clearer, more colloquial front.

He continues, 'I've come to the conclusion, as you said, that no matter what you are doing, it's focusing on here and now, the everyday things, that matters. Life is lived on a second-to-second basis and if you can't take care of the now, then I think it's a bit of an illusion, a dream. I sat down to do some exercises I've been doing for years, and it suddenly occurred to me — why am I doing them if I don't try to do them properly, rather than rushing through them, because, I'm not sure quite how to express what I mean, but in everything that you do, in every second, surely there has to be a level of happiness and fulfilment with God, or whatever. It has to really mean something.'

'Yes,' I reply, 'you are not just looking for some eventual salvation; if there is some eventual enlightenment, that is almost secondary. What you are doing in the here and now is creating heaven on earth. Past lives and future lives are of little importance. Which isn't to say that they are ultimately not important. Of course they are. They are products and causes. But all action is effective, in the here and now. What really matters is the quality of what you are doing at the moment, not what you plan or intend to do in the future, or even what you are doing for the future. All of those things may matter, but the moment matters too, often far more. Realising that is crucial.'

Astrology as a predictive device, and clairvoyance, have played a significant part in Henry's past. I want to talk to him about them. 'I think there are problems with looking into the future. For me, the relation between what's preordained and what you create yourself is not simple, or clear at all. One of the problems about having a glimpse of the future, or listening to what somebody else has to say about what will happen, is that you wait for it to happen without doing anything yourself. You can feel relieved of the responsibility for doing anything.

'Or you can go the other way, and work to make what you think might happen, based on what's been told to you, actually happen. Then, your interpretation of what you've been told will happen could be right or wrong. I'm not going to debate the truth of prediction here. Obviously I believe that in some circumstances it is possible to know the future — for someone else to tell it to you, for you to dream it, to hear it in your head, or something else.

'But the caveats are endless. For example, which clairvoyant works for whom? How to understand what you're told? How does the clairvoyant interpret what he or she is told, for that matter? It's difficult enough dealing with information you receive yourself, but when someone else becomes involved, further complexities enter. The central point for me is that relying on someone else to predict your future disempowers you. It removes your ability to create, or participate in creating, your future. It reduces you to the puppet in the hands of another, human, puppet master.'

'Yes, I can see that. But so much of life is lived anticipating the future. And it's hard to know how to decide what to do for the best. Or what is the best.'

'Of course, we all long for certainty, and there are times where some form of prophecy, or your interpretation of what you hear, will help provide that. But for me it is immensely important never to give up your own sovereignty. You own power to choose and to act is one of the most precious you have. It is your link with God. It is you as God'

Henry is plagued by what he sees as his inability to use his intuition. His own judgment too, I suggest. After years of spiritual study aimed at hearing the inner voice and developing himself, I feel he's deprived.

'Deprived of what?' he asks. My speech comes out too quickly to make it simple.

'Most fundamentally of all, you deprive yourself of the essence of your intelligence. You defer to another or a given or a received truth. You have immense resources. And you have the sharpest of minds. You understand the importance of respecting others and you have every ability to see truth for yourself. The denial and the deprivation, particularly the deprivation, is in following a set of limits laid down by another, following a set of rules that you perceive to be correct but in a narrow mechanistic form that avoids the sensations coming to you from your own body. You have not been listening to your own messages.'

'Could you amplify that? It seems very fundamental.'

'Your sensory input tells you what is good. It tells you what you would like, which direction to go in. But you are bound and wrapped, or perhaps I should say that you have been bound and wrapped, in a serious of 'oughts' and 'shoulds'. They constrain you to the point where they destroy your own sensibility. So that indeed there is little that you can do, except tread on a path that is outlined for you by another. You deprive yourself of the effects of your intuition, the very thing that you wish to cultivate.'

For years, Henry has tried to work out what to do, how to live, with his mind. I urge him to follow his senses. 'Following where you are led is not a mental exercise. It is a physical one. See with your feet. Follow the body. Trust in the body. Trust in the truth that you contain. Trust in your own innate goodness, which ultimately will be trusting the goal, the divine spark or the divinity in you. As long as you continue to say "I need a set of rules from elsewhere, somebody else will tell me what to do," you are undermining not only yourself, but God. Because you are saying, "I don't contain any God, somebody else does." I'll follows, as long as it's all laid out for me. And that is the denial of God.

'You have reached the place where you reach within yourself to be your own teacher. To discriminate yourself. In discriminating, making choices, it is your truth that speaks to you. You are capable of humility. Your ego is not about to run away with you. You are not about to say "all teachers are irrelevant to me, I know everything that there possibly is to know, I'll never hear anything that anybody else says". You are in much greater danger of doing the opposite: "I will hear everything and only everything that other people say. And what comes to me from myself – well, I'm not hearing it. I can't hear it. Maybe somebody else will bring me to a place where I can hear it." And I say no. You are capable of choice. Stop now. Listen to yourself. Start with listening to the things that you can most easily hear. And continue.'

'It's a radical departure from how I've understood things.'

Henry questions me about education and the need to learn principles to live by. I agree it's very important to establish certain ground rules. Do no harm, a most complex concept. Respect others. Respect difference. The fact — so difficult for so many to truly grasp — that we are all interrelated. No one individual, no one section of society, can ultimately benefit at the expense of another. As well as more obvious, but equally important, the role of qualities like kindness and humility.

'But,' I say, 'I'd like to think of education as a reinforcement of your inner truth, so that an education system doesn't present a foreign set of values, but rather works on the inner. So you don't tell a child "don't hit somebody else because its bad", you tell a child "if somebody hits you, it hurts, doesn't it? So before you hit somebody else remember what it feels like to you and don't do it." Of course, the message you present yourself is crucial, as is the message from the culture. And obviously not everyone will respond, to begin with, to teaching in this way; for those who need them, there must be certain rules. That's why we all need laws.

'But it's this constant ability to put yourself in the other's shoes that I think is the essence of understanding, of living as a community, of the sense of all beings as one, of our links with others, of the unity of the whole. Of morality and ultimately finality. Cruelty is only possible because of the inability to empathise. External belief structures that separate 'us' from 'them' undermine that ability to put yourself in the other's shoes.'

Most of the time there is no longer a separate voice in my head. Just my own sense, or the sense that's given to me, which from time to time takes over. Often I feel what I have to say is so obvious, so simple, that it seems presumptuous to say it. I learn constantly from what I am teaching. Then I teach what I know. But there is so much to learn.

In January 1997, I give a talk, On Relationships, which the Circle Group organises.[2] In February, I answer questions from a group of Buddhists. It's some time since I have been consulted by a practising Buddhist and I wonder what will happen. On arrival, they present me with a sheaf of detailed complex questions, all couched in Buddhist terminology. I am a little taken aback. I have no Buddhist learning — many of the words they use are quite unknown to me.

However, I determine to start at the beginning and simply allow whatever comes to come. To my surprise, the answers flow confidently. They're pithy, direct and deal with Buddhist concepts I have no conscious knowledge of. It's an intense session and the audience seem very pleased. Afterwards, a middle-aged man, a client and a Buddhist student for many years, comes to talk to me.

'It's Dzogchen you're teaching,' he says. 'Some of us have been talking about it and we don't think there's any doubt.' I smile. I do.

In March, the Circle Group arrange another talk; this time I choose Truth and Illusion as the subject. My eye is playing up, so we have to cancel. It's rescheduled for April, and I make a great effort to be present in what I am saying. To allow the words to flow, but somehow to be closer to them. In June, I am due to talk on Integration, what it means to me to try to integrate spiritual principles, as I understand them, into the everyday.

2. A tape of this, and most of Michal Levin's talks, is available from 10 Bamborough Gardens, London W12 8QN.

Some days now I see all life in each quiet instant, hold the world in my hand. Then there's no need to move beyond the confines of my small private space. The boundaries have disappeared. For the first time, I truly understand how a physical prison could offer absolute freedom. Yet life remains to be lived. I don't wish to go to prison. I am not a nun, nor do I aspire to be a religious recluse. I am glad for everyday life. I am glad to party. A colour, let alone a skyline, can still have me in raptures. My physical body goes on improving. There are ups and downs. I dig my feet deeper in the soil. Life continues.

July, August, September. Joy. Without my recognising it, joy, in a new form, has triumphed. Speaking 'the words that come' has bound me closer and closer to their source, to myself and all others. Still it does not stop. October and November. Finally, I do what I have found so difficult. I speak publicly about myself, I speak not just from the effects of this journey, but of the journey. Of the way I now understand some of the forces I encountered. Of what I have learnt from the forces of Light and Darkness and how they presented themselves to me.

I speak of 'Angels and other inhabitants of the deeper dimension' and then 'Death, the dark, demons and beyond — again a talk from personal experience.' The force running through me is stronger and stronger. I am so grateful and so glad to be alive. I am the river returning to the sea, the red of the bishop bird's breast, the cliffs above the ocean in V's domain, the phosphorescent depths of the sacred pool, the light of the mountain, force of the wheel, all those I have known and will know, the pain and pleasure of birth, certainty of death. And life again.

Now, I feel the next stage stirring.